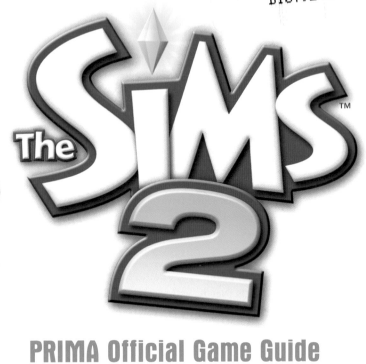

The Sims 2 ™

PRIMA Official Game Guide

Greg Kramer

Prima Games
A Division of Random House, Inc.

3000 Lava Ridge Court, Ste. 100
Roseville, CA 95661
1-800-733-3000
www.primagames.com

Product Manager: Jill Hinckley
Editor: Alaina Yee

Important:

ISBN: 0-7615-5209-X
Library of Congress Catalog Card Number: 2005906155
Printed by Butler & Tanner Ltd, England
05 06 07 08 LL 10 9 8 7 6 5 4 3 2 1

Table of Contents

Chapter 1
Game Modes, Controls, and Special Features

The wide new world of the Sims awaits with all the richness of life at your fingertips. First, however, there are a few mechanical considerations that you should know.

This section lays out the different game and control modes, the console-specific special features, and the mechanics of two-player action.

> **note** Throughout this guide, we use the term "lots" to mean locations.

Game Modes

The Sims™ 2 can be played in two distinct modes.

In the main menu, select between Story mode and Freeplay mode.

Story Mode

Story mode is a linear, goal-based game in which you must help your Sims (and the Sims on the lots) satisfy their most dearly-held desires. Success on one lot enables your Sims to access further lots, until they eventually reach the lofty height of their personal Aspiration at the mysterious Biodome.

In Story mode, your focus is on satisfying Gold Wants and progressing through a series of lots.

Story mode has several other unique features.

◆ There is only one player-created Sim per player.
◆ You have full control over the player-controlled Sim, as well as at least one additional resident of all lots (except on the first lot).
◆ Visitors to the lots come from any Story mode lot you've unlocked.

Freeplay Mode

Freeplay mode has no Gold Wants and, thus, no defined goals besides battling the constant disorder of life to make your Sim's existence easier and more efficient.

Create up to four Sims and move them into any of four lots. Some of these lots contain prebuilt but empty houses, and some are raw and undeveloped, ready for your architectural imagination.

◆ 8 Rockpile Road, Strangetown: Inhabited by the Freebers, a four-Sim family. This lot is developed and furnished.
◆ 14 Arbor Grove, Pleasantview: Inhabited by the Newbies, a two-Sim family. This lot is developed and furnished.
◆ 96 Largess Lane, Pleasantview: This lot is uninhabited and undeveloped.
◆ 87 Yamoto Crest, Melbourne: This lot is uninhabited and undeveloped.

> **note** In Freeplay mode, stick to the basics when building your home. Starting funds can be easily drained on decorations, rugs, and wall coverings, leaving nothing for the more important objects that feed your Sims' Needs and build their skills. Wait until your Sims are pulling in reliable income before spending any significant money on their home.

Once settled in a lot, your Sims can pursue their Wants, avoid their Fears, and climb the career ladder for as long as you like.

Choose your household in Freeplay mode.

Freeplay mode is distinct in several ways.

> **note** Saved game slots preserve data from both Freeplay and Story mode. And Sims in both modes contribute to the same pool of accumulated Aspiration points and, therefore, share object unlocks. You can, consequently, accelerate the unlocking of objects in Story mode by satisfying Wants in Freeplay mode. Being able to get some of these unlockable objects early in the game in Story mode is a real boon.

- Sims only leave the Freeplay lot to go to work and cannot visit any other lots.
- Objects, clothing, and objects unlocked in Story mode are available in Freeplay mode lots.
- Visitors include any residents of other Freeplay mode lots.
- You may freely switch control between any resident of a lot.
- To control Sims of your creation who reside on other lots, select their home lots from the "Places to Go" Freeplay menu.

Game Modes and This Guide

The bulk of this guide applies equally to both Story and Freeplay modes. Where any concept applies to only one mode or functions differently between modes, it's noted so you'll be aware.

> **note** Needless to say, the part of this book entitled "Story Mode" does not apply to Freeplay mode.

Control Modes

There are two ways to control your Sims, the second of which is brand new to the console incarnation of this storied franchise.

> **note** To switch between control modes, press the Toggle Control Mode button. To cycle through all controllable Sims, press the Switch Sims button.

In classic control mode, you don't control your Sims as much as you control what you want them to interact with by choosing it with the cursor.

1. Classic Mode: Control your Sims indirectly by using the cursor to select an object or Sim you want your Sim to interact with, then choosing among the available interactions.
2. Direct Control: Control your Sims directly by moving them around the lot. Approach an object or Sim and press X to interact with it.

Each method of control has its advantages and its compromises.

In direct control mode, you control your Sim rather than a cursor. Want to interact with that trampoline? Walk right up to it and press X to start bouncing.

> **tip** Though you could certainly play exclusively in either classic or direct control mode, the most efficient and effective way to play is by switching between the two modes for activities best done in each.
>
> For instance, you could do most of your Need satisfaction (except Hunger) and skill work in classic mode, but use direct control to socialize, prepare food, or use specifically designed direct control objects (fire extinguisher, vacuum, metal detector).

Classic Control Mode

Traditionally, Sims move at your command, but you have no direct control over the route they take or the way they opt to do things. As in direct control mode, the currently controllable Sim is highlighted with a green crystal (known as the "plumb bob") over his or her head. By contrast, however, moving the control stick moves not your Sim but rather a green cursor (like a pillar of light) that you use to select an object or Sim to interact with.

Icons down the right side of the screen indicate the actions your Sim will do in order.

The benefits of the classic system, however, substantially make up for this slight relinquishment of control. You can, for instance, queue up several activities for your Sim to perform in order and leave him or her to them. Moreover, you can see queued icons for actions your Sim has chosen autonomously.

tip When trying to keep multiple controllable Sims busy, use classic control to queue up several interactions, then switch to another Sim and repeat, and so on.

note Another benefit of classic mode is a bit more subtle but does make a difference for some players. In this mode, all queued activities are shown in a column down the right-hand side of the screen. When you cancel a task, you get visual feedback of what interaction has been cancelled (it turns red). In direct control mode, by contrast, you can't queue up more than one action at a time. To experienced players, this feels a bit unnatural at first.

You may certainly continue to play in classic mode when queuing up actions is your most effective method, but you may find queuing isn't so essential once you've spent some time in direct control. In the end, the choice is yours.

Direct Mode

With direct Sim control, you control your Sims, well, directly. Want them to use the TV? Direct them to the TV and push the Select Interaction button. Any available interactions for the TV appear for your selection.

note When interacting with or holding an object in direct control mode, your Sims' have easier access to several special subinteractions. They can, for instance, read a magazine while luxuriating on the toilet or search the cushions of a sofa for loose change or other surprises.

In classic control, you'd have to position your indicator over the object to activate these additional interactions.

There are three instances in which direct control provides substantially greater command over your Sims' actions than classic control.

◆ Social interaction
◆ Food preparation
◆ Use of direct control objects: fire extinguisher, vacuum cleaner, and metal detector.

Socializing in direct control mode is an entirely different experience.

tip Another advantage of direct control over classic control is your Sim's tendency to run. A classic controlled Sim only runs when late for the carpool. Direct control mode's speed of foot is much more time efficient and makes moving around the lot in direct control mode a must.

Food preparation is much easier to control in direct control mode since you choose what steps to take, rather than trying to override your Sim's own choices.

Each of these instances is either inaccessible or more difficult in classic control mode, depending more heavily on fast button pushing.

For example, in food preparation, when Sims remove ingredients from a refrigerator, the surface or object they prepare the food with dictates what dish results. In classic mode, you've only a brief time to direct this choice, requiring fast adjustment of the interaction indicator before your Sim makes a decision. In direct mode, however, when the Sim closes the fridge, a new interaction selector pops up awaiting your preference on what to do with the food.

Console Special Features

Though the core game is the same for all versions of *The Sims™2*, the Xbox and PlayStation 2 come with exclusive features.

Xbox

See more of the world with your Xbox and a high-definition TV.

The Xbox version of the game features HDTV support. This is more than just bells and whistles, however—it provides a much wider view of the action.

PlayStation 2

PlayStation 2 owners can harness the power of the Sony EyeToy™, plastering their custom images all over their Sims' homes.

Add your own images to the poses of your Sims by placing Sony EyeToy™ shots in the image slots.

You may store up to five images taken with your EyeToy™ and display them on a variety of decorative objects used in the game.

Sony EyeToy™ images adorn:

◆ Moodscape Painting
◆ Opticluster Promotional Painting
◆ Opticluster 360
◆ Easel paintings created by your Sims

Sony EyeToy™ images can adorn the walls of your Sims' lots.

note Players of other consoles or PlayStation 2 players who don't use the EyeToy™ instead see images of their Sim in the designated EyeToy objects. As with EyeToy™ images, there are five poses to choose from when Sims interact with the objects. These images update whenever you alter your Sim's fashion or appearance.

When the object is first placed, a random picture is displayed. Interact with the object and use the Change Picture interaction, and you may specify which picture slot is used in that specific instance of that object.

Your Sims may even be inspired to paint your Sony EyeToy™ images.

note In two-player mode, Sony EyeToy™ is not available for player two.

Fun Frames

Two-Player Mode

Two players can work together in either Story or Freeplay mode.

Two-player mode features a horizontal split screen.

Regardless of the mode you're playing, several rules apply.

◆ Aspiration points and family funds are collective. Each player's Sim contributes or deducts money or Aspiration points to or from these common pools.

◆ Both Sims can have careers. If their carpools arrive at the same time, they share a car.

◆ If the two players' Sims interact socially in direct control mode, the player who initiates the contact selects all interactions. The other player may, of course, exit the interaction at any time.

◆ If in classic control mode, on the other hand, player two may queue up social interactions with player one's Sim at any time, and Sims take turns in the order interactions are selected.

◆ Whichever player calls up the Pause menu gets exclusive control over the menu.

◆ All items in the Unlock Progress panel are shared between the players.

◆ The game speed can only be accelerated to double speed if *both* players press and hold their respective Fast Forward buttons.

◆ If one player's Sim departs the lot to another lot (not to work), the other player's Sim immediately stops all activity and joins the departure. The transition occurs even if the second Sim hasn't reached the taxi.

◆ If one player's Sim dies on a lot, he or she must be resurrected before the other player's Sim can leave the lot.

◆ Only player one's Sim's likeness or Sony EyeToy™ images appear in Sony EyeToy™ objects on the lots.

Story Mode

In story mode, player one controls the primary Sim throughout the game, and player two controls an additional controllable Sim, who moves from lot to lot with the primary Sim.

Functionally, player two is playing the primary Sim's roommate. If player one wants the primary Sim to get married, he or she can either marry player two's Sim (converting that Sim from roommate to spouse) or marry any NPC Sim. In the latter case, player two's Sim departs the lot, and player two thereafter controls the new spouse.

note Second players can join Story mode games already in progress by plugging in a second controller, loading a saved game, and initiating a two-player game. They then create their own Sim and join the primary Sim wherever the game was saved.

The secondary Sim has no Gold or Platinum Wants but can switch to any controllable resident Sim on a lot.

Neither player may switch control to a Sim being controlled by the other player. If, therefore, there's only one controllable resident on the lot, the player not directing that Sim is limited to his or her own Sim.

Freeplay Mode

In Freeplay mode, either player can control any household Sim that the other player isn't currently directing.

When entering an existing lot, player two initially takes control of a random Sim. If there's only one Sim in the household, it can't be played as a two-player game unless the single-Sim family is moved out and a new one with two or more Sims is created.

Chapter 2
Creating Your Sim

Birth is the first step in all new Sims' lives. What kind of people they are, however, depends heavily on the choices you make at your Sims' inception. The decisions you and your Sims make later matter too, but most of what comes is shaped by how a Sim is constructed.

This section looks at how a Sim is built in Create-a-Sim, including the steps, the considerations, and the implications of every choice you're asked to make. Turn your mind, therefore, to your new creation's appearance, Aspiration, personality, interests, and all the other attributes that define a Sim.

Sim Generation

We are all an assembly of bits and pieces of those who came before us, and their genetic material, traits, and features combine to form our outward appearance. This is why the first step in creating any Sim is to generate his or her forebears and then, in turn, combine these ancestors into the Sim you control.

> **note** Each gender features a basic, default Sim that you are welcome to use instead of generating a new Sim. You may, of course, adorn these Sims how you like, tune their personalities, etc. in the screens to come.

Those who came before make a Sim (initially) who she is.

Choose which gender Sim you want to use and start the generation process. First, your Sim's four grandparents are randomly selected. Second, these Sims' genetic traits are combined to create your Sim's parents. Finally, these last two Sims are mated to form your new Sim.

> **note** Of course, if you don't like the result, generate new Sims until you're satisfied.

When decades of history and genetic intermingling have been simulated in but a few seconds, the result is a unique Sim that's all your own.

Create-a-Sim

The next phase of the process is Create-a-Sim, where you change and tune your Sim's:

◆ Bodily Features
◆ Fashion
◆ Aspiration
◆ Personality
◆ Name

Body

Though genetics defined what your Sim initially looks like, you can alter many of these attributes in the Body section of Create-a-Sim.

Your Sim's body is shaped here.

Skin Tone

Choose from among 11 skin tones, including green alien skin.

Body Type

Your Sim may take shape as thin, medium, or stout.

Morph Body

Choose different body features and move the sliders to adjust.

The thickness and shapeliness of your Sim's legs, arms, and torso can be adjusted by shifting the morphing slider.

Morph Head

Head morphing can change your Sim's whole look.

The narrowness of the skull, thickness of the jaw, and the shape of the eyes, nose, and mouth can also be adjusted with a slider.

Hair

The style and color of your Sim's hair can be adjusted by choosing from all unlocked hairstyles.

note If a hairstyle has a closed lock icon on it, you can't use it until you unlock it in Story mode. This also applies to locked facial hair and tattoos.
Hairstyles are unlocked by building relationships with certain Story mode resident Sims to 100.

Pick from all unlocked hairstyles.

Once a hairstyle is chosen, you may specify its color and apply any accessory sets (like headbands, propped sunglasses, etc.) designated for that style.

Facial Hair (Male Only)

Men can select facial hair.

As with hair, facial hair can be chosen from all unlocked styles. The color of the facial hair automatically matches the hair color you selected.

Tattoos

Tattoos can be applied to a variety of body parts.

With your Sim considerably stripped to his or her undies, you can apply tattoos to the arms, torso, or legs.

Fashion

Fashion categories correspond to different parts of your Sim's body.

What your Sim wears is as important as the form from which the clothes hang. As such, fashion choices abound. Start by selecting which part of the body you want to adorn.

note Fashion items are unlocked in Story mode by building relationships with resident Sims to 100 relationship points or reaching certain levels in each career track. Only when relationships with every Sim have been maxed to 100 and every career track is conquered is every fashion option available.

Fashion Item Counts by Sim Gender

CATEGORY	MALE	FEMALE	CATEGORY	MALE	FEMALE
Hats	21	21	Pants/Skirts	17	18
Glasses	21	21	Shoes	23	21
Undershirts	6	13	Arm	13	17
Overshirts	18	22	Waist	10	10
Jackets	20	20	Jewelry	26	31

> **note** Many items are unisex, so there's some overlap in the counts between men and women.

Head

On your Sim's head, you can add hats or glasses.

Hats come in many shapes, sizes, and colors.

Each selected hat can be adjusted for material (to change pattern and/or color) and style (how it's worn). For example, a baseball cap can come in a variety of colors and shapes and can be worn forward, backward, sideways, etc.

Glasses can be changed in color only.

Tops

Tops come in three kinds.

- Undershirts
- Overshirts
- Jackets

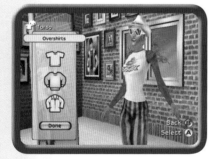

Choosing tops in each category creates the layered look.

Your Sim can wear one shirt of each type or any combination of the types. There's no requirement to wear all three. The different kinds simply allow for a more flexible "layered" look that is the key to great fashion.

Adjusting sleeve length is very important in achieving the right layering.

Depending on the type, each kind of top can be adjusted in its material (color and pattern), sleeve (length and style), torso (whether a jacket is worn open or closed), and collar (worn up or down).

Bottoms and Shoes

The lower half of your Sim's body is covered by pants/skirt (depending on gender) and shoes.

You can judge a Sim by the shoes she wears.

Pants and skirts are adjustable for material (color and pattern) and style (length or style of wear).

Accessories

Accessories go on the wrists, around the waist, and on the head.

Accessories include adornments to the arm and waist and jewelry (including neckties, scarves, and piercings) for various body parts. All accessories can be modified for materials (color and design), and arm accessories can be adjusted for style (on which arm they're worn).

Aspiration

Sims are so much more than just the sum of their physical and psychological needs. Any Sim sociologist would tell you (it isn't a career track yet, but you never know) that what really makes life worth living for Sims is getting what they *want*. Conversely, what makes life so treacherous is realizing their deepest *fears*.

Your Sim's Aspiration is one of your most crucial choices.

And what Sims want (and what they fear) is pretty rich and complex. Much of it is a matter of personality, but most is in some way directed by one overarching factor, their life's goal or Aspiration.

Game Impact

Satisfying your Sims' Wants, preventing realization of their Fears, and fulfilling their Aspirations significantly affects many aspects of *The Sims™ 2*.

◆ Affects which Green Wants and Fears your Sim sees in the Wants and Fears panel.

◆ Earns Aspiration points that unlock a long and illustrious list of locked objects.

◆ Modifies the speed of Need satisfaction.

◆ Slows decay of Needs, allowing your Sim to go longer between meals, potty breaks, sleep, etc.

◆ Dictates which final Platinum Want your Sim receives in the final Story mode lot (Biodome).

The crux of the Aspiration challenge is to combine meeting your Sim's Needs and climbing up the career and earning ladder while satisfying specific Wants and avoiding Fears. This, in turn, makes meeting the Sim's Needs and career advancement easier, which facilitates satisfying Wants, and so on.

note If a different approach appeals to you, you can make it your mission to visit every horrible Fear upon your Sims to make them all jagged wrecks on the rocky shores of life. It's your call.

Wants and Fears

A Want is an experience the Sim sees as positive and desirable. A Fear is an experience the Sim sees as negative and undesirable. An experience that's a Want for one Sim can be a Fear for another.

What Sims want and fear tells you a lot about them.

At any given moment, every Sim may have dozens of Wants and Fears, but the Wants and Fears panel only shows the top four Wants and the top three Fears. The displayed Wants and Fears are the only ones that matter for Aspiration scoring.

Wants can be as simple as the desire to cook food or buy a TV or talk to another Sim, or be as complex as a quest to completely master a skill or get very physical with several Sims.

Fears can be just as simple or just as remote. They can even be unavoidable or just seem so. Sims can fear being rejected for a social interaction, losing a job, or suffering a fire.

The goal is to do everything in your power to help your Sim get many of the displayed Wants and avoid the displayed Fears. The more difficult the Want/Fear, the longer or more work it takes and the more points at stake.

Want Types

There are three kinds of Wants, each designated by a color.

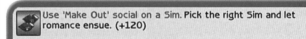

Green Wants are non-goal Wants that appear in both Story and Freeplay mode.

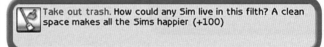

Gold Wants are goals your Sim must satisfy in Story mode.

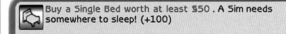

Platinum Wants are the final goals in each lot in Story mode. Satisfying them unlocks the next lot.

◆ Gold: These represent game tasks that must be performed to move on to the next game task. Not all Sims have Gold Wants—only your Story mode primary Sim and designated resident Sims whose Gold Wants are either part of your Sim's Help Gold Want (see following) or are required to unlock bonus lots.

◆ Platinum (white): This is the final game task Want on a lot after all the primary Sim's Gold Wants have been satisfied. Once it's achieved, the next Story mode lot is unlocked. Completing the very last Platinum Want in the game unlocks and plays a secret reward movie—a blooper reel featuring the characters from the game.

◆ Green: These nonessential Wants are worth Aspiration points, like Gold and Platinum. The harder these Wants are to achieve, the more points they're worth. Generally, Green Wants are desires common to all Sims, but a Sim's personality and Aspiration affect which Wants are the highest priority. For example, a Creativity Sim may want to paint a "great painting" while a Wealth Sim would more desperately desire to get a job promotion. Green Wants can change without being satisfied when the Wants and Fears panel is refreshed (see "Refreshing" later).

Fears

Fears are all colored red and are, for the most part, pitfalls to avoid in your quest to maintain a high Aspiration score and unlock Buy Catalog objects.

Fears must be avoided, but that can be difficult when they're connected to one of your Sim's Wants.

Fears, like Green Wants, are chosen based on their priority to your specific Sim (generally based on personality and Aspiration).

Sometimes, however, a Fear arises that's connected to a Gold or Platinum Want. Such a Fear can never be eliminated by

a refreshing of the Wants and Fears panel and only goes away when the Gold or Platinum Want to which it's tied is fulfilled.

Sample Wants and Fears Categories

Wants and Fears come in several general categories.

◆ Socials and Relationships: These pertain to the desire to do a specific social interaction on or achieve a certain relationship level with any Sim or a specific Sim. Fears revolve around being rejected for socials, losing relationships, and the death of Sims with high relationships.

◆ Career: These are Wants regarding job promotions, acquisition of skill points, earning money, or going to work. Fears center on getting fired, demoted, or missing work.

◆ Build/Buy: Sims want to purchase a general class of object or a specific object or change the structure of a lot.

◆ Sightseeing: Sims may want to travel to another lot just for fun. Alternatively, Sims may have a Gold Want to visit a new lot immediately after unlocking the next lot in the chain.

◆ Food Creation: Sims may want to cook general or specific meals or prepare meals with certain effects and serve these meals to others.

◆ Help: When a Sim wants to help another Sim, this is actually your cue to switch control to another resident Sim and help satisfy his or her Gold Wants. Finishing all of a resident Sim's Gold Wants satisfies the primary Sim's Help Want and allows you to move on to the next Gold or Platinum Want in the sequence.

How Displayed Wants and Fears Are Chosen

At any given moment, your Sim probably has more than four Wants and more than three Fears, but only the most important appear in the Wants and Fears panel. These are the only ones that are visible and can score Aspiration points.

Gold and Platinum Wants appear in Story mode by virtue of what lot the Sim is on and which goals have already been completed. They have *nothing* to do with your individual Sim. These remain in the Wants and Fears panel indefinitely until satisfied and can't be changed by a refreshing of the panel.

Your Sims' array of Wants and Fears reflects much about them and their current situation.

When your Sim awakens, his or her Wants and Fears scramble to reflect any life changes.

Green Wants and almost all Fears, on the other hand, are more dynamic and personal to your Sim and his or her current situation. At any given moment, there are dozens of things your Sim could potentially want or fear, but only the four highest-ranking Wants and three strongest Fears can appear in the panel. Which ones are ranked the highest can be affected by three factors.

◆ Current Circumstances: Relationships, skill levels, etc. can trigger Wants in your Sims. For instance, having a very strong Crush relationship with a Sim may make your Sim want to take that relationship up to Lover status.

◆ Personality: Your Sim's specific personality can change which potential Wants and Fears are most pressing. A very Neat Sim has an increased desire to clean up messes while a very Sloppy Sim assigns such concerns a very low priority. Active Sims raise the appeal of physical fun activities while Lazy Sims give higher priority to sedentary activities.

◆ Aspiration: Which Aspiration your Sim strives toward also aids in selecting your Sim's strongest Wants and Fears. Romance Sims give the top positions to wants relating to amore while Knowledge Sims fill their Wants and Fears panel with various desires for more skills and cerebral experiences.

Each of these factors contributes to how important a Want or Fear is to your specific Sim and affects how it's ranked. Whenever the Wants and Fears panel is refreshed (see following), the currently top ranked Wants and Fears are selected to fill all available slots (slots not occupied by Gold or Platinum Wants or any Fears tied to them).

Refreshing Wants and Fears

Wants and Fears are constantly and invisibly changing in their ranking, based on circumstances, but you don't see all these fluctuations in the Wants and Fears panel. It only changes when it's refreshed.

When the panel refreshes, it replaces not only the satisfied Wants and Fears but any others that no longer rank in the top available positions. Wants and Fears that have dropped out of the top spots are replaced with whichever Wants and Fears are at that moment the most important.

note Wants and Fears while your Sim is a ghost obey different rules than those explained here. This is covered in the "Death" section.

The Wants and Fears panel refreshes only when certain triggers occur. Fortunately, one of these triggers is completely within your control.

◆ Your Sim wakes from sleep.
◆ A Want or Fear (of any kind) is fulfilled.
◆ All Platinum Wants are fulfilled.
◆ You direct your Sim to use the telephone Services menu to "Call Therapist."

note Wants and Fears don't refresh when you load a saved game. You find everything exactly the way it was when you last left the game.

Call Therapist

At any moment you desire, you can refresh your Sim's Wants and Fears panel by using the telephone to "Call Therapist." Doing so forces new Wants and Fears to replace any that are outdated or have been outranked by other Wants and Fears.

Calling the Sim Therapist instantly refreshes Wants and Fears.

If nothing has really changed since the last refresh, the call to the Therapist results in the same set of Wants and Fears.

note Gold/Platinum Wants and the Fears tied to them are unaffected by a call to the Therapist.

Satisfying Wants and Realizing Fears

Wants and Fears are fulfilled in several ways. The satisfaction of a Want or realization of a Fear can arise from a random occurrence, a specific interaction, a sequence of actions that lead to a more complex result, or just about anything else that occurs in the game.

Full descriptions of Wants and Fears appear in the "Goals: Wants and Fears panel" in the Pause menu.

Be sure to read the description of a Want or Fear closely to understand precisely what conditions will fulfill it. If it's a Want, make those conditions happen. If it's a Fear, do everything in your power to make sure those things don't occur.

note Sims never autonomously act to fulfill their Wants and Fears. They may do things that, by chance, end up doing so, but they never choose their actions based on what's in the Wants and Fears panel.

Aspiration Score, Meter, and Points

All playable Sims have constantly changing Aspiration scores that represent how many Wants they've recently fulfilled and Fears they've avoided.

This score is shown in the Aspiration meter (displayed alongside the Wants and Fears panel). The meter's height and color indicate the Sim's current level of Aspiration success.

- Red: Very low negative Aspiration score
- Green 1: Positive but low Aspiration score
- Green 2: Very good positive Aspiration score
- Platinum: Excellent Aspiration score

The Aspiration meter appears on the left side of the screen when the Wants and Fears panel is visible.

Aspiration Score Effects

Each level of Aspiration score on the meter affects two aspects of gameplay.

- Rate of Need decay
- Rate at which Needs are satisfied

Effect of Aspiration Level on Gameplay

Asp. Level	Need Decay	Need Satisfaction
Red	Normal	15% slower
Green	Normal	Normal
Gold	15% slower	15% greater
Platinum	25% slower	25% greater

Changing Aspiration Score

Aspiration score is raised and lowered by two things.

note You don't see these values in the game, but Aspiration score ranges from -100 to 900. Therefore, a Want worth 100 points raises Aspiration score by 10 percent.
Aspiration levels correspond to this scale:
- Red: -100–-1
- Green 1: 1–500
- Green 2: 501–800
- Platinum: 801–900

Knowing these values will give you a sense of proportion when judging how important a Want or Fear is.

Realization of Wants and Fears

Every Want and every Fear carries a point value that is added to or subtracted from Aspiration score if the Want or Fear comes to pass. This value is also added to or subtracted from your accumulated Aspiration points (see following).

Aspiration Decay

Aspiration score is high now, but if no more Wants are satisfied for a while, it decays back to zero.

Every hour, Aspiration score drops by 12.5 points (2.5 percent) until it reaches 0 (the line between red and green levels). Therefore, a Sim with a full Aspiration meter is, if no more Wants or Fears are realized, reduced back to zero in 36 game hours. Decay *does not* affect accumulated Aspiration points, only the Aspiration meter.

Accumulated Aspiration Points

Separate but related to the Aspiration meter is your accumulated Aspiration points. This number controls the unlocking of all the Buy Catalog's locked objects. When you accumulate the required points for an object, it becomes available for purchase in both Story and Freeplay mode.

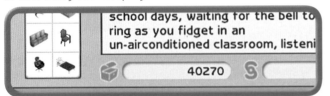

Accumulated Aspiration points can be viewed in the Buy Catalog.

This count, like Aspiration score, is raised and lowered by points assigned to satisfied Wants and realized Fears, but the similarity ends there.

Unlike the Aspiration meter, the count in accumulated Aspiration points does not decay over time. Once points are earned, the only way to lose them is to realize a Fear.

Also, points in the Aspiration meter affect only the individual Sim to whom the meter belongs. Accumulated Aspiration points, on the other hand, are (like family funds) a common pool for all controllable Sims on a lot. Any time any controllable Sim (even one you're not currently playing) satisfies a Want or realizes a Fear, this count is changed to reflect it.

This commonality makes it deeply in your interest to make sure all controllable Sims on the lot are getting what they want and avoiding what they fear.

> **note** Once the number of points needed to unlock an object is amassed, the object is unlocked for good. Dropping below the object's unlock score due to Fear deductions does not relock it.

The Five Aspirations

Sims can aspire to five goals.

- Creativity
- Popularity
- Wealth
- Romance
- Knowledge

Creativity

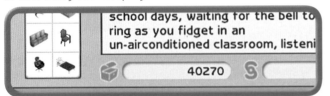

- Preferred Careers: Artist, Fashion
- Skill Bent: Creativity, Cooking
- Sample Wants: Make Food, Give Food, Create Group Meal, Change Clothes, Paint a Picture

- Sample Fears: Make Food with Nauseous Effect, Vomit, Be Mocked
- Final Platinum Want: Make a Meal with a Special Effect

A Creativity Aspiration Sim wants to live the inspired life—painting beautiful paintings, cooking powerful food, and building Creativity skill.

Buy this type of Sim easels, musical instruments, and harvesting objects.

Creativity Sims are happiest cooking and harvesting food.

Personality for Creativity Sims should be very heavy on Playful since it impacts how quickly they develop Creativity skill.

Wealth

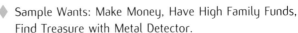

- Preferred Careers: Business, Athletics, Crime, and Medicine
- Skill Bent: Only whatever needed for career
- Sample Wants: Make Money, Have High Family Funds, Find Treasure with Metal Detector.
- Sample Fears: Get Fired, Have Object Stolen, Break an Object
- Final Platinum Want: Get Family Funds to §30,000

Wealth Sims are all about the Simoleons. Anything that doesn't involve the acquisition of money or stuff isn't really on their radar.

Going to work (and buying stuff) are what Wealth Sims are all about.

Career is more important for this Aspiration than any other; Wealth Sims are the only Sims who won't sacrifice career success for other Wants.

Personality for Wealth Sims should be geared toward career. They should be very Sloppy (unless Medicine is their field) because personality points can be better used elsewhere. For the creation of valuable paintings and novels, Wealth Sims should always have high Playful/Serious to maximize their Creativity. Creativity can do double duty if you limit your Wealth Sims to the Crime and Business fields that also require this skill. Wealth Sims can, but probably shouldn't, be Lazy. Lazy Sims want to quit their job when their Mood is bad, and this would be damaging to a Wealth Sim.

Knowledge

◆ Preferred Careers: Science, Medicine

◆ Skill Bent: All

◆ Sample Wants: Master a Skill, Find a Comet, Be Abducted by Aliens, Read a Book

◆ Sample Fears: Be Teased, Be Fired

◆ Final Platinum Want: Master All Skills

The Knowledge Sim wants experiences that involve learning, even if the lessons are some of life's darker ones.

Skill building is a major preoccupation of Knowledge Sims, and they get their best Aspiration scoring from maxing out several, and eventually all, their skills.

Knowledge Sims also want to experience the truly bizarre. They hanker to see the ghosts of Sims and be abducted by aliens (several times if possible).

Keep peering through the expensive telescope, and maybe the Knowledge Sim will get her dearest wish. Hello aliens.

When they have a low Mood, Knowledge Sims want to buy items that feed their thirst for knowledge—bookcases and telescopes.

Knowledge Sims are attracted to the Medicine and Science professions but want to quit or stay home from work to pursue their general love of learning. Their desire for all skills means they learn three skills mostly by doing: Cooking, Cleaning, and Mechanical. It helps (for Cleaning at least) if they're very Neat.

A good Personality profile for Knowledge Sims is 10 Neat/Sloppy, 10 or 0 in Playful/Serious, 5 in Nice/Grouchy, and (if Playful/Serious is 0) 10 in Outgoing/Shy or Active/Lazy. This gives them accelerated learning in three skills.

Popularity

◆ Preferred Careers: Politics, Military, and Athletics

◆ Skill Bent: Charisma

◆ General Wants: Make a Friend, Make a Best Friend, Make Multiple Friends

◆ General Fears: Lose a Friend, Make an Enemy, Have Socials Rejected

◆ Final Platinum Want: Have 20 Friends

Popularity Sims crave companionship and collect friends like trading cards.

Popularity Sims want notoriety and to be liked. Their Wants/Fears, therefore, revolve around making and keeping as many best friends as possible and throwing successful parties.

Their career ambitions fit their desire for fame. Politics, Military, and Athletics careers meet this need.

Popularity Sims already spend much of their time making friends, so having enough for a career is no extra work.

Popularity Sims want to get the party started and keep it going.

Personality traits for Popularity Sims should center on those that help them make friends, develop Charisma, and succeed in one of the Aspiration's favored careers. They should certainly have 10 Outgoing/Shy and probably 10 Nice/Grouchy. Beyond that, it depends on career choice. If they stay at home, a high Neat/Sloppy score is helpful.

Romance

- Preferred Careers: Fashion, Art
- Skill Bent: Creativity, Charisma
- Sample Wants: Make a Lover, Get a New Crush, Make Multiple Lovers, Have WooHoo with Multiple Sims
- Sample Fears: Be Rejected for WooHoo, Lose a Lover, Make an Enemy
- Final Platinum Want: WooHoo with Five Sims

Romance Sims are all about romantic conquest and want nothing to do with anything smacking of commitment. Their biggest desires involve experiencing love and making WooHoo with as many Sims as possible. They're even happier if they can maintain more than one love at once.

Romance Sims like to keep things hot, heavy, and busy.

Their Fears involve being rejected in romantic interactions. They save their greatest Fears, however, for the conventions of family life. They deeply fear marriage. If you force them into it, their Aspiration score may drop irretrievably low. To make matters worse, once married, they eventually have a powerful desire to meet someone new.

> **note** Logistically, the hardest part of playing a Romance Sim is avoiding jealousy. Doing this means going to great lengths to keep lovers from being in the same room or even on the same lot. The more intricate a Romance Sim's web of paramours becomes, the harder it is to fulfill his or her greatest Wants.

Jealousy is a major pitfall for the Romance Sim.

Romance Sims don't mind work, but the only *specific* career they desire is the Fashion career. They're comfortable being jobless but fear the commitments that would allow them to live the unemployed life. Popularity Sims make good roommates for them, however, because of their different but similarly met goals. A Popularity Sim wants friends while a Romance Sim wants lovers. Because these two relationships aren't incompatible and don't lead to jealousy, one third-party Sim can satisfy the Wants of both a Romance and a Popularity Sim in one visit. He or she can be the Romance Sim's lover and the Popularity Sim's friend without causing any static.

Personality-wise, a Romance Sim should be very high in the traits that facilitate Romance: Outgoing and Nice.

Personality

The very core of your Sims' being is their personality. It drives countless things they do in their daily life. Here are but a few of the things personality can affect.

Skill Acquisition Speed

Some skills are learned more quickly (up to twice as fast) by Sims with certain personality traits. The more points a Sim has in a trait, the less time it takes to gain a point in that skill.

The time it takes to gain skill points can be cut significantly if your Sim has the right personality.

Most skills have an aligned personality trait that makes the skill easier to learn.

- Body: Active
- Charisma: Outgoing
- Cleaning: Neat
- Cooking: None
- Creativity: Playful
- Logic: Serious
- Mechanical: None

Only a Sim of the specified personality extreme sees any difference in skill speed. Sims with Active/Lazy of 0–5, for example, increase Body skill at the normal rate while Sims of Active/Lazy 6–10 do it faster (increasing how Active they are). Among Active Sims, the increase is gradual. A 6 gets a slight increase while a 10 works at double the normal rate.

Need Decay Rate

Some personality traits alter the rate at which Needs decay. In other words, they shorten or lengthen how long a Sim can go without satisfying a specific Need.

- Hunger: Active decays faster; Lazy decays slower
- Bladder: None
- Energy: Lazy decays faster; Active decays slower
- Hygiene: Sloppy decays faster; Neat decays slower
- Fun: Playful decays faster; Serious decays slower
- Social: Outgoing decays faster; Shy decays slower
- Comfort: Lazy decays faster; Active decays slower

In each case, a neutral Sim (5 points) decays at the standard rate, while those above and below decay faster or slower. The farther from neutral, the greater the effect.

Career Affinities

Some personality traits make a Sim more likely to succeed in certain careers. Each career focuses on three skills that must be developed for the Sim to advance. Sims whose personality allows them to build those skills more easily advance more quickly in any career that requires the skill.

A Sim with extreme scores in one or more personality traits has an easier time in these careers:

- Artist: Outgoing, Playful
- Athletics: Active, Outgoing
- Business: Serious or Playful, Outgoing
- Crime: Active, Serious, Outgoing
- Fashion: Outgoing, Playful
- Law: Serious, Active, Neat
- Medicine: Serious, Neat
- Military: Active, Serious, Neat
- Politics: Serious or Playful, Outgoing
- Science: Serious, Neat

note Some careers benefit from conflicting traits (for example, Politics has both Serious and Playful). Obviously, a Sim may only be one or the other, so any score other than neutral provides some advantage in the career.

Other Effects

Personality impacts many parts of Sim life.

Sloppy Sims are, well, sloppy.

- Whether they accept certain social interactions
- What they do when left to their own devices
- Whether they clean up after themselves or others
- Whether special object interactions are available
- Whether they get in a hot tub in the buff
- Which Sims they get along with and which they clash with
- How successful they are at prank calls
- How much they enjoy music when dancing
- What they like to watch on TV
- Which Aspiration best suits them
- Which Fears they harbor, such as fire, Bladder failure, etc.

Personality Traits

A Sim's personality is the sum of five traits. These traits are expressed in terms of their extremes.

- Neat/Sloppy
- Outgoing/Shy
- Active/Lazy
- Playful/Serious
- Nice/Grouchy

Each trait has 10 settings—0 represents the "negative" extreme, and 10 represents the "positive." The more toward one extreme or the other Sims lean, the more often they autonomously behave in accordance with that extreme. For example, a Sim with Nice/Grouchy of 8 exhibits sweet and helpful behavior toward other Sims, Nice/Grouchy of 5 is neutral, and Nice/Grouchy of 2 is very surly indeed. The higher or lower the number, the more frequently these behaviors occur.

Personality is more than a Sim's autonomous mindset. It also affects which interactions a user-directed Sim will accept.

> **note** The term "negative" is a bit of a misnomer regarding personality traits. Being Serious, for example, merely means your Sim tends toward reading, finds gregarious Sims insufferable, and learns Logic very quickly. A Serious Sim can make friends and find love too, although perhaps not with extremely Playful Sims.

Assigning personality points, however, requires choices. Every Sim has only 25 Personality points that can be distributed between these five traits. Unless you construct a perfectly balanced Sim with five points in each trait, you must put one trait in the negative to get another in the positive.

In the game, a playable Sim's personality and zodiac sign can be viewed in the Careers, Skills & Personality panel of the Pause menu.

Strategically, this means that you must make decisions about what you want your Sim to be. If you want a social butterfly with Outgoing 10, you may have to make your Sim a total slob or extremely slothful. Understanding the consequences of these choices is what this section is all about.

Neat/Sloppy

- Modify Need Decay: Hygiene (Neat: Slower/Sloppy: Faster)
- Speeds Skill: Cleaning (Neat)
- Career Tilt (Neat): Medicine, Science, Law, Military

Neat Sims (6–10) pick up after themselves and others. Sloppy Sims (0–4) rarely put anything away, make messes whenever possible, and never clean up things left by others.

Neat Sims LOVE to clean.

Neutral Sims (5) show weak tendencies toward both extremes.

- Hygiene decays much more quickly for Sloppy Sims than for Neat ones, meaning they require more showers/baths to keep their Mood high.
- Neat Sims develop Cleaning skill much more quickly than Sloppy ones. As such, much of the time Neat Sims "waste" cleaning things is offset by their impressive speed at doing it, the Fun they receive, and the further acquisition of skill (cleaning things actually bestows Cleaning skill).
- Because of their acumen at Cleaning skill, Neat Sims advance faster in Law, Medicine, Military, and Science careers.
- The Sloppier Sims are, the faster they *create* messes. For example, a very Sloppy Sim can foul a shower with a few visits while a Neat Sim's shower doesn't need cleaning for several uses. They're also messier in the kitchen.
- Neat Sims get Fun from cleaning while Sloppy Sims lose Fun when forced to tidy.
- Sloppy Sims gobble their food, causing Neat Sims nearby to react.

Outgoing/Shy

- Modify Need Decay: Social (Outgoing: Faster/Shy: Slower)
- Speeds Skill: Charisma (Outgoing)
- Career Tilt (Outgoing): Artist, Business, Crime Politics, Fashion, Athletics

Outgoing Sims are the life of the party.

Outgoing Sims (6–10) thrive on social interaction; the more other Sims around the better. Shy Sims don't like to attract attention to themselves and are visibly uncomfortable with it, even if they actually like the interest. Because, on the other hand, Shy Sims (0–4) require less social interaction, they can spend more time in seclusion, working on skills or fulfilling their Aspirations. Neutral Outgoing/Shy Sims (5) have neither the benefits nor drawbacks of either extreme, which is not a desirable setting for any purpose.

- Outgoing Sims crave social interaction, so their Social motive decays at an accelerated rate. Shy Sims need less contact, and their Social need decays at a slower rate.

◆ If a high Outgoing Sim gets into a hot tub, he or she enters in the pixilated buff.

Active/Lazy

◆ Modify Need Decay: Hunger (Active: Faster/Lazy: Slower), Energy (Lazy: Faster/Active: Slower), Comfort (Lazy: Faster/Active: Slower)
◆ Speeds Skill: Body (Active)
◆ Career Tilt (Active): Crime, Athletics, Law, Military

Active Sims (6–10) have the undeniable benefit of needing less sleep and less time sitting, but they require a lot more visits to the feed bag. For the more physical professions, Active Sims build Body skill at a higher rate.

Neutral Sims (5) show weak tendencies toward both extremes.

Active Sims gravitate to physical pursuits.

Lazy Sims (0–4) actually require less food than others but must sit, nap, and sleep more frequently.

◆ There's a random chance that Lazy Sims will turn off their alarm clock, go back to sleep, and miss work.
◆ Active Sims tend toward Fun activities and objects that are more physical while Lazy Sims tend toward the sedentary.
◆ Lazy Sims take longer to get out of bed, making their prework routine take even longer.

Playful/Serious

◆ Modify Need Decay: Fun (Playful: Faster/Serious: Slower)
◆ Speeds Skill: Creativity (Playful), Logic (Serious)
◆ Career Tilt (Serious): Science, Medicine, Law, Business, Politics, Crime, Military
◆ Career Tilt (Playful): Crime, Business, Politics, Artist, Fashion

Playful Sims (6–10) can find Fun in the oddest places where no other Sim can, but they need a heck of a lot more of it than their Serious counterparts. They are extremely well suited for creative endeavors.

Neutral Sims (5) show weak tendencies toward both extremes.

Serious Sims (0–4) can go longer between Fun activities and are naturally attracted to quieter, more cerebral endeavors (reading, playing chess, etc.). Serious is the only "negative" trait that speeds the learning of a skill; Serious Sims are very adept at Logic.

◆ Fun decays faster for Playful. Serious Sims decay more slowly, requiring only occasional Fun interactions.

Nice/Grouchy

◆ Modify Need Decay: None
◆ Speeds Skill: None
◆ Career Tilt: None

Nice Sims (6–10) are very considerate toward the feelings of others, autonomously engaging in social interactions that benefit both parties.

Grouchy Sims (0–4), on the other hand, bring down almost any relationship if left to their own devices. Sometimes Grouchy Sims even derive a positive benefit (Social, Relationship, or Fun) from being mean to others.

Generally, socializing is easier for Nice Sims because they can do stronger interactions earlier in relationships.

Nice/Grouchy is also a major factor in the acceptance of many social interactions. Which way a Sim tilts can change the difficulty of relationship building, but not fatally so.

Strategically, Nice/Grouchy is not a factor in either skills or career, so it's a theoretically expendable trait. That doesn't, however, mean that it should be set to zero; Grouchy Sims can do a lot of damage to hard-won relationships. Unless a surly Sim is what you want, never set Nice/Grouchy below 5.

◆ Grouchy Sims watching other Sims compete are more likely to taunt the contestants while Nice Sims cheer.
◆ Grouchy Sims autonomously cheat at slot machines.

Zodiac Signs

Every Sim sports one of the 12 astrological signs. Each star sign represents a set of personality settings that approximates the real-world astrological character of the sign.

note A Sim's zodiac sign can be set in Create-a-Sim and viewed in the game in the Personality tab of the Career, Skills, & Personality screen (next to the Personality bars).

As you change each personality trait, the Sim's sign changes to fit an astrological profile. It also works the other way—change the sign, and all personality traits change to the following settings.

Personality Presets by Zodiac Sign

ZODIAC SIGN	NEAT	OUTGOING	ACTIVE	PLAYFUL	NICE
Aries	5	8	6	3	3
Taurus	5	5	3	8	4
Gemini	4	7	8	3	3
Cancer	6	3	6	4	6
Leo	4	10	4	4	3
Virgo	9	2	6	3	5
Libra	2	8	2	6	7
Scorpio	6	5	8	3	3
Sagittarius	2	3	9	7	4
Capricorn	7	4	1	8	5
Aquarius	4	4	4	7	6
Pisces	5	3	7	3	7

These values are the default for each sign, but they aren't precise. You can tweak them up to a point without changing the sign. Extreme changes eventually cause the sign to shift.

Sims may befriend and fall in love with anyone, but due to inherent differences in personality types, some combinations are harder or easier than others. Keep the following affinities/aversions in mind to discover who's a more likely friend and who poses an interesting challenge.

Zodiac Sign Compatibility

ZODIAC SIGN	ATTRACTED TO	REPELLED BY
Aries	Gemini/Taurus	Cancer/Libra
Taurus	Aries/Libra	Virgo/Cancer
Gemini	Pisces/Virgo	Capricorn/Aries
Cancer	Taurus/Scorpio	Gemini/Aries
Leo	Sagittarius/Cancer	Capricorn/Gemini
Virgo	Aquarius/Sagittarius	Leo/Taurus
Libra	Virgo/Cancer	Pieces/Scorpio
Scorpio	Pieces/Leo	Libra/Aquarius
Sagittarius	Pisces/Capricorn	Libra/Scorpio
Capricorn	Aquarius/Taurus	Leo/Gemini
Aquarius	Capricorn/Sagittarius	Scorpio/Virgo
Pisces	Scorpio/Gemini	Leo/Aries

Interests

Upon a Sim's creation, interest points are randomly distributed among the 18 interests. An interest can be assigned 0–10 points: 0 indicates no interest, 5 moderate interest, and 10 intense interest. The level in each interest guides the Sim in Talk interactions.

Sims' interests become apparent during Talk interactions. If they bring up or like a topic raised by another Sim, they flash that interest's symbol. If not, they look bored or offended.

note Unlike personality points, interest points are distributed randomly and automatically at creation or birth.

- ◆ Animals
- ◆ Crime
- ◆ Culture
- ◆ Entertainment
- ◆ Environment
- ◆ Fashion
- ◆ Food
- ◆ Health
- ◆ Money
- ◆ Paranormal
- ◆ Politics
- ◆ School
- ◆ Sci-Fi
- ◆ Sports
- ◆ Toys
- ◆ Travel
- ◆ Weather
- ◆ Work

Interest in Talk

The number of points in an interest dictates how likely the topic is to arise in a Talk initiated by your Sim. The choice of topic in a given conversation is random, but the higher an interest's level, the more likely it is to be picked.

> **note** In direct control mode, Talk interactions aren't extended by each Sim's interest in the topics. Each Sim takes one turn talking, then the other takes over. The level of interest dictates how many relationship points result.
>
> In classic control mode, Talk volleys back and forth between the Sims with level of interest dictating the chances of another round.

When your Sim's on the receiving end of a conversation, interest level in the other Sim's chosen topic determines how likely your Sim is to continue the conversation (if interest is high) or end it (if interest is low).

Using Interest Strategically

Neither your own Sims' interests or those of the various resident Sims are directly visible in the game. The resident Sims' interests are, however, specified in this guide.

Since your Sims' interests are chosen at random, it may seem as if there's no certain way to know what interests your Sims and, thus, no way to guide them to Sims they share interests with. Well, that's not exactly true.

If you observe your Sims in Talk interactions and examine the interest bubbles they use, you can determine which topics interest them and which don't. With that info in hand, you can compare these interests to those of the NPCs to see who would make the most fruitful conversation partners.

Name

Finally, give your Sim a name.

The final step is to give your Sim a name. It can be anything you like, but note that it can't be changed once the Sim is moved in.

> **tip** If you want your Sim to have a middle name or initial, make it part of the first name.

And Go

That's it. Your Sim is complete, and you have all the insight you need to be ready for how your choices will affect your Sim's ability to function in the world.

Chapter 3
Facts of Sim Life and Death

Higher callings and professional achievement are all for naught if Sims can't take care of their physical and emotional necessities. All Sims must spend time every day fulfilling their Needs, or they quickly find themselves unable to function. If, however, they can satisfy these Needs with maximum efficiency, their rise in the world becomes a speedy one.

If, on the other hand, they fail to meet their Needs, or something untoward befalls them, the afterlife awaits. Fortunately, the opportunities to see the Grim Reaper are relatively rare, and the road back to the full bloom of Sim life is an easy one. It's just possible, however, that your Sim may have a bit of fun before returning to the living.

This section discusses both Needs and the dark realm of death, along with a few other miscellaneous issues that govern how Sims live their lives.

Needs

Every Sim is driven, at the most fundamental level, by his or her common physical and psychological *Needs*. This section examines how those Needs function, how to most efficiently satisfy them, and how to enable Sims to take care of them autonomously.

Taken together, the level of a Sim's Needs dictates overall *Mood*.

Mood and Needs drive and impact several important elements of the game.

- Sims' performance at work is largely dictated by their Mood when they leave the lot.
- Mood affects the availability of social interactions.
- The acceptance of social interactions depends on Mood and Needs.
- Mood and Needs affect a Sim's willingness to build skills.
- Mood and Needs affect a Sim's willingness to use Fun objects.
- Certain special behaviors and interactions are triggered by the level of individual Needs or overall Mood.
- Many Wants and Fears arise based on Mood.
- Visitors stay only as long as they can fulfill certain Needs.
- Time management depends largely on your Sims' ability to quickly and efficiently tend to their Needs.

Needs Defined

Every Sim has eight basic Needs.

- Hunger
- Comfort
- Bladder
- Energy
- Fun
- Social
- Hygiene
- Environment

The Needs Panel

Needs are measured on a scale of -100 (fully depleted) to +100 (fully satisfied).

> **note** The numbers mentioned in this section, and others that describe the level of a Need or Mood, are not seen in the actual game, but they should provide a guide to where on the meter the numbers would be. For example, if a Need is at 0, the meter is dead center (50 percent full). If it's at -50, it's at 25 percent full. If it's at +50, it's at 75 percent full.

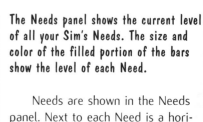

The Needs panel shows the current level of all your Sim's Needs. The size and color of the filled portion of the bars show the level of each Need.

Needs are shown in the Needs panel. Next to each Need is a horizontal bar. When a bar is filled with green, the Need is fully satisfied (+100). When it's in the middle (yellow), the Need is partially satisfied. When the bar is orange, the Need is said to be "in distress" (around -60 to -80). When the bar is all red, the Need is in "failure" (-100).

Arrows next to the bars indicate that something is pushing a Need's level either up or down. This can be due to an interaction, normal decay, or passive influence of some nearby object.

When a Need is changing, arrows appear next to the bar. If they're pointing up, the Need is being satisfied by whatever the Sim is doing. If they're pointing down, the Need is decaying. The number of triangles indicates the speed of the change. Three triangles mean a fast change, and one indicates a gradual change.

> **note** If you see Fun rising for no apparent reason, look to see if your Sim is near a stereo or TV. If so, the Sim is feeling the pull of those objects' passive influence, gaining Fun just from being near them.

Mood

Sims' overall sense of well-being is reflected in their Mood. Mood, in turn, is the sum effect of all Needs (except Energy).

Mood (without regard for any of the individual Needs) dictates which social interactions are accepted, whether a Sim looks for a job or develops skills, how well a Sim is doing at work, and whether the Sim is eligible for a job promotion.

Not all the Needs impact Mood to the same extent. The level of each Need dictates how much it affects overall Mood. If, for example, Hunger is just below fully satisfied, it affects Mood just a little. If it's in the middle, it affects Mood more, but at only a minimal level. Once Hunger gets very low, however, its effect is multiplied several times, growing stronger as the Need creeps lower.

The Mood Meter

This is the Mood meter. If it's all green, your Sim is in a super Mood. The more red there is, the worse your Sim's Mood.

Mood is represented by the Mood meter (on the Needs panel), a curved bar running along the top of the onscreen control wheel in the lower-left corner of the screen. The meter decays from right to left and fulfills from left to right. If the bar is mostly green, Mood is positive. If it's mostly red, Mood is negative.

Need Decay

All Needs (except Environment) decay over time. If left unsatisfied, they eventually drop to their lowest value (-100).

The speed of this decay dictates how often a Sim has to tend to a Need and is influenced by several factors.

◆ Personality: Many Needs are tied to certain personality traits that accelerate (if at one extreme) or slow (if at the other) decay. A Sim with 10 Active/Lazy decays Hunger the fastest, 5 is normal, and 0 is slowest.

◆ Sleep: Many Needs decay at a slower rate or not at all when a Sim is asleep. Energy and Comfort replenish during sleep.

◆ Objects and Interactions: Many objects or interactions speed the decay of certain Needs.

Distress and Failure

When Needs get very low, they enter two stages, distress and then failure.

Distress

Need distress occurs in two stages, at -60 and -80. At -60, Sims gesture about their dwindling Need and display blue thought bubbles indicating the Need that's getting low.

Sims with dwindling Needs start to signal their distress.

If a Need is below -80, Sims indicate their trouble in red thought bubbles and their general behavior. Tired Sims sag in posture, and Sims in Bladder distress pin their knees together. Either of these behaviors significantly slows Sims' speed.

Sleepy Sims walk very slowly like they're, well, extremely sleepy.

Desperate for food and low on cash? Have a seat on the couch and search the cushions. Your Sim may just find a treat. It won't help much, but every little bit counts.

> **note** Sims with low Energy, Hunger, Fun (skill only), Comfort (if not seated for the activity), or Bladder (regardless of overall Mood) automatically exit out of or refuse to enter skill or Fun objects, wake from sleep, and refuse to look for a job.
>
> Other Needs don't have this effect, though they bring down overall Mood as they decline. Low Mood causes some of the same kickouts as Energy, Hunger, Fun, Comfort, or Bladder distress.

> **note** For all the minute details on making the most satisfying food, see the "Food Creation" section.

Failure

Failure occurs when a Need reaches -100. What happens then depends largely on the specific Need.

Hunger

Hunger is the physical Need for food and drink.

Sims satisfy Hunger by eating. The more nourishing the food, the more the satisfaction a meal contains.

Depletion

Hunger depletes at a steady rate all day, though it slows when the Sim is asleep. The speed of Hunger depletion depends also on personality.

Hunger can also be depleted by social interactions. For example, a session of WooHoo can make a Sim pretty peckish.

Satisfaction

Hunger is satisfied by eating food or drinking liquid. The more satisfying a meal, the more Hunger it refills. The more Hunger is fulfilled, the fewer servings Sims Need to become full, and the less time they must spend eating.

Personality

Active Sims lose Hunger more quickly than other Sims. The more Active they are (more personality points they have in Active/Lazy), the more quickly Hunger depletes.

Mood Impact

Hunger has a low impact on Mood when it's high or even moderate. As the Need descends into negative territory, Hunger's impact on Mood grows quickly. By the time it nears failure, Hunger has more impact on Mood than any other Need.

Therefore, satisfied Sims don't give much thought at all to having a full stomach, but they care plenty when it starts to growl.

If Hunger declines too low, Sims either exit or refuse to use skill building or Fun objects, even if Mood is still positive.

Distress and Failure

When Hunger gets low, Hunger icons appear above Sims' heads.

If Sims are prevented from eating and Hunger reaches -100, they go into Need failure. In the case of Hunger, and no other Need, this means a slow and horrible death. It's OK, though. They can come back.

Comfort

Comfort is the physical Need to get off your feet and the emotional Need to feel safe, well, and cared for.

A nice, expensive chair is just the thing for flagging Comfort.

PRIMA OFFICIAL GAME GUIDE

Depletion

Comfort is steadily depleted every minute a Sim is not sitting, reclining, or lying down. Like Energy, Comfort is satisfied when the Sim is sleeping anywhere but the floor.

Passing out on the floor? That's not so comfortable.

Comfort is also decreased by doing certain activities.

- Sleeping on the floor
- Standing
- Dancing
- Being electrocuted
- Using exercise equipment

Satisfaction

Comfort is satisfied by sitting, reclining, using comfortable objects, and engaging in comforting activities.

Lounging in the hot tub brings back lost Comfort too.

- Sleeping or relaxing in bed
- Doing anything on a sofa
- Sitting or reclining in chairs
- Using a hot tub
- Taking a bath
- Using an expensive toilet
- Looking into a fireplace

note The main difference between a shower and a bath is that the bath provides Comfort in addition to Hygiene—hence the higher price of a bathtub with the identical Hygiene of a cheaper shower.

Any Comfort object or interaction has a speed of satisfaction and a cap. The more expensive an object, the more quickly it satisfies Comfort, and the higher it allows Comfort satisfaction to climb.

note Sims with desk jobs rather than more physical occupations come home with increased Comfort.

Personality

Lazy Sims lose Comfort more quickly than other Sims. The lazier they are (fewer personality points they have in Active/Lazy), the faster Comfort depletes.

Mood Impact

Like Hunger, Comfort has no exaggerated effect on Mood until it gets very low. Unlike Hunger, however, this moment comes only after Comfort drops just shy of halfway into the red zone. As it drops farther and eventually empties, however, its effects are increasingly multiplied.

At its lowest point, Comfort has its greatest influence on Mood, though it's still considerably less than extremely low Hunger.

Low Comfort can knock a Sim out of skill building if the Sim is standing for the activity.

Distress and Failure

Sims in Comfort distress signal with a comfy chair thought bubble and look generally uncomfortable (stretching, fighting back pain).

There is no failure state for Comfort; Sims just waste a lot of time telling you how uncomfortable they are. Plus, their Mood is thoroughly tanked until you allow them to sit.

Bladder

Bladder is the physical Need to use a toilet.

Depletion

Bladder decreases steadily all the time, albeit more slowly when a Sim is sleeping.

Depletion can be accelerated if a Sim eats food or drinks liquid (especially coffee and espresso).

Satisfaction

There's nothing complicated about how to satisfy the Bladder Need.

Bladder can be satisfied anywhere (though most places aren't by choice), but there's only one place that doesn't simultaneously cause a total depletion of Hygiene—a toilet. All toilets fulfill the Bladder Need at the same rate, but more expensive ones also give Comfort.

Personality

All personalities have identical Bladder motives.

Mood Impact

Bladder has no heightened effect on Mood until it gets very low. At that point, its effect becomes quickly and profoundly serious.

If Bladder declines too low, Sims either exit or refuse to use skill building or Fun objects, even if Mood is still positive.

Distress and Failure

Sims with low Bladder walk like they're "holding it."

Around the time Bladder begins to seriously affect Mood, Sims start to show their distress by displaying toilet thought balloons.

> **note** Sims "holding it" walk very slowly, making the trudge to the bathroom an arduous process that may end in a wet floor before reaching the toilet.

At -100, failure occurs, and Sims wet themselves. This completely refills the Bladder Need but also decimates the Hygiene Need. Sims who've gone through Bladder failure don't need a toilet until Bladder decays again, but they need a bath or shower.

When Bladder failure occurs, nearby Sims react and get a Disgust memory.

For some Sims (particularly if they're Shy or have the Popularity Aspiration), it's likely that Bladder failure is a Fear that brings down Aspiration score.

Energy

Energy is the basic physical Need for sleep and rest.

Depletion

Every waking moment, Sims use Energy, though the rate varies by personality.

Energy is depleted more quickly when Sims engage in physically demanding activities.

> **note** If using any objects or doing any interaction drops Sims' Energy too low, they automatically stop interacting.

Satisfaction

A bed is inarguably the best way to restore Energy.

When Sims sleep, the Energy Need is refilled at a rate defined by what they're sleeping on.

- Couch: Power naps on couches refill Energy, but at a slower rate than beds. They are also, unlike beds, capped with a maximum Energy restoration. The speed of and caps on Energy restoration generally rise with the cost of the couch.

  Another benefit is that unlike with a bed, you waste no time changing clothes when you get up.

- Bed: Beds are the primary engine for fulfilling Sims' Energy Need. They tend to fill Energy more quickly than other furniture and fill the Need to its top. The speed with which a bed restores Energy is generally tied to its cost, and the difference can be dramatic.

- The Floor or Standing: If Sims can't get to a bed or couch before their Energy Need fails, they fall asleep on the ground. Not surprisingly, the ground provides very slow Energy satisfaction. Give them a few minutes to recharge, wake them up, and get them into a real bed.

tip Spending Simoleons on a bed is a sound investment. A cheap bed provides full rest in about nine game hours, a medium bed requires seven and a half hours, and an expensive bed Needs only six hours.

tip Some Sims (particularly Active Sims and Sims with the Popularity Aspiration) have a Fear of passing out, so failing to meet their Energy Need can have the added penalty of reducing their Aspiration score.

A frothy cup of espresso is just the thing for flagging Energy, but it means a trip to the bathroom.

There is a less-obvious way to gain Energy, drinking espresso. This strong, brown brew adds a fixed amount of Energy but takes time to drink and causes Bladder to deplete.

Personality

Lazy Sims lose Energy more quickly than other Sims. The lazier they are (fewer Personality points they have in Active/Lazy), the faster Energy depletes.

Mood Impact

Energy has no effect on Sims' overall Mood. Therefore, for job performance, it doesn't matter how high Energy is when they go to work. If it's too low, however, they collapse on the sidewalk when they return home.

If Energy declines too low, Sims either exit or refuse to use skill building or Fun objects, even if Mood is still positive.

Distress and Failure

Sims in Energy distress show red thought balloons. This behavior wastes time.

When Energy reaches rock bottom, Sims instantly fall asleep on the ground or where they're standing. Passed out Sims can't be revived until they gain sufficient Energy to get to a bed (about five game minutes).

If there isn't room to collapse, Sims fall asleep standing up. After a few moments, they can be awakened with the Wake Up interaction. Take the opportunity to get them to bed.

Fun

Fun is the psychological Need for amusement and relaxation.

Depletion

Fun decays steadily while a Sim is awake. No decay occurs during sleep.

Satisfaction

Anything amusing feeds the Fun Need.

Fun is satisfied by engaging in any interaction with a Fun rating. The higher the rating, the more Fun it imparts. This rating is typically a measure both of the speed of satisfaction and the maximum to which Fun can rise.

tip You know a Fun object has a maximum limit if the meter stops filling even if the Sim is still doing the activity. Sims also declare that an object is no longer or not sufficiently Fun once they exceed or reach that maximum.

This warning means Sims will do the directed interaction but they won't get any Fun satisfaction because the object is capped lower than the current Fun level.

A very expensive Fun object, for example, gives Fun quickly all the way up to 100. Less pricey diversions might get a Sim to max Fun but do it very slowly, or they might work quickly but only raise Fun to a fixed level. And still others might offer a fixed dose of Fun but allow Sims to go back for additional doses until Fun hits maximum.

Viewing a decorative object is an easy dose of Fun—small but easy.

Fun can be had from interactions with both objects and other Sims. In the latter case, many social interactions (in addition to Relationship and Social Need benefits) also give Fun.

tip Arcade machines are super fun objects and money well spent.

Spectators can get Fun too.

Fun can also be had from watching other Sims engaged in a Fun activity.

Personality

Playful Sims lose Fun more quickly than other Sims. The more Playful they are (the more personality points in Playful/Serious), the faster Fun depletes.

note Neat Sims receive Fun from cleaning while Sloppy Sims lose Fun.

note Playful Sims (Playful/Serious more than 5) need about two hours of Fun per day while Serious Sims require only about an hour to be fully satisfied.

Mood Impact

Fun has its greatest impact on Mood when it's very high (about 50 to 100) or very low (about -50 to -100). Sims are never in a top-notch Mood unless their Fun is totally satisfied, but only truly bored Sims allow a lack of Fun to dampen their otherwise positive Mood.

Fun can, by itself, knock a Sim out of skill building if it gets too low. Less dire levels of Fun can indirectly have the same effect if they lower Mood below 0.

Distress and Failure

Sims without Fun slouch, look depressed, and show TV thought bubbles, all of which waste time. They're also likely to be in a pretty sour overall Mood.

There is no failure state for Fun; the effects of distress simply worsen.

Social

Social is the psychological Need to interact with other Sims.

No Sim is an island, so Sims must interact in some way to feed their Social Need.

tip Whenever possible, get Sims to eat, watch TV, use the hot tub, etc. together so they can feed their Social Need along with whatever else they're doing.

Depletion

Any time Sims aren't directly interacting with another Sim, Social is decaying at a steady rate.

Social is also reduced by negative social interactions. If the outcome of an interaction (mostly rejected ones but some positive too) is negative, it probably reduces Social.

Satisfaction

Social is satisfied by having positive social interactions. In most such interactions, both sides receive some increase in the Social Need.

tip If the Social Need is very low, focus social interactions on Sims with high-level relationships. The interactions that come with these relationships satisfy far more Social Need than even the best low-level interactions.

Chatting on the computer gives Sims a good boost to their Social Need when other forms of interaction are scarce.

There are more ways to interact, however, than face-to-face. Sims can talk on the phone; chat over a computer; or talk in groups at meals, on the couch, or in hot tubs.

When Sims join an activity (like talking, watching TV, etc.), that activity usually gains a Social benefit for all involved.

Personality

Outgoing Sims lose Social more quickly than other Sims. The more Outgoing they are (the more personality points they have in Outgoing/Shy), the more quickly Social depletes.

note Shy Sims Need about an hour of Social per day (on top of what they get at work) while Outgoing Sims Need about two hours of interaction.

Mood Impact

Like Fun, Social has its strongest influence on Mood when it's very high and very low. Also as with Fun, Social's baseline impact on Mood is higher than for the physical Needs. Social's "normal" effect is twice that of the other Needs. This means when all Needs are high, Social and Fun are actually the strongest determinants of Mood.

Distress and Failure

Sims in Social distress show red socializing thought bubbles. These displays waste time and reduce efficiency. Really low Social is also a serious drag on Mood.

There is no failure state for Social.

Hygiene

Hygiene is the physical Need to feel clean.

Depletion

If Sims are awake, they're gradually losing Hygiene. When they're sleeping, this rate is slowed but not stopped.

This porta-potty is not for the fastidious; it depletes Hygiene at an alarming rate.

Many activities accelerate the loss of Hygiene, especially ones involving physical exertion.

Satisfaction

Showers are the quickest way to full Hygiene.

Hygiene is satisfied by several objects, primarily showers and bathtubs. Tubs provide slower Hygiene than showers but provide simultaneous Comfort. Hot tubs have even slower Hygiene satisfaction but also provide Comfort, Fun, and Social (if there's more than one soaking Sim).

Personality

Sloppy Sims lose Hygiene faster than other Sims. The sloppier they are (less personality points in Neat/Sloppy), the faster Hygiene depletes.

Mood Impact

Hygiene doesn't begin to seriously affect Mood until it reaches -40. At this point, its impact quickly multiplies (though not as much as the other physical Needs).

Hygiene does not, by itself, knock a Sim out of skill building except to the extent that it may lower Mood below 0.

Distress and Failure

When Sims' Hygiene is in distress, they're followed by a swarm of flies, and nearby Sims react to the odor.

Whew! This Sim Needs a bath.

Low Hygiene doesn't directly affect Sims' ability to work on skills (unless it brings Mood down below medium), but it does make it difficult to interact socially. The clouds of flies are unpleasant, and the self-sniffing and scratching waste valuable time.

There is no failure state for Hygiene. Your Sim is just in a pretty bad Mood, stinks to high heaven, and is unable to interact (no Sim wants to get close enough to talk) or (if Mood is low enough) have Fun or work on skills.

Environment

Environment is the psychological need for order and cleanliness in one's surroundings. This Need is unique in both the way it works and how it influences Mood.

An untidy home makes a full good Mood impossible.

The Environment Need doesn't decay like other motives. Rather, it exists as a score in a given location that pushes the Environment Need of any nearby Sim either up or down.

Generally, Environment score is based on the quality and cleanliness of each room, though the amount of light and whether the Sim is indoors or out creates more localized effects.

note Indoors, a "room" is defined as a place enclosed by walls with access only via doors. If two spaces are connected by a gap in the wall rather than a door or archway, the two spaces together form a single "room" for Environment score purposes.

Calculating Environment Score

Environment score defines where Sims' Environment Need is set when they are in that room.

Two elements make up Environment score.

◆ The "niceness" of the room (including presence of plants and decorative objects)

◆ The presence of any messes (including trash, dirty dishes, ashes, or dead plants)

The final score is determined by subtracting messiness from niceness. Which things influence these elements provide the strategy behind Environment score.

note Environment score scales to the size of the room. Therefore, it takes more total Environment score (and money) to top out a large room than a small one.

Niceness

Niceness reflects three elements.

◆ Purchase price of objects in the room (including lights)

◆ Purchase price of flooring

◆ Purchase price of wallpaper

Nice decorations from the Buy Catalog and floor and wall coverings from the Build Catalog contribute to Environment.

Each of these elements has only a partial impact on Environment. The bulk of the score comes from objects, but the rest comes from sizeable allotments for each of the rest.

In other words, a room packed with expensive objects but no wall coverings or floor coverings offers only about 60 percent full Environment score.

Objects

The combined purchase prices of all objects in a room dictates the first portion of the niceness calculation.

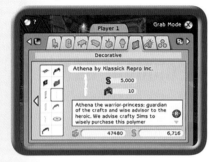

The more expensive a decorative object, the greater its positive effect on Environment.

Every object is assigned a "niceness" factor that raises Environment score in the room in which it's placed.

note Every object has a niceness factor, but the factor is minimal for ordinary objects. Only the more expensive and decorative objects have really significant Environment scores.

Each object in the room contributes its niceness to the room's overall Environment score.

note Given the strong but limited effect of objects on Environment score, there always comes a point when spending money on decorative objects shows no further increase in Environment score. The precise Simoleon amount of this point rises with the size of the room.

If, therefore, you're trying to improve Environment score, and adding a new object doesn't show any effect, consider returning it and instead upgrading the lighting, flooring, or wall covering.

The cost of an object largely determines how much effect it has on Environment, but decorative objects have a far greater effect per Simoleons spent.

Wall and Floor Covering

The plywood floors and sheetrock walls that you put up in Build mode contribute nothing to Environment score. This leaves two massive chunks of niceness empty, making a full score impossible.

The quality (read: purchase price) of the coverings you place on walls and floors determines how much these two elements add to niceness. The more expensive they are, the more they contribute.

note Each of these elements is scored as an average for the room. Therefore, if a room is mostly expensive wallpaper with some sections of the cheap stuff, top score isn't possible.

Messiness

Niceness is, however, only part of the Environment equation. What separates overall Environment score from niceness is the element of messiness.

A messy object in the room deducts a fixed amount from Environment score everywhere in the room. Messy objects hold down Environment score until they are cleaned or removed.

Dirty dishes and puddles mean low Environment score for this room.

Messy objects include:
- Ash piles
- Books left out
- Broken objects
- Dirty dishes
- Flies (in addition to dirty object's messiness)
- Full trash cans
- Old newspapers
- Puddles
- Spoiled food
- Soiled objects (dirty sinks, toilets, countertops)
- Trash piles
- Uncovered floor sections
- Uncovered wall sections
- Unmade beds

note Messiness can be a result of noise too. A ringing alarm clock pulls down Environment score in its room until it's turned off.

Dirty objects detract from Environment only if they're *visibly* dirty. Therefore, an object may show a "Clean" interaction before it actually begins to bring down Environment.

Flies

Flies appear in Sims' homes in response to certain messes.

Flies appear above dirty dishes, spoiled food, or trash piles (including full trash cans) after a few hours. They create an additional Environment reduction beyond the dirty object itself.

To get rid of flies, clean up the object that attracted them.

Environment Outdoors

Outdoor environment works the same as indoor. Keep it clean and add nice decorations.

The game considers any outdoor space as one big "room" for Environment score purposes. Just as in indoor spaces, nice objects raise Environment score outdoors, and dirty things decrease it.

Personality

Environment affects all personality types equally.

Mood Impact

Environment is the least Mood influencing of all the Needs (other than Energy, of course). Like Fun and Social, it exerts greater effect when it's very high or very low.

Distress and Failure

Maybe maid service isn't such a waste of money after all.

When Sims suffer Environment distress, they flash a door-shaped thought balloon. This wastes time, and the effect of low Environment somewhat depresses overall Mood.

There is no failure state for Environment.

Needs at Work

Every job has a distinctive effect on a Sim's Needs. When Sims are off the lot at a job, their Needs when they return is altered by this effect. So a Sim with a physical job returns home with a large deduction from Energy. Some of these effects are positive too—Sims with desk jobs return home with higher Comfort. Most jobs, except really solitary ones (security guard), increase Social.

Passive Influence and Needs

Some objects satisfy Sims' Needs even when the Sims aren't directly interacting with them. This effect is called "passive influence."

Just being near a TV passively gives your Sim Fun.

Such objects raise or lower a Need up to a limit for as long as the Sim is physically within the object's area of effect.

tip For efficient satisfaction of both Energy and Fun, power nap near a switched-on television. The nap doesn't provide complete Energy satisfaction, but it's fast, and you can get the passive Fun boost from the TV.

Objects that exert passive influence and the Need they impact are:

◆ All switched-on televisions passively *increase* Fun. Sim watches interestedly.

◆ All switched-on stereos passively *increase* Fun. Sim dances slightly.

◆ Trashcans or piles of trash passively *decrease* Hygiene. Sim makes stinky gestures.

Awareness and Memories

Various social interactions and events can cause memories in Sims who participate in or witness them. These memories can cause the Sims to react to the memory whenever they're near your Sim. This behavior is called "awareness."

Sims can develop eight different memories.

◆ Crush   ◆ Hate

◆ Disgust   ◆ Jealousy

◆ Fear   ◆ Love

◆ Friend   ◆ P.O.'d

Memories range in strength from 0 to 15 points. Interactions and events add or subtract points to the memories of your and other Sims involved in the event that creates a memory.

If Sims have strong memories about another Sim, they show it anytime the Sim is near.

For example, a Sim who witnesses another Sim vomiting or having a Bladder failure develops a Disgust memory about the unfortunate Sim. Until the memory fades with time, that Sim reacts with a disgusted gesture whenever the other Sim is near.

The intensity of the awareness reaction depends on the strength of (number of points in) the particular memory.

◆ Memory 0–1: No reaction

◆ Memory 2–5: Minor reaction, turn head to look at Sim

◆ Memory 6–10: Higher reaction, Sim turns to face the other Sim, throws a thought balloon of the memory, and uses a gesture for that memory

◆ Memory 11–15: Highest reaction, Sim stops and turns full attention to the object of the memory and does a high-intensity gesture for the memory

> **note** Sims react to the highest-scoring memory they have for the other Sim. If they have two of equally high score, they choose randomly.

> **note** Full details on memories can be found in the "Social Interactions" section.

Death and Ghosts

Satisfying your Sims' Needs makes life possible. What, however, about the opposite? What about death? Well, there is death in *The Sims™ 2*, but it may be some comfort to know it's pretty fun, and, moreover, it's curable.

How Sims Die

Sims can die by three causes: starvation, object disaster, or fire.

Starvation

As described previously, if Sims' Hunger Need goes into total failure and stays that way (they're unable to find any food source, or you actively prevent them from doing so), they eventually expire from starvation.

Hunger is the only Need that, if allowed to completely deplete, can kill your Sim.

Object Disaster

Using certain objects carries a chance for an early demise. For most, however, this is usually a function of low skill. For others, the chance of death is either completely random or heightened by some condition (like a dirty fireplace), but the chances are usually very small.

Low Skill

Some objects require skill to use properly, and using them with too little of a certain skill can be fatal.

◆ Bad Food: Food poisoning results from poorly prepared food—depends on Cooking skill.

◆ DJ Booth: When using fireworks or lasers, there's a chance of electrocution if Creativity skill is low.

- Slot Machine: When cheating, there's a chance of fatal mangling if your Sim has low Mechanical skill.
- Stove: Chance of fire depends on Cooking skill. Sim can die in the fire.
- Television: When repairing a broken TV, there's a chance of electrocution if Mechanical skill is low.

Cheaters never prosper, and sometimes they just die. This guy better watch out if his Mechanical skill is low.

The probability of death in every instance drops with each skill level, becoming nonexistent once your Sim reaches level 5.

- 0: 20%
- 1: 10%
- 2: 5%
- 3: 3%
- 4: 1%
- 5 and higher: 0%

Random Object Death

Some objects just bear the mark of random misfortune. Still, it's not *completely* random. Each of these objects has a risk factor that alters the probability.

Don't use the Genie Lamp when Aspiration is low, unless you wish to meet the Grim Reaper.

- Fireplace: All fireplaces can cause fires if there's a flammable object nearby, but the chances increase with the dirtiness of the fireplace. The dirtier it is, the greater the chance of an out-of-control fire and, if further misfortune ensues, death.
- Genie Lamp: In general, the lower your Sim's Aspiration score, the greater the odds of a bad wish. The worst possible wish is instant death. This, however, occurs *very* rarely. Additionally, another bad wish is a randomly placed fire on the lot. This blaze can, if it gets out of control, kill someone.

Fire

Sims can die if the space they're standing on catches fire. Most often, this occurs while Sims are standing around a fire, gawking and panicking. Suddenly, the fire is no longer in the next tile but rather right under the Sims' feet. If they don't move, poof.

Fires can be started by cooking, fireplaces, or a genie wish gone bad.

Tombstones and Urns

At the spot of a Sim's demise, a memorial marker is left behind. Depending on whether the location is outdoors or in, the Sim site is marked by either a tombstone or an urn, respectively.

Dead Sims leave behind a marker with which the living can interact.

note Tombstones and urns can be moved via the Buy Catalog or even deleted entirely. The markers, however, have no monetary value.

The living can perform several interactions on these markers.

note Moving a marker from outside to inside or vice versa changes its form.

- Dance: Satisfies the dancer's Fun but lowers relationship with the deceased.
- Eulogize: Develops the speaker's Charisma skill.

◆ Mourn: Adds relationship points with the owner of the marker and depletes Fun. If the deceased is currently showing a "Be Mourned" Want, directing another Sim to mourn at the grave satisfies this Want, raises the deceased's Aspiration score, and increases the chances of resurrection via the fiddle contest with the Grim Reaper. The degree of mourning and the amount of Fun depleted by it depends on the level of relationship with the deceased. The higher the relationship, the more intense the weeping and the greater the drop in Fun.

> **note** Markers remain after a Sim comes back to life. Sims attempting to mourn, however, simply shrug and move on.

Ghost Life

Ghosts are now controllable Sims, but their interactions are limited.

As ghosts, Sims are still controllable but have many new abilities and handicaps.

◆ Ghosts can walk through walls and objects.
◆ Ghosts can't interact with other ghosts.
◆ Ghosts can't interact with objects.
◆ Ghosts' Needs don't decay.
◆ Ghosts can't satisfy their Needs.
◆ Ghosts can interact with the living, but only with special ghost interactions (see following).

Ghost Interactions

When ghosts socialize with the living, they have a special set of interactions that only ghosts may perform. These interactions don't impact the ghost's relationship with the living Sim but do increase the recipient's Fear response when the ghost is nearby (see "Awareness" previously and "Memories" in the "Social Life" section).

Dude, gross!

Each ghost interaction negatively impacts one of the recipient's Needs, and each can be avoided if the other Sim rejects the interaction.

> **note** Rejection of ghost interactions depends on the living Sim's Logic skill. The higher the Logic skill, the more likely the Sim can avoid the interaction.

◆ Possess: Depletes target's Energy.
◆ Puke: Depletes target's Hygiene.
◆ Spook: Depletes target's Bladder.
◆ Wail: Depletes target's Energy.

Ghost Wants

Ghosts don't have your typical Wants and Fears. Instead, their Wants and Fears are completely replaced by ones that revolve around doing ghost socials, wanting their memorial markers interacted with, and returning to life.

Ghost Wants revolve around their few but powerful influences on the living.

Just as with normal Wants and Fears, however, the realization of any of these Wants and Fears impacts both the Sim's Aspiration score and accumulated Aspiration points.

> **tip** If a ghost wants to be mourned, switch control to a living Sim and do the mourn interaction on the correct memorial.

Keeping a ghost's Aspiration score high, as you'll see later, is critical to its chances of returning to life.

The Grim Reaper

As soon as a Sim dies, the Grim Reaper shows up and ushers the Sim into the ghostly life.

Anytime there's a ghost on a lot, you find the Reaper.

As long as there's at least one ghost on the lot, the Reaper remains, roaming the lot and occasionally watering the plants. He lingers to be available if any ghost wishes to attempt to return to life.

Returning to Life

There are two ways to return a Sim ghost to life: bribery or fiddle playing.

Pony up the cash for an easy resurrection.

The quickest and surest way to return to life is to pay the Reaper a fee of §100. Upon payment, your Sim is instantly returned to life as good as new.

If you don't have the money, can't spare it, or just want to "live" dangerously, you can instead direct your Sim to challenge the Grim Reaper to a fiddle contest.

He's got a fiddle of gold against your soul 'cause he thinks he's better than you. Actually, if you lose, you just have to try again.

Success in the fiddle contest depends on two factors.

◆ Creativity skill
◆ Ghost's Aspiration meter

The higher each is, the greater the chance of defeating the Grim Reaper.

As a ghost, there's nothing you can do about skill since your Sim can't interact with any skill objects. You can, however, change the Sim's Aspiration score by satisfying ghostly Wants. The ghost Sim may, for example, want to make a Sim have a Bladder failure, so find the lowest Logic Sim on the lot and do the Spook interaction to satisfy the Want and increase Aspiration score.

If your Sim wins over death, he or she is immediately returned to life with his or her Needs set to neutral and a refresh of the Wants and Fears panel.

NPC Sims and Death

If an NPC Sim (either a resident or a visitor) dies, he or she automatically challenges the Grim Reaper and wins, thus returning to life.

Chapter 4
Skills and Careers

What Sims do for a living is at least equally important to what they need and want. Skills enable Sims to have more of an impact on the things around them. Work defines Sims to themselves and the world, and more importantly, it pays the bills.

To become successful in both skills and career, it's crucial to understand how this finely balanced mechanism works and how you can use this knowledge to tilt it to your advantage.

Skills

Whether Sims are climbing the career ladder, staying home to pursue their Aspirations, or living a life of self improvement, they need skills.

Skills can impact many things:

◆ To advance in any career, Sims must develop three defined skills. Career advancement increases Sims' income and provides fulfillment of career-related Wants.

◆ The Wants of many Sims are tied to the acquisition of a skill or all skills. Aspiration points increase with each skill level and pay off big time if the skill is maximized.

◆ Some skills provide the opportunity for extra income.

◆ Doing certain activities with high or low skill can elicit reactions from nearby Sims.

◆ Some skills make household chores faster and easier.

◆ Skills determine who wins a fight or many physical games.

◆ High household skills lessen the need for hired help.

◆ Skills dictate how safe it is for a Sim to use certain objects.

This section introduces you to the seven basic skills and details how they impact your Sims' everyday lives and entire lifetimes.

The Basic Skills

Your Sim's level in all skills can be viewed in the Careers, Skills & Personality panel of the Pause menu.

Seven basic skills appear in the Careers, Skills & Personality panel. Basic skills affect many aspects of the game, including career and homemaking. The basic skills are:

◆ Cooking   ◆ Logic

◆ Mechanical   ◆ Creativity

◆ Charisma   ◆ Cleaning

◆ Body

Skill Building

Skill levels can also be seen in the in-game Skill panel. When skills are being developed, both the skills button and the icon for the skill being developed blink.

Each basic skill is broken down into 10 increasingly difficult levels. Each level takes longer to master than the one before. For example, without any personality-based acceleration, it should take a Sim one game hour to earn the first level of any skill. The 10th level of that skill should require 12 hours.

The Skill Meter

While working on a skill, the Skill meter shows your Sim's progress to date on the current level in development.

Progress in each skill level is displayed in the Skill meter that appears above the Sim's head while skill building. This meter fills, from bottom to top, as the Sim trains in the current skill level. When the meter reaches the top, the number of the new skill level briefly appears, the Sim graduates to the next level, and he or she begins working on the following level. The meter

resets to empty, and the process begins anew (more slowly with each more difficult level).

> **note** If you stop skill building in the middle of a level, the Sim's progress in that level is preserved the next time he or she returns to build that skill.

Skills and Aspirations

Skills play a prominent role in the Aspirations game. Sims of all Aspirations want to gain skill levels, though some desire it more intensely and often than others. The higher the skill level, the more points the Aspiration bestows.

Eventually, some Sims want to get to the top of a skill or (in the case of Knowledge Sims) maximize *all* skills. The big payoffs for these Wants reflect how difficult a feat that is.

Intimately understanding the course of each Aspiration can guide you in how much to engage your Sims in skill building. For some Aspirations, it's central, and for others, it's a minor pursuit.

Skills and Careers

As detailed in the following "Careers" section, Sims need skills for their careers. Each career requires development in three skills. With each level of the career, the skill requirements increase.

 In the Careers, Skills & Personality panel, the skill level required for the next promotion is shown as a white border around the target skill level.

> **tip** When choosing a career, consider how many of the career's required skills can be learned faster, thanks to your Sim's personality. Having at least one skill match the Sim's personality substantially aids career advancement.

Career Tracks, Featured Skills, and Helper Personalities

CAREER TRACK	SKILL 1 (PERS.)	SKILL 2 (PERS.)	SKILL 3 (PERS.)
Art	Creativity (Playful)	Mechanical (None)	Charisma (Outgoing)
Athletics	Body (Active)	Mechanical (None)	Charisma (Outgoing)
Business	Logic (Serious)	Creativity (Playful)	Charisma (Outgoing)
Crime	Body (Active)	Charisma (Outgoing)	Logic (Serious)
Fashion	Charisma (Outgoing)	Creativity (Playful)	Mechanical(None)
Law	Logic (Serious)	Body (Active)	Cleaning (Neat)
Medicine	Logic (Serious)	Mechanical (None)	Cleaning (Neat)
Military	Body (Active)	Logic (Serious)	Cleaning (None)
Politics	Logic (Serious)	Creativity (Playful)	Charisma (Outgoing)
Science	Logic (Serious)	Cooking (None)	Cleaning (Neat)

How Basic Skills Are Learned

Every basic skill can be learned in two ways: by interacting with objects and/or, for a few skills, by doing an activity that falls under a skill's domain ("practical skill building").

Object Interaction

Many objects impart skill building with certain interactions. Object skill building is the most common and effective method. The amount of skill building an interaction gives depends on the object. Normally, the more expensive a skill object is, the faster it provides skill.

Expensive skill objects build skill more quickly than cheaper versions.

Practical Skill Building

Cooks learn to cook by cooking. The Skill meter proves it.

Three skills offer skill building while performing the skill itself: Cooking, Mechanical, and Cleaning. Whenever Sims cook a meal, fix an object, or clean a mess, they're increasing their acumen in the skill. This increase is marked by the Skill meter over the Sim's head.

Practical skill training is equal in speed to object-based training, but the activities themselves don't last indefinitely. Sims can sit and study for as long as their Needs and Mood allow, but cleaning the toilet or cooking a meal lasts only a short time, after which skill building is over.

In two primary ways, however, practical skill building is preferable to object-based skill building.

◆ Efficiency: Sims have to either clean and repair things themselves or pay someone to do these things for them. Learning a skill by doing it means Sims get the job done and improve a skill at the same time, without having to spend money. On the flip side, they're spending some-thing more valuable than money: time. This is, therefore, only an advantage if you intended the Sim to learn these skills anyway.

♦ Always Available: As described later, Sims can't skill build with objects if Mood or certain Needs are too low. They can still get skill from cooking and cleaning (but not repairing) no matter what their Mood or Needs. On the other hand, there isn't always something to clean or someone to feed.

As noted later (see "Skills and Personality"), another major difference between practical and object-based skill building arises when a Sloppy Sim gains practical Cleaning skill. The lower the Neat/Sloppy score, the more slowly the Sim learns Cleaning. This can be as low as one-third the rate that a Sim with a Neat/Sloppy of 10 would learn.

Speeding Skill Building

Two things accelerate skill building.

♦ Personality traits

♦ Cheering by other Sims

Skills and Personality

Many basic skills are learned (whether using an object or learning by doing) more easily by Sims of a certain personality trait. The more extreme Sims are in the trait, the faster they learn the skill.

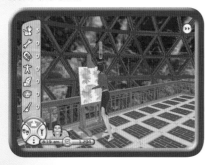

Put a Playful Sim in front of an easel, and the Creativity points just roll in.

The skill/personality alliances are:

♦ Cooking: None   ♦ Logic: Serious
♦ Mechanical: None   ♦ Creativity: Playful
♦ Charisma: Outgoing   ♦ Cleaning: Neat
♦ Body: Active

A Sim with an extreme personality trait (such as 10 points in Active) trains at double the normal speed.

In each case, skill speed increases with every point toward the aligned skill. Therefore, a Sim with Outgoing/Shy of 0–5

would take a game hour to get the first level of Charisma skill, and one with Outgoing/Shy 10 would take only 30 game minutes. A Sim with 7 Outgoing/Shy would not gain full speed but would still do better than a neutral or Shy Sim: about 48 minutes.

There is one exception to this system—Sloppy Sims and practical Cleaning skill. In most cases, a Sim of the opposite personality extreme trains at the same normal rate as a neutral Sim (5 points). However, in the case of practical Cleaning skill, the fewer points in Neat/Sloppy (0–4), the more slowly the Sim learns to clean. To gain the first level of Cleaning skill, for example, an extremely Sloppy Sim (Neat/Sloppy 0) would take about 90 minutes.

Cheering

For some Body skill objects (see each skill object's description in the "Objects" section for details), the skill of the Sim using the object can be accelerated if another Sim uses the object's cheer interaction. The adoration of the crowd seems to spur training Sims on to greater heights.

Directing other Sims to cheer your Sims while they train further speeds skill development.

Such objects include:

♦ Exerto Self-Spot Exercise Machine

♦ Fists of Spite Punching Bag

♦ Rat Race Executive Power Wheel

Skills, Mood, and Core Needs

Sims may build skills only when they're in a good Mood and their core Needs are reasonably satisfied.

Low mood or low levels in the core Needs prevent Sims from skill building.

If Mood drops below 0, regardless of individual Need levels, a Sim refuses to do object-based skill building and immediately ceases skill building if already engaged with a skill building object.

Even if Mood is OK, five individual core Needs can, by themselves, forestall or end skill building.

- Energy
- Fun
- Hunger
- Comfort (if Sim isn't sitting to work on skill)
- Bladder

Other than these, no other Need automatically bumps a Sim out of skill building. If the other Needs are low enough, however, they quickly reduce Mood to negative.

It's important to note that practical skill building in Cooking and Cleaning (but not Mechanical) is *not* affected by motive or Need level. A Sim gains skill building from practical avenues even if Mood is rock bottom and Needs are dwindling. It may not be the best choice of actions when Bladder is about to bottom out, but Sims do clean and learn the Cleaning skill if you tell them to.

Skill Loss

Skill levels, once acquired, can't be lost.

Skills in Detail

Cooking Skill

- Personality Acceleration: None
- Careers Used: Science
- Objects: Bookshelves, Refrigerators/Counters/Cooking Appliances, "White Fire" Teppanyaki Table
- Practical: Cooking

> **tip** In Story mode, your primary Sim should get Cooking skill 10 as soon as possible so you always have someone on the lot who can make nutritious food.

Being skilled in Cooking is critical to making great meals and lowers the chance of your Sim's food being poisonous.

Cooking influences how quickly Sims can cook, how nourishing (in terms of Hunger satisfaction) their efforts are, and the likelihood that that food has positive extra effects. Also, recipes are unlocked on attainment of each of the 10 Cooking skill levels.

Finally, Cooking skill determines the odds of Sims starting a cooking fire (the lower the skill, the greater the chances) and the chances that food they create is fatally poisonous.

> **tip** A Sim with no Cooking skill using any cooking appliance other than a microwave often starts a fire. Be sure to have a smoke alarm somewhere in the same room as the stove.

Mechanical

- Personality Acceleration: None
- Careers Used: Athletics, Fashion, Medicine, Art
- Objects: All bookshelves (Study), chess tables (Play Paper Football), "Jimmy Three Fingers" Rocket Bench
- Practical: Repair any broken object

Mechanical skill dramatically speeds the time required to repair broken objects. It also decreases the chance of electrocution when repairing electronic objects or of your Sim being fatally mangled while cheating on the slot machines.

Mechanical skill can save your Sim oodles in repair costs.

> **note** When repairing an object, the Repair meter covers the Skill meter. The meter you see, therefore, is not reflecting progression to a new skill but rather the progress of the repair itself.

Mechanical can be learned using the study interaction on any bookshelf, using objects that develop Mechanical skill, or by repairing any broken object. When the Sim is low in Mechanical skill, repairs take a very long time, and the Sim gives up frequently (requiring you to reactivate the interaction). On the upside, the Sim is learning Mechanical skill the entire time.

Charisma

- Personality Acceleration: Outgoing
- Careers Used: Business, Politics, Athletics, Art, Fashion, Crime
- Objects: All mirrors (Practice Speech, Practice Kissing), tombstones/urns (Eulogize), computers (Blog)
- Practical: N/A

Practicing kissing is one of the more flamboyant ways to build Charisma skill.

Charisma is primarily useful for careers that require it and is learned by practicing speeches or kissing in any mirror. You can also build Charisma through eulogizing a deceased Sim.

Working on a blog on the computer also develops Charisma.

Body

◆ Personality Acceleration: Active
◆ Careers Used: Athletics, Law, Military, Crime, Law
◆ Objects: Exerto Self-Spot Exercise Machine, Fists of Spite Punching Bag, Rat Race Executive Power Wheel
◆ Practical: N/A

Body is one of the most important skills because it impacts so many little things (too many to list here). It's most prominently important as a career skill, but there's more.

To build your Sim's physique, pick an exercise machine and have someone cheer your Sim on.

Body skill affects which Sim wins in a fight, what tricks Sims can do on the surfing simulator, and who wins in foosball or air hockey games.

Build body skill by using exercise equipment.

Logic

◆ Personality Acceleration: Serious
◆ Careers Used: Business, Law, Medicine, Crime, Politics, Science, Military
◆ Objects: Computers (Design Video Game), chess sets (Play Chess), Astrowonder Telescope, Prof. Feather's Chicken Checkers (Practice)
◆ Practical: N/A

Logic is important primarily as a career skill.

> **tip** Time invested in building Logic skill eventually pays off. Designing video games can make your Sim a good living with top skill and a time commitment.

Cerebral activities build Logic skill.

Logic is developed using several objects; sometimes it can be built up while tending to your Sim's Needs. Chess, for example, allows you to build Logic while taking care of Comfort (being seated while playing) and Social (if your Sim plays against another Sim).

Logic affects how easily your Sims are scared by ghosts, how often the massage table malfunctions when your Sim programs it, whether stargazing Sims discover a comet, and how well your Sim plays chicken checkers.

Creativity

◆ Personality Acceleration: Playful

◆ Careers Used: Business, Politics, Art, Fashion

◆ Objects: Pianos, Bonsai Tree (Prune), Bookcases (Write in Journal), Independent Expressions, Inc. Easel, "Does it Rock!" Electric Guitar

◆ Practical: N/A

Creativity is important in several careers, but it has other applications as well, some of them financially beneficial.

Painting on an easel teaches Creativity—and you can sell the paintings the Sim produces. The greater the Sim's Creativity, the higher the painting's sale price.

A Sim's performance of music is also affected by Creativity. Low Creativity Sims just bang away on the piano while high Creativity Sims play lovely music. Nearby Sims react to music's quality.

Along with Aspiration score, Creativity helps you in fiddle contests with the Grim Reaper.

Creativity also impacts your Sims' ability to safely use DJ pyrotechnics and beat the Grim Reaper in a fiddle contest.

Cleaning

◆ Personality Acceleration: Neat

◆ Careers Used: Law, Medicine, Science, Military

◆ Objects: All bookshelves (Study)

◆ Practical: Cleaning any object

Cleaning is a very important skill for Sims in careers that call for it and those who don't want to hire a maid.

Sure you can get Cleaning skill from a book, but multitasking is the way to glory.

The better Sims are at cleaning, the faster they perform cleaning tasks. Faster cleaning means more free time for other things.

> **note** High Cleaning skill doesn't make Sloppy Sims clean more often; it just makes them clean more quickly. If you want Sloppy Sims with high Cleaning skill to tidy up after themselves, you must direct them to the messes.

Careers

Learning to play the career game is absolutely essential if Sims are to have a reasonably efficient and successful life.

> **tip** In Story mode, immediately get every playable resident Sim employed. Since all money earned by resident Sims goes into a common pot of family funds that your Sim carries from lot to lot, everyone is essentially working for you.

Without a regular and substantial income:

◆ Bills don't get paid.

◆ The refrigerator is empty.

◆ Environment score is hopelessly mediocre.

◆ Hired help is unaffordable.

As such, have a look at the mechanics of the working life.

Getting a Job

Sims find job listings in two sources, the newspaper and the computer.

Each day at 7:00 am, the newspaper is delivered to the Sims' front walk. Select "Find Job" and you're presented with *three* job openings. The computer offers more variety, serving up *five* job openings a day.

More and better job listings are found on the computer than the newspaper.

When a Sim with few skills or friends enters a new career track, he or she starts at level 1.

Sims who leave or are fired from a track can get back into the career track at two levels below their previous job. For example, Sims fired at level 5 and still qualified for the job would reenter at level 3. If performance is good, they quickly regain their former position.

> note The job level boost for previously held careers only shows in computer job listings. All jobs in the newspaper are always level 1 positions, regardless of previous experience.

Career Structure

Every job has certain common attributes that tell you all you need to know about what is required of your Sim.

Skill Requirements

Every career features *three* skills that must be developed in order to climb the ladder.

With every job level, the skill requirements may increase, requiring the Sim to meet all the skill thresholds before even being eligible for promotion.

Friends Requirement

In the Careers, Skills & Personality panel of the Pause menu, the number of friends needed for promotion is shown in the number on the right.

Many jobs require, as a condition for promotion, that a Sim have a certain number of friends. What this means, though, isn't as clear as it seems.

> note The friend count on the Careers, Skills & Personality panel shows the current number of the individual Sim's friends, then the number NEEDED for promotion.

For promotion purposes, a "friend" is any Sim with whom your individual Sim has a relationship of 40 points or higher. Friendships with housemates also count for promotion purposes.

> note Whether it's in Story or Freeplay mode, job promotion only counts each individual Sim's friendships—not, as in previous versions, the friendships of housemates, roommates, or spouse ("family friends").

> note Falling below the friend requirement for a Sim's current job doesn't result in demotion, but further promotion is impossible until the friend count is up to the next job's demands.

Hours

Jobs vary in their hours (both the start and quitting times and number of hours per shift).

> note Carpools arrive one hour and fifteen minutes before the job's start time and wait until the job's exact start time.
> Sims return home 10 minutes after quitting time.

Unless your Sim is in a rockin' good mood with all skills and friends needed for a promotion, spend the hour and a quarter the carpool waits getting more qualified.

Generally, higher-level jobs require fewer hours than lower-level jobs.

> tip Put a night table and an alarm clock next to your Sim's bed and set it (only needs to be done once). The clock automatically goes off one hour before the carpool arrives—two hours before the shift starts—awakening your Sim and, if needed, automatically taking the game out of triple speed.

To get to work on time, you may catch the carpool the instant it arrives (one hour before the shift begins) or use the hour it waits to feed Needs and work on skills. Don't cut it too close, however, or you'll miss work.

> **tip** If it looks like your Sim won't make the carpool, hold the pause button, switch to classic control, and use the indicator on the car to select "Go to Work." The car won't pull away—even if it's after work start time—as long as "Go to Work" is the only item in your Sim's queue.

Daily Salary

With each higher job level, daily salary increases.

Needs Effects

Sims' Needs don't stand still while they're at work. When Sims return home, their Need levels at their departure time are adjusted by fixed amounts.

> **note** If Sims' Energy or Bladder is near failure when they leave for work, it's possible that the at-work Need adjustment will cause them to go into Need failure upon their return. Send them to work too tired, and they'll come home and pass out on the sidewalk.

Every job decreases Energy of course (none permit napping on the job, sadly). More physical jobs decrease Energy more.

Not all Needs are, however, diminished at work. Some jobs increase Fun, and particularly cushy ones increase Comfort. All jobs, except the most solitary (like Security Guard), increase Social.

Promotion

Come home with a promotion, and you get your Sim's new salary, work hours, and a nice fat promotion bonus.

Each day Sims go to work, there's a chance they'll be promoted to the next level. But whether a promotion's available and a Sim's odds of getting it depend on several factors.

Skills and Friends

As described previously, to be eligible for promotion, a Sim must meet the next level's skill and friends requirements. If the Sim lacks these, there is no chance of promotion.

> **note** In the Careers, Skills & Personality panel, needed skill levels are highlighted by a white oval on the indicator for the level. The second of the two friend numbers shows how many friends your Sim needs to be eligible for promotion (the first is the number of friends you have). If the left-hand number is larger than the right, you're set.

Job Performance

The other variable in promotion is job performance. The higher it is, the greater the odds of promotion. High job performance isn't a guarantee of promotion, but it tilts the odds in the Sim's favor.

> **note** Going to work with all skill and friend qualifications and a Mood at least 75 percent positive guarantees a promotion.

Job performance is a product of Sims' Mood when they leave for work. The higher their Mood when they get in the car, the better their job performance for that day.

Promotion Bonus

On the happy day when a Sim rises to a new job level, he or she receives the daily salary for the old job, plus a promotion bonus of twice the daily salary of the new job level.

Uniform Unlocks

When Sims are promoted to career levels 2, 3, 5, 7, 9, and 10, they unlock parts of a uniform for their career. These items are thereafter available in Create-a-Sim or in the dresser for all Story and Freeplay mode Sims.

Reach the top of the Military career and this cool infrared helmet.

45

Several careers share common uniform pieces, so if a piece is unlocked in one career and your Sim gets a promotion to another career that uses the same piece, there isn't any new item unlocked. Level 10 in each career, however, is always an item unique to that career, so it's always worthwhile to climb to the top.

Getting Fired

Sims get fired from their job if they miss two consecutive days of work.

In order to regain their prior position, they must use the computer (not the newspaper) to find a job listing in their previous career. This listing is two slots below the job they had when they were terminated.

> **tip** When going for the more difficult higher-level promotions, it pays to skip one day of work to develop skills and friends. If your Sim goes to work the day after a "mental health day" in a very good Mood, he or she will likely get the promotion.

Career Directory

Artist

Level	Job Name	Friends	Cooking	Mechanical	Charisma	Body	Logic	Creativity	Cleaning	Daily Salary	Hours	Shift Length
1	Nude Model	0	0	0	0	0	0	0	0	§126	2pm–6pm	4
2	House Painter	0	0	0	0	0	0	0	0	§154	9am–2pm	5
3	Studio Assistant	0	0	1	0	0	0	0	0	§210	9am–3pm	6
4	Museum Guard	0	0	1	1	0	0	0	0	§252	10am–3pm	5
5	Studio Artist	2	0	1	2	0	0	1	0	§385	11am–4pm	5
6	Resident Artist	4	0	3	2	0	0	1	0	§392	6pm–1am	7
7	Art Critic	5	0	4	2	0	0	2	0	§613	11am–5pm	6
8	L'Enfant Terrible	7	0	4	3	0	0	3	0	§788	2pm–7pm	5
9	Gallery Owner	10	0	4	4	0	0	4	0	§933	10am–3pm	5
10	Museum Director	13	0	4	5	0	0	5	0	§1,500	11am–3pm	4

Athletics

Level	Job Name	Friends	Cooking	Mechanical	Charisma	Body	Logic	Creativity	Cleaning	Daily Salary	Hours	Shift Length
1	Mascot	0	0	0	0	0	0	0	0	§154	3pm–9pm	6
2	Ball Collector	0	0	0	0	1	0	0	0	§238	9am–3pm	6
3	Rookie	0	0	0	0	2	0	0	0	§322	9am–3pm	6
4	Starter	1	0	0	1	2	0	0	0	§420	9am–3pm	6
5	All-Star	2	0	0	2	6	0	0	0	§539	9am–3pm	6
6	MVP	3	0	1	3	8	0	0	0	§893	9am–3pm	6
7	Superstar	4	0	2	4	10	0	0	0	§1,190	9am–4pm	7
8	Head Coach	5	0	4	5	10	0	0	0	§1,500	9am–2pm	5
9	Hall of Famer	6	0	7	7	10	0	0	0	§1,750	9am–3pm	6
10	Living Legend	8	0	7	10	10	0	0	0	§2,033	11am–5pm	6

Business

Level	Job Name	Friends	Cooking	Mechanical	Charisma	Body	Logic	Creativity	Cleaning	Daily Salary	Hours	Shift Length
1	Traveling Salesman	0	0	0	0	0	0	0	0	§250	9am–3pm	6
2	Used Car Dealer	0	0	0	0	0	0	0	0	§300	9am–4pm	7
3	Telemarketer	0	0	0	2	0	0	0	0	§350	9am–4pm	7
4	Junior Executive	1	0	0	2	0	0	1	0	§448	9am–4pm	7
5	Executive	3	0	0	4	0	2	1	0	§560	9am–3pm	6
6	Senior Manager	4	0	0	4	0	3	3	0	§728	8am–5pm	9
7	Vice President	5	0	0	5	0	4	3	0	§924	8am–4pm	8
8	President	6	0	0	5	0	6	4	0	§1,400	9am–4pm	7
9	CEO	7	0	0	6	0	7	6	0	§1,665	9am–4pm	7
10	Business Tycoon	8	0	0	9	0	9	7	0	§2,100	10am–4pm	6

Crime

Level	Job Name	Friends	Cooking	Mechanical	Charisma	Body	Logic	Creativity	Cleaning	Daily Salary	Hours	Shift Length
1	Vandal	0	0	0	0	0	0	0	0	§168	9am–3pm	6
2	Shoplifter	0	0	0	1	0	0	0	0	§252	9am–5pm	8
3	Burglar	0	0	0	2	0	0	0	0	§350	8am–4pm	8
4	Car Thief	1	0	0	2	0	1	0	0	§448	9am–4pm	7
5	Mugger	3	0	0	3	1	1	0	0	§560	9am–4pm	7
6	Body Guard	4	0	0	4	2	1	0	0	§728	3pm–11pm	6
7	Arsonist	5	0	0	5	2	2	0	0	§924	9am–3pm	6
8	Extortionist	6	0	0	5	3	5	0	0	§1,400	9am–3pm	6
9	Hit Man	7	0	0	6	3	7	0	0	§1,665	2pm–8pm	6
10	Mob Boss	8	0	0	9	3	9	0	0	§2,100	5pm–11pm	6

Fashion

Level	Job Name	Friends	Cooking	Mechanical	Charisma	Body	Logic	Creativity	Cleaning	Daily Salary	Hours	Shift Length
1	Hand Model	0	0	0	0	0	0	0	0	§200	7am–12pm	5
2	Lingerie Model	0	0	0	0	0	0	0	0	§230	3pm–9pm	6
3	Body Waxer	0	0	0	0	0	0	2	0	§300	9am–3pm	6
4	Fingernail Painter	0	0	1	0	0	0	3	0	§365	10am–3pm	5
5	Wig Designer	2	0	2	0	0	0	4	0	§400	11am–4pm	5
6	Hair Stylist	4	0	3	1	0	0	5	0	§540	6pm–1am	7
7	Makeup Artist	5	0	4	2	0	0	6	0	§700	11am–5pm	6
8	Runway Model	7	0	4	3	0	0	7	0	§900	2pm–7pm	5
9	Centerfold	10	0	4	4	0	0	9	0	§1,200	10am–3pm	5
10	Super Model	13	0	4	5	0	0	10	0	§1,400	10pm–2am	4

Law

Level	Job Name	Friends	Cooking	Mechanical	Charisma	Body	Logic	Creativity	Cleaning	Daily Salary	Hours	Shift Length
1	Security Guard	0	0	0	0	0	0	0	0	§336	7pm–2am	7
2	Cadet	0	0	0	0	1	0	0	0	§448	9am–3pm	6
3	Patrol Officer	0	0	0	0	2	0	0	0	§552	3pm–11pm	8
4	Desk Sergeant	1	0	0	0	2	1	0	0	§616	9am–3pm	6
5	Vice Squad	2	0	0	0	3	1	0	0	§686	10am–4pm	6
6	Detective	2	0	0	0	3	4	0	2	§756	9am–3pm	6
7	Lieutenant	3	0	0	0	4	5	0	4	§826	9am–3pm	6
8	SWAT Team Leader	4	0	0	0	4	6	0	6	§875	11am–6pm	7
9	Secret Service Agent	6	0	0	0	7	9	0	7	§910	8am–4pm	8
10	Sim in Black	7	0	0	0	10	9	0	8	§1,225	10am–4pm	6

Medicine

Level	Job Name	Friends	Cooking	Mechanical	Charisma	Body	Logic	Creativity	Cleaning	Daily Salary	Hours	Shift Length
1	Emergency Medical Technician	0	0	0	0	0	0	0	0	§280	8am–2pm	6
2	Paramedic	0	0	0	0	0	0	0	1	§385	8pm–2am	6
3	Nurse	0	0	0	0	0	1	0	2	§476	7am–2pm	7
4	Intern	1	0	2	0	0	2	0	4	§574	9am–6pm	9
5	Resident	2	0	2	0	0	3	0	5	§672	6pm–1am	7
6	General Practitioner	3	0	4	0	0	4	0	6	§770	10am–6pm	8
7	Specialist	4	0	7	0	0	5	0	7	§875	10am–4pm	6
8	Surgeon	5	0	9	0	0	7	0	8	§980	10am–4pm	6
9	Medical Researcher	7	0	9	0	0	8	0	9	§1,356	11am–6pm	7
10	Chief of Staff	9	0	9	0	0	10	0	10	§1,499	9am–4pm	7

Military

Level	Job Name	Friends	Cooking	Mechanical	Charisma	Body	Logic	Creativity	Cleaning	Daily Salary	Hours	Shift Length
1	Latrine Cleaner	0	0	0	0	0	0	0	0	§250	7am–1pm	6
2	Boot Polisher	0	0	0	0	1	0	0	0	§300	9am–3pm	6
3	Drill Instructor	0	0	0	0	2	0	0	0	§552	3pm–11pm	8
4	Paratrooper	1	0	0	0	2	1	0	0	§616	9am–3pm	6
5	Chopper Pilot	2	0	0	0	3	1	0	0	§686	10am–4pm	6
6	Covert Ops	2	0	0	0	3	4	0	2	§756	9am–3pm	6
7	Secret Agent	3	0	0	0	4	5	0	4	§826	9am–3pm	6
8	Code Breaker	4	0	0	0	4	6	0	6	§875	11am–6pm	7
9	"Cleaner"	6	0	0	0	7	9	0	7	§910	8am–4pm	8
10	War Monger	7	0	0	0	10	9	0	8	§1,225	10am–4pm	6

Politics

Level	Job Name	Friends	Cooking	Mechanical	Charisma	Body	Logic	Creativity	Cleaning	Daily Salary	Hours	Shift Length
1	Campaign Worker	0	0	0	0	0	0	0	0	§245	9am–6pm	9
2	Intern	0	0	0	1	0	0	0	0	§310	9am–4pm	7
3	Lobbyist	0	0	0	2	0	0	0	0	§350	9am–4pm	7
4	Campaign Manager	2	0	0	4	0	0	0	0	§448	9am–4pm	7
5	City Council Member	4	0	0	5	0	2	0	0	§560	9am–3pm	6
6	State Assemblyperson	6	0	0	5	0	3	1	0	§728	8am–5pm	9
7	Congressperson	7	0	0	5	0	4	2	0	§924	8am–4pm	8
8	Judge	8	0	0	6	0	6	3	0	§1,400	9am–4pm	7
9	Senator	10	0	0	7	0	6	4	0	§1,665	9am–4pm	7
10	Mayor	12	0	0	10	0	7	5	0	§2,200	10am–3pm	5

Science

Level	Job Name	Friends	Cooking	Mechanical	Charisma	Body	Logic	Creativity	Cleaning	Daily Salary	Hours	Shift Length
1	Lab Cleaner	0	0	0	0	0	0	0	0	§217	11am–5pm	6
2	Potion Tester	0	1	0	0	0	0	0	1	§332	4pm–10pm	6
3	Pyro	0	1	0	0	0	1	0	3	§448	9am–3pm	6
4	Virus Breeder	1	2	0	0	0	1	0	5	§525	9am–3pm	6
5	Chemist	2	3	0	0	0	2	0	6	§630	10am–5pm	7
6	Vivisectionist	3	4	0	0	0	4	0	6	§756	10am–7pm	9
7	Gene Splicer	3	5	0	0	0	5	0	7	§896	8am–1pm	5
8	Robotician	3	6	0	0	0	8	0	7	§1,036	8am–1pm	5
9	Space-Time Tinkerer	5	6	0	0	0	8	0	8	§1,522	10am–2pm	4
10	Death Ray Inventor	8	9	0	0	0	10	0	10	§2,333	10pm–2am	4

Chapter 5

Social Interactions

For Sims, heaven is other people—well, other Sims, that is. Therefore, socializing is very possibly the SimNation national pastime.

This is fitting, given the new social tools that arrive in *The Sims™ 2*. This section introduces you to the social scene and delves into the very powerful issues of direct control socializing, socializing interest, and relationship memories. Plus, there's a full index of social interactions.

Other than a constant good Mood, Platinum Aspiration score, and enough skills for a level 10 promotion, what else could you want?

General Principles

note Interactions are always between two Sims: the Sim who initiates the interaction and the Sim who is the target of it. For clarity, the initiator is referred to as "Sim A," and the target is referred to as "Sim B."

Relationship Score

Each Sim has some degree of relationship with every Sim he or she has met. Relationship scores are measured on a scale of 100 to -100. The higher the score, the stronger the relationship and the more powerfully positive or negative available interactions are.

Relationship scores for every Sim your Sim knows are viewable in the Relationships panel of the Pause menu.

It's important to understand that the relationship score between two Sims is usually reciprocal for both Sims. If Sim A has a relationship of 35 towards B, then Sim B's relationship to Sim A is also 35. You can, therefore, rely on your Sim's relationship to another Sim to determine if the other Sim will accept the interaction.

Relationship Score Decay

Relationships decay toward zero with time (down if positive and up if negative). Every day that two Sims don't interact, the relationship score shifts toward zero by three points. If the relationship drops below a relationship threshold (below 40 for a Friend), the relationship shifts to the next level (from Friend to Acquaintance).

tip Decay occurs every day at 4:00 pm and only if the Sim with whom your Sim has a relationship is not on the lot with your Sim. Therefore, if a Sim and his roommate or a Sim and a visitor are both on the lot at 4:00 pm (even if they're not interacting), their relationship doesn't decay for that day.

note Losing a friend through neglect is particularly problematic since you need certain numbers of friends to get job promotions. If, just before going to work fully qualified for a promotion, your Sim loses a friend due to decay, your Sim won't get the promotion.

As friendships near the point of falling to a lower level, you receive an onscreen warning reminding you to touch base with the endangered Sim. Heed it if you want to be ready when that next promotion is in sight.

tip Because of relationship decay, you shouldn't stop socializing with a Sim when you reach Friend status. Finish the job by building the score to as close to 100 as possible. This provides ample cushion so you aren't required to socialize with that Sim for a while, and it unlocks the Sim's signature appearance item.

Keeping in Touch

The way you keep relationships going is to interact with anyone your Sim knows on a regular basis. Whenever they're around, direct your Sim to chat for a while and get the relationship score as high as possible. As long as you stay ahead of the pace of decay, the relationship will grow.

Simply picking up the phone may be all you need to keep a relationship from falling.

Finding time for friends is hard enough. Sometimes just finding them at all is a challenge. There are four ways to meet up with Sims to work on your relationship.

◆ Chat on the phone or computer: You don't have to be together to talk, thanks to the wonders of modern communication. A few relationship points can be gleaned by calling a Sim on the phone or chatting on the computer for a few minutes. This doesn't make a friendship grow, but a daily call can easily overcome decay.

◆ Invite over: The phone and computer are also your means to bringing your friends and acquaintances to you. They don't always accept an invitation to drop by, but they usually do if you invite them during civilized hours. Once they're at the house, your Sim can interact freely, building the relationship as much as possible.

◆ Go visiting: If you're playing Story mode, call a cab and take your Sim to visit another Sim's lot. You can visit any place you've unlocked in the game and interact with anyone who's there.

◆ Drop bys: You hear the doorbell ringing all day; that's the sound of other Sims popping by to say hello. They wait for a while before giving up, so greet them at the first opportunity. Once in your home, they stay until you ask them to leave, or until a Need or the hour forces them to, so make use of your time together.

Social Need

The Social Need is, as discussed, a Sim's need to be interacting with other Sims in any way. Interactions sway this Need one way or the other.

Even most failed social interactions feed the Social Need.

tip Higher relationships lead to better social interactions. Better social interactions give more Social Need points.

Memories

Interacting with other Sims and witnessing certain acts feed your Sim's memories.

note There's nowhere to see the current status of your Sim's memories.

There are eight types of memories.

◆ Crush   ◆ Hate

◆ Disgust   ◆ Jealousy

◆ Fear   ◆ Love

◆ Friend   ◆ P.O.'d

The strength of a memory is measured in points on a scale of 0 to 15. The more points a memory has, the stronger it is.

Memories are mostly affected by the acceptance or rejection of social interactions. A caress, for example, increases the Love memory points but doesn't, by itself, create a Lover relationship. The two Sims need to do a few more interactions with Love memory points to attain that.

note When memories are changed by a social interaction, the change is equal for both Sims. Thus, two Sims should have mostly identical memories regarding each other.

A cuckolded Sim is haunted by the Jealousy memory whenever the cheater is in the room.

Some memories are affected also by witnessing other events or conditions. If, for example, a Sim's lover is in the room when the Sim kisses a third Sim, the lover receives several Jealousy memory points. In another case, any Sim who witnesses another Sim having a Bladder failure receives Disgust memory points that, if enough are collected, affect how the witnessing Sim behaves when the other Sim is nearby.

An interaction or event's impact on a memory can be either positive or negative. A generally positive interaction can, for example, undo the damage of a Hate or Fear memory. Apologizing, for example, deducts five points from the Hate memory.

Very few interactions or events feed only a single memory; most impact several at once. The influence on each memory can be either positive or negative, serving several purposes at once.

Memory Decay

Memories can be weakened by interactions that deduct their points, or they can weaken naturally over time through decay.

Every day, each memory decreases in strength by two points. Without any interactions or events to affect a memory, therefore, a very strong memory disappears due to decay in eight days. Therefore, Lovers who spend more than a week apart eventually become just Best Friends purely by virtue of memory decay, and two Sims who currently hate each other due to a fight eventually stop shaking their fists at one another if they spend enough time apart.

Memory Functions

Love and Crush memories add up to convert Friends into Crushes and Best Friends into Lovers.

Memories serve two functions.

◆ Along with relationships score, they define the kind of relationship two Sims have. For example, two Sims with a relationship score of 85 and no Love memories from romantic interactions are Best Friends while two with the same relationship score and several Love memory points become Lovers. This difference changes what interactions are available between the Sims and can impact each Sim's Wants and Fears if they have desires for specific kinds of relationships.

◆ They command a Sim's awareness reactions to other Sims. If, for example, a Sim has several Hate memories toward your Sim, he or she may stop and shake a fist angrily when your Sim is nearby.

tip Certain interactions available in platonic stances or relationships carry enough Crush or Love memory points to bring on amore. If romance is not what you're after, avoid the following:

◆ Check Out (Neutral) ◆ Kiss (Best Friend)
◆ Hit On (Friend) ◆ Kiss (Friend)
◆ Hug (Best Friend) ◆ Smooch (Crush)

Relationship Levels

Sims have some kind of relationship with every Sim they meet. What level of relationship it is, however, depends on relationship score and (for romantic relationships) memories.

tip Make food with aphrodisiac effects and serve it to your Sim and, if possible, the other Sim. For a limited time, all socializing your Sim does is with Love interactions (Lover stance), regardless of actual relationship score. This is valuable only when the relationship score with the other Sim is high, but you can't quite get the love relationship established.

There are seven relationship levels.

Relationship Levels and Requirements

RELATIONSHIP	RELATIONSHIP SCORE RANGE	MEMORY REQ.	ICON
Lover	75–100	Love > or = 4	
Best Friend	75–100	None	
Crush	40–74	Crush > or = 4	
Friend	40–74	None	
Acquaintance	-10–39	None	
Enemy	-30–-11	None	
Archenemy	-100–-31	None	

The kind of relationship two Sims have dictates the slate of available interactions, though not all are immediately available.

> **note** There are also several generic interactions that are available regardless of the relationship level.

Icons in the Relationships panel highlight significant relationships.

The level of relationship is reflected in the Relationships panel of the Pause menu by the relationship icon next to the Sim's picture (see the previous table). Beyond relationship type, each interaction has its own set of Mood, relationship, and personality availability requirements.

> **note** There's no panel to view your Sim's memories regarding any certain Sim, so it can sometimes be confusing when a romantic relationship doesn't form as expected. If reaching the correct threshold and doing a single romantic interaction doesn't do the trick, do the same interaction (or another, see previous) until enough Crush or Love memories are set to engender the relationship.

In classic mode socializing, a change in relationship level changes the slate of interactions but has no other visible impact.

In classic control mode, socializing is done like any other interactions.

In direct control mode, however, Sims change their social "stance" in relation to one another, providing a powerful visual indication of the relationship they share.

> **note** See "Direct Control Mode Socializing" later for full details on stances.

Availability

Whether interactions are available to you depends on *your* Sim and has nothing to do with the other Sim. Each interaction appears on your Social menu based on a combination of factors.

- ◆ Relationship type/stance
- ◆ Mood
- ◆ Relationship toward Sim B
- ◆ Personality traits

Availability, however, is no guarantee of acceptance. Normally, the qualifications for availability are likely to arise before the conditions for acceptance. So don't try an interaction as soon as it arises because it's unlikely to be accepted. Instead, precede newly available interactions with safe interactions to build relationship score a bit more.

Acceptance

Interactions are accepted based on several possible attributes *of Sim B* and not on anything to do with your Sim. Sims accept or reject interactions based on several factors.

How an interaction is received is out of your hands, but you can make educated guesses and take calculated risks.

note Most interactions carry a base probability of success to which Sim B's various factors are added or subtracted. Every interaction also includes a random chance that it will be rejected even if Sim B is otherwise guaranteed to accept. Though it is extremely rare, it does happen. The more completely the Sim fulfills the interactions requirements, the smaller this chance of a random rejection becomes. Therefore, a Sim who is well qualified for a Make Out may very rarely reject, but a Sim who just barely meets the qualifications stands a larger chance.

- Relationship to Sim A
- Outgoing/Shy personality
- Neat/Sloppy personality
- Playful/Serious personality
- Active/Lazy personality
- Nice/Grouchy personality
- Mood

tip If it helps to think about these things in more aggressive terms, think of socializing as a battle to get to 100 over the Mood defense of the other Sim. The lower Mood is, the more resistant Sim B is to interactions. If possible, therefore, engage Sims when you suspect or can verify that their Mood is high. For playable Sims, you can simply switch to them and check their Mood. For NPC Sims, observe them for signs of Need distress and approach them after they've satisfied a Need and seem to be gravitating toward other interactions.

Positive or Negative Interactions

Every interaction is either positive or negative, and every relationship type, no matter how loving or vitriolic, has both varieties. In other words, every relationship comes with the tools to damage it (negatives for positive relationships and positives for negative relationships).

Positive interactions tend to raise relationship and Social Need for both Sims, increase good memories, or undo the damage of bad memories. Negatives do the opposite, though only a few actually deplete the Social Need.

Interaction Effects

Most interactions impact both Sims' relationship score toward the other Sim, their Social Need, and various memories.

The effect, however, depends on whether the interaction is accepted or rejected. In most cases, the result varies dramatically.

Positive interactions flash green plus signs to indicate an increase in relationship points. Double plus signs mean a big change.

note Only a few interactions actually deplete the Social Need. Pretty much any interaction, positive or negative, satisfies the Social Need.

You can see some of these effects in action if you watch your Sim and his or her socializing partner carefully.

- Relationship: When an interaction finishes, icons indicate the level of change to the relationship. Single plus signs mean a small positive change, and double plus signs mean a large shift. Minus signs and double minus signs signify negative changes small and large.
- Social Need: If the Needs meters are visible during the interaction, arrows indicate the direction of the effect. Up is good, down is bad.

Boredom

If you do the same interaction five times in a row, the other Sim gets bored and automatically rejects it, even if he or she would otherwise accept. Sim B continues to reject it until you successfully attempt another interaction; you can then go back to the repeated interaction.

tip If there's one interaction you know to be effective and powerful, do it four times, pick another interaction that's extremely likely to work, then do the preferred interaction four times. Repeat.

Proposing Marriage or Moving In

Nearly any Sim can become a spouse or roommate if you develop the relationship correctly.

Weddings are lovely but quick affairs with little fanfare but cool outfits.

note Roommates are handy to provide an extra money/Aspiration point earner for your primary Sim. Get them jobs, wind them up, and let them earn while your Sim tends to more demanding duties.

Either of these living arrangements converts the other Sim into a playable Sim on all lots. The cohabitating Sim also accompanies your Story mode Sim from lot to lot.

In fact, roomies and spouses only differ in two ways.

◆ Acceptance Chances: Not surprisingly, the relationship and Mood requirements for marriage are quite a bit higher than for roommates.

◆ Kicking Out: Both kinds of Sims living arrangements are undone by using the Kick Out interaction. What happens next, however, differs between the two. Roomies just move out with no hard feelings. Kicked out spouses, on the other hand, take rejection less gracefully. Relationship drops by 30 for the dumper and 60 for the dumpee. Furthermore, the dumpee's Love and Crush memories are set to zero, and the dumpee's Hate memory toward the dumper is boosted.

note Each controllable Sim can accommodate one roommate OR spouse. These arrangements are tied to the Sim, not the lot or household. As such, a Sim with either a roomie or a spouse can't ask another Sim without jettisoning the existing companion.

When playing in two-player mode, player two's Sim inhabits the roomie slot of player one's Sim.

Acceptance

Whether a Sim rejects a roommate invitation or a marriage proposal depends on both Mood and relationship to the asking Sim.

Roommates are guaranteed to accept if their Mood is positive and relationship to your Sim is above 60.

Marriage is a bit more demanding. Guaranteed acceptance is only possible if the other Sim has a Mood and relationship of +90 or better.

note Sims whose marital status is important in Story mode reject all proposals, regardless of relationship and Mood, until their role has been fulfilled. They are effectively unable to marry until that time.

note Married relationships are indicated by an interlocked ring icon in the Relationships panel.

Marriage in Two-Player Games

Player two's Sim serves as player one's roommate. If, therefore, player one successfully directs his Sim to propose marriage or moving in to another Sim, player two must approve. With approval, player two switches control from his or her original Sim (who departs) to the new roomie/spouse.

Classic Control Mode Socializing

In classic control mode, socializing is a simple but somewhat loosely controlled undertaking. Using the interaction indicator, select the Sim with whom you want your Sim to socialize, then choose among the available interactions.

Repeating the same interaction is easy in classic control mode since you can queue up several repetitions and let them play out in order.

The benefit of classic mode socializing is that you can queue up several interactions to occur in succession. This, if skillfully employed, can be an efficient way to quickly build relationship but at the cost of control.

The available interactions, their availability, and their base outcomes are identical to direct control mode, but there are several direct control features you can't utilize. In classic mode, you don't see the visual clues and body language that you do in direct control, and the bonuses provided by the Interest meter are not awarded either.

Direct Control Mode Socializing

The most lively and efficient means of socializing is through the new direct control mode. You can't queue up interactions like you can in classic mode, but you have much more control over the interaction and better visual feedback of the relationship (thanks to "stances") and can benefit from your Sim's ability to get and keep the other Sim's "interest."

Stances Defined

Stances are physical manifestations of the relationship as it exists between two Sims. The game camera zooms in on the socializing Sims and softens focus on everything around them.

Stances are visual representations of the type of relationship shared by two Sims and the selection of possible interactions between them.

Stances correspond to the seven different kinds of relationships (Lover, Best Friend, Crush, Friend, Acquaintance, Enemy, Arch Enemy) and are visually indicated in several ways.

Body Language

Sims in Lover or Crush stances stand very close and can't keep their hands off each other.

Sims stand and move differently depending on the level of relationship and, therefore, the current stance. Lovers touch and lean toward each other while acquaintances keep a polite distance.

Background Color

The background tint of the screen when you're engaged in socializing is a strong clue of what stance your Sim is in.

- Lovers: vivid purple
- Crush: light purple
- Best Friend: vivid yellow
- Friend: light yellow
- Acquaintance: no color
- Enemy: light red
- Archenemy: vivid red

Available Interactions

With each stance, most of the available interactions change. As non-stance availability requirements are met, other interactions tied to that stance may appear as well.

Generic interactions (talk, gossip, etc.) appear regardless of stance.

Interest Defined

Interest measures the other Sim's level of enthusiasm about your Sim in general and the current session of socializing in particular.

Interest acts as both a bonus for social interactions, amplifying the effect of positive interactions and minimizing the impact of negative ones, and a timer that forces you to exit the session of socializing if you don't adequately maintain the other Sim's interest.

Current interest is displayed to the left of the portrait of the Sim your Sim is socializing with.

note In addition to dwindling interest, Sims exit socializing if no interactions are initiated for 30 seconds. This has nothing to do with interest, just boredom.

Interest Bonus

After an interaction, the interest number is added to whatever relationship change your Sim receives and this modified amount shifts to the right side of the portrait where it's added to the current relationship score.

A Sim's level of interest at any given moment is added to the relationship effect of an interaction. If, therefore, interest is 2 and the interaction adds 5 to relationship score, the actual change in relationship is 7. If, conversely, interest is 4 and the interaction reduces relationship by -2, the final outcome is actually a net increase of 2.

Interest ranges from 0 to 8 points per interaction. Your Sim's existing relationship with the other Sim sets starting interest level, and socials drive it up (if accepted) or down (if rejected).

Initial Interest

A Sim's initial interest in socializing with your Sim is dictated by the relationship toward your Sim. The higher the initial relationship, the greater the initial interest.

Relationship to A	Starting interest
Below 20	0
20–29	+1
30–49	+2
50–100	+3

Interest Decay

While your Sim is socializing, interest slowly decays with time. With no positive interactions to "add time" to the session, the other Sim eventually loses interest and exits.

Starting interest due to an existing relationship, therefore, provides a substantial time cushion for socializing. New acquaintances don't have much patience for slow or fitful socializing and are quick to exit if things aren't going well.

note Regardless of interest, if a Sim rejects three straight interactions, he or she exits the session.

The goal is to do enough accepted interactions to counter the diminishing of interest by decay. A very successful session can go on for a long time, as long as it's getting regular infusions of positive socializing.

tip To get things started, use simple, always-accepted interactions like talk and gossip. Mix them up to avoid repetition and keep doing them until relationship climbs over 10 or so.

When two Sims are not engaged in socializing, their interest in each other is rebuilding. Over time spent not socializing, interest eventually rebuilds (or declines) to the starting interest dictated by the relationship (see previous table).

Social Interaction Directory

Interaction	Relationship Level/Stance	Pos/Neg	Availability	Base Prob%	Accept Based on B's	Rel A Accept	Rel A Reject	Rel B Accept	Rel B Reject	Social A Accept	Social A Reject
Admire	Best Friend	Positive	Mood, Neat/Sloppy	0%	Rel, Mood, Outgoing/Shy, Neat/Sloppy, Nice/Grouchy	3	-9	3	-9	12	-10
Apologize	Enemy	Positive	Always	75%	Rel, Mood, Neat/Sloppy, Nice/Grouchy	10	-5	10	-5	5	5
Argue	Crush	Negative	Mood, Rel, Neat/Sloppy	0%	Rel, Mood, Neat/Sloppy, Playful/Serious, Nice/Grouchy	3	-5	3	-5	5	1
Ask to Move in	Generic	Positive	Mood, Rel, Outgoing/Shy	0%	Rel, Outgoing/Shy, Mood	4	-2	4	-2	7	2
Back-Crack	Friend	Positive	Mood, Rel, Active/Lazy	20%	Rel, Mood, Neat/Sloppy, Active/Lazy, Nice/Grouchy	4	-8	4	-8	10	-8
Best Friend Hug	Best Friend	Positive	Rel, Mood, Nice/Grouchy	0%	Rel, Mood, Neat/Sloppy, Nice/Grouchy	4	-12	4	-12	12	-10
Best Friend Kiss	Best Friend	Positive	Rel, Mood, Outgoing/Shy	0%	Rel, Mood, Neat/Sloppy, Playful/Serious, Nice/Grouchy	6	-18	6	-18	12	-10
Blackmail	Archenemy	Negative	Mood, Rel, Neat/Sloppy	50%	Rel, Mood, Outgoing/Shy, Neat/Sloppy, Playful/Serious, Nice/Grouchy	-1	-10	-1	-10	5	5
Burp In Face	Enemy	Negative	Mood, Neat/Sloppy	50%	Rel, Mood, Outgoing/Shy, Neat/Sloppy, Playful/Serious, Active/Lazy, Nice/Grouchy	-10	-5	-10	-5	5	5
Card Trick	Acquaintance	Positive	Mood, Rel, Neat/Sloppy	50%	Rel, Mood, Neat/Sloppy, Nice/Grouchy	4	-2	4	-2	8	-5
Caress	Crush	Positive	Mood, Rel, Outgoing/Shy, Nice/Grouchy	0%	Rel, Mood, Outgoing/Shy, Playful/Serious, Nice/Grouchy	4	-7	4	-7	10	-8
Challenge to Fiddle	Ghost	N/A	Always	0%	= A's Aspiration and Creativity	0	0	0	0	0	0
Charm	Friend	Positive	Mood, Rel, Nice/Grouchy	-30%	Rel, Mood, Outgoing/Shy, Playful/Serious, Active/Lazy, Nice/Grouchy	3	-5	3	-5	10	-8
Check Out	Acquaintance	Positive	Mood, Rel, Outgoing/Shy	50%	Rel, Mood, Outgoing/Shy, Playful/Serious	7	-5	7	-5	8	-5
Chill Out	Enemy	Positive	Always	75%	Rel, Mood, Neat/Sloppy, Active/Lazy	5	-5	5	-5	5	5
Compliment	Acquaintance	Positive	Mood, Rel, Nice/Grouchy	50%	Rel, Mood, Outgoing/Shy, Nice/Grouchy	6	-5	6	-5	8	-5
Confide	Friend	Positive	Mood, Rel, Outgoing/Shy	0%	Rel, Mood, Outgoing/Shy, Nice/Grouchy	5	-5	5	-5	10	-8
Dirty Joke	Friend	Positive	Mood, Rel, Neat/Sloppy	25%	Rel, Mood, Outgoing/Shy, Neat/Sloppy, Playful/Serious, Active/Lazy, Nice/Grouchy	4	-8	4	-8	10	-8

Social B Accept	Social B Reject	Fear Accept	Hate Accept	Jealousy Accept	P.O.'d Accept	Disgust Accept	Love Accept	Crush Accept	Friend Accept	Fear Reject	Hate Reject	Jealousy Reject	P.O.'d Reject	Disgust Reject	Love Reject	Crush Reject	Friend Reject
12	-10	-2	-2	-2	-2	-2	0	0	2	0	0	0	0	0	-1	-1	-1
5	5	-5	-5	-5	-5	-5	0	0	0	0	1	0	0	0	-1	-1	-1
5	1	0	0	0	1	0	-1	-1	-1	0	3	0	1	0	-2	-2	-2
7	2	0	0	0	0	0	0	0	3	0	0	0	0	0	-1	-1	-1
10	-8	2	-1	-1	-1	-1	0	0	1	4	0	0	0	0	-1	-1	-1
12	-10	-2	-2	-2	-2	-2	0	0	-1	0	0	0	1	0	-2	-2	-1
12	-10	-2	-2	-2	-2	-2	3	1	-1	0	0	0	1	0	-2	-2	-1
5	5	5	-5	-5	-5	-5	-5	-5	5	0	5	0	0	0	-5	-5	-5
5	5	0	0	0	0	6	-2	-2	-2	0	4	0	0	2	-2	-2	-2
8	-5	-1	-1	-1	-1	-1	0	0	1	0	0	0	1	0	-1	-1	-1
10	-8	-1	-1	-1	-1	-1	3	0	-1	0	0	0	2	0	-1	-1	-1
0	0	0	0	0	0	0	0	0	0	0	0	0	0	0	0	0	0
10	-8	-1	-1	-1	-1	-1	1	1	0	0	2	0	0	0	-1	-1	-1
8	-5	-1	-1	-1	-1	-1	0	5	-3	0	1	0	1	0	-1	-1	-1
5	5	-5	-5	-5	-5	-5	0	0	0	0	1	0	0	0	-1	-1	-1
8	-5	-1	-1	-1	-1	-1	0	0	1	0	0	0	1	0	-1	-1	-1
10	-8	-1	-1	-1	-1	-1	0	0	1	0	2	0	0	0	-1	-1	-1
10	-8	-1	-1	-1	-1	1	0	0	2	0	1	0	5	0	-1	-1	-1

Social Interaction Directory continued

Interaction	Relationship Level/Stance	Pos/Neg	Availability	Base Prob%	Accept Based on B's	Rel A Accept	Rel A Reject	Rel B Accept	Rel B Reject	Social A Accept	Social A Reject
Dis	Best Friend	Negative	Mood, Nice/Grouchy	0%	Rel, Mood, Playful/Serious, Nice/Grouchy	-8	-3	-8	-3	-8	-7
Draw Portrait	Acquaintance	Positive	Mood, Rel, Outgoing/Shy	50%	Rel, Mood, Playful/Serious, Active/Lazy	5	-3	5	-3	8	-5
Electro-Hand	Archenemy	Negative	Mood, Playful/Serious	100%	Rel, Mood, Outgoing/Shy, Playful/Serious, Nice/Grouchy	5	-5	5	-5	5	5
Elicit Comfort	Best Friend	Positive	Mood, Outgoing/Shy	0%	Rel, Mood, Outgoing/Shy, Nice/Grouchy	3	-9	3	-9	12	-10
Fight	Archenemy	Negative	Mood, Nice/Grouchy	50%	Mood	-12	-12	-12	-12	5	1
Flying Hug	Crush	Positive	Mood, Rel, Active/Lazy	0%	Rel, Mood, Outgoing/Shy, Playful/Serious, Active/Lazy	5	-8	5	-8	10	-8
Friend Kiss	Friend	Positive	Mood, Rel, Nice/Grouchy	0%	Rel, Mood, Outgoing/Shy, Playful/Serious, Nice/Grouchy	5	-10	5	-10	10	-8
Give Daisy	Archenemy	Positive	Always	75%	Rel, Mood, Outgoing/Shy, Neat/Sloppy, Nice/Grouchy	7	-5	7	-5	5	5
Give Finger	Enemy	Negative	Mood, Nice/Grouchy	100%	Rel, Mood, Outgoing/Shy, Neat/Sloppy, Playful/Serious, Nice/Grouchy	5	-10	5	-10	5	5
Gossip	Generic	Positive	Mood, Rel, Outgoing/Shy	100%	Random	2	2	-2	-2	7	2
Greet	Universal	Positive	Always	100%	Random	2	0	2	0	3	0
Gross Out	Friend	Negative	Mood, Rel, Neat/Sloppy	50%	Rel, Mood, Neat/Sloppy, Playful/Serious, Active/Lazy	5	-12	5	-12	5	0
Grovel	Archenemy	Positive	Always	75%	Rel, Mood, Neat/Sloppy, Playful/Serious, Nice/Grouchy	8	-4	8	-4	5	5
Hit On	Friend	Positive	Mood, Rel, Outgoing/Shy	0%	Rel, Mood, Outgoing/Shy, Neat/Sloppy, Playful/Serious	5	-10	5	-10	10	-8
Hold Hands	Crush	Positive	Mood, Rel, Outgoing/Shy	15%	Rel, Mood, Outgoing/Shy, Neat/Sloppy, Nice/Grouchy	3	-5	3	-5	10	-8
Impress	Acquaintance	Positive	Mood, Rel, Outgoing/Shy	50%	Rel, Mood, Outgoing/Shy, Neat/Sloppy, Playful/Serious	5	-6	5	-6	8	-5
Insult	Friend	Negative	Mood, Rel, Nice/Grouchy	51%	Rel, Mood, Outgoing/Shy, Neat/Sloppy, Playful/Serious, Nice/Grouchy	5	-5	-5	-5	0	0
Kick Out	Universal	Positive	Always	100%	Random	-30	-5	-30	-5	0	0
Kicky Bag	Acquaintance	Positive	Mood, Rel, Active/Lazy	50%	Rel, Mood, Outgoing/Shy, Playful/Serious, Active/Lazy	4	-3	4	-3	8	-5
Lover Hug	Lover	Positive	Mood, Active/Lazy	0%	Rel, Outgoing/Shy, Active/Lazy, Nice/Grouchy	4	-12	4	-12	15	-12

SOCIAL B ACCEPT	SOCIAL B REJECT	FEAR ACCEPT	HATE ACCEPT	JEALOUSY ACCEPT	P.O.'D ACCEPT	DISGUST ACCEPT	LOVE ACCEPT	CRUSH ACCEPT	FRIEND ACCEPT	FEAR REJECT	HATE REJECT	JEALOUSY REJECT	P.O.'D REJECT	DISGUST REJECT	LOVE REJECT	CRUSH REJECT	FRIEND REJECT
-8	-7	3	0	0	0	0	-1	-1	-1	0	3	0	0	0	-1	-1	-1
8	-5	-1	-1	-1	-1	-1	0	0	1	0	0	0	1	0	-1	-1	-1
5	5	3	0	0	0	0	-2	-2	-2	0	0	0	5	0	-5	-5	-5
12	-10	-2	-2	-2	-2	-2	0	0	2	0	0	0	1	0	-1	-1	-1
5	1	5	0	0	0	0	-5	-5	-5	0	5	0	0	0	-5	-5	-5
10	-8	-1	-1	-1	-1	-1	3	0	-1	0	0	0	2	0	-1	-1	-1
10	-8	-1	-1	-1	-1	-1	4	4	-3	0	0	0	5	0	-3	-3	-3
5	5	-3	-3	-3	-3	0	2	2	0	0	0	0	5	0	-1	-1	-1
5	5	0	3	0	0	0	-2	-2	-2	0	5	0	0	0	-2	-2	-2
5	2	0	0	0	0	0	0	0	0	0	0	0	0	0	0	0	0
2	0	0	0	0	0	0	0	0	0	0	0	0	0	0	0	0	0
5	0	0	0	0	0	3	-1	-1	-1	0	1	0	0	6	-5	-5	-5
5	5	-5	-5	-5	-5	0	0	0	0	0	3	0	0	0	-1	-1	-1
10	-8	-1	-1	-1	-1	-1	2	2	-3	0	0	0	2	0	-1	-1	-1
10	-8	-1	-1	-1	-1	-1	3	0	-1	0	0	0	2	0	-1	-1	-1
8	-5	-1	-1	-1	-1	-1	0	0	1	0	2	0	0	0	-1	-1	-1
0	0	3	0	0	0	0	-1	-1	-1	0	3	0	0	0	-2	-2	-2
0	0	0	0	0	0	0	0	0	0	0	0	0	0	0	0	0	0
8	-5	-1	-1	-1	-1	-1	0	0	1	0	2	0	0	0	-1	-1	-1
15	-12	-2	-2	-2	-2	-2	3	0	-2	0	1	0	1	0	-2	-2	-1

Social Interaction Directory continued

Interaction	Relationship Level/Stance	Pos/Neg	Availability	Base Prob%	Accept Based on B's	Rel A Accept	Rel A Reject	Rel B Accept	Rel B Reject	Social A Accept	Social A Reject
Make Out	Lover	Positive	Mood, Outgoing/Shy	20%	Rel, Outgoing/Shy, Neat/Sloppy, Nice/Grouchy	4	-12	4	-12	15	-12
Mock	Friend	Negative	Mood, Rel, Nice/Grouchy	50%	Rel, Mood, Outgoing/Shy, Neat/Sloppy, Playful/Serious, Nice/Grouchy	3	-8	3	-8	5	0
Poke Chest	Enemy	Negative	Mood, Neat/Sloppy	75%	Rel, Mood, Outgoing/Shy, Neat/Sloppy, Nice/Grouchy	-5	-5	-5	-5	5	5
Portable Gaming	Best Friend	Positive	Mood, Playful/Serious	0%	Rel, Mood, Outgoing/Shy, Playful/Serious, Active/Lazy	4	-12	4	-12	12	-10
Possess	Ghost	N/A	Always	0%	= inverse of B's Logic	0	0	0	0	0	0
Propose	Lover	Positive	Rel, Mood, Nice/Grouchy	25%	Rel, Mood	4	-12	4	-12	15	-12
Puke	Ghost	N/A	Always	0%	= inverse of B's Logic	0	0	0	0	0	0
Punch Arm	Best Friend	Negative	Mood, Active/Lazy, Nice/Grouchy	0%	Rel, Mood, Outgoing/Shy, Neat/Sloppy, Playful/Serious, Active/Lazy, Nice/Grouchy	5	-15	5	-15	12	-10
Reminisce	Best Friend	Positive	Rel, Mood, Outgoing/Shy	0%	Rel, Mood, Outgoing/Shy, Playful/Serious, Active/Lazy	3	-9	3	-9	12	-10
Secret Handshake	Generic	Positive	Mood, Rel, Outgoing/Shy	0%	Rel, Playful/Serious, Mood	2	-3	2	-3	7	0
Serenade	Crush	Positive	Mood, Rel, Outgoing/Shy	0%	Rel, Mood, Outgoing/Shy, Playful/Serious, Active/Lazy, Nice/Grouchy	3	-7	3	-7	10	-8
Sexy Growl	Lover	Positive	Mood, Playful/Serious	0%	Rel, Outgoing/Shy, Playful/Serious, Mood	4	-12	4	-12	15	-12
Shove	Enemy	Negative	Mood, Active/Lazy	75%	Rel, Mood, Outgoing/Shy, Active/Lazy, Nice/Grouchy	-4	-8	-4	-8	5	5
Show Sock Puppet	Acquaintance	Positive	Mood, Rel, Neat/Sloppy	40%	Rel, Mood, Outgoing/Shy, Neat/Sloppy, Playful/Serious, Nice/Grouchy	7	-8	7	-8	8	-5
Slap	Acquaintance	Negative	Mood, Rel, Nice/Grouchy	80%	Rel, Mood, Outgoing/Shy, Nice/Grouchy	-5	-10	-5	-5	3	0
Slap Game	Friend	Negative	Mood, Rel, Active/Lazy	50%	Rel, Mood, Playful/Serious, Active/Lazy	4	-8	4	-8	5	0
Smooch	Crush	Positive	Mood, Rel, Playful/Serious	0%	Rel, Mood, Outgoing/Shy, Neat/Sloppy, Playful/Serious	5	-12	5	-12	10	-8
Spook	Ghost	N/A	Always	0%	= inverse of B's Logic	0	0	0	0	0	0
Squeeze	Lover	Positive	Mood, Neat/Sloppy	0%	Rel, Mood, Neat/Sloppy, Playful/Serious, Active/Lazy	4	-12	4	-12	15	-12
Talk	Generic	Positive	Mood, Playful/Serious	100%	Random	3	-2	3	-2	5	2
Tease	Lover	Negative	Mood, Nice/Grouchy	40%	Rel, Mood, Playful/Serious, Nice/Grouchy	4	-12	4	-12	15	-12

Social B Accept	Social B Reject	Fear Accept	Hate Accept	Jealousy Accept	P.O.'d Accept	Disgust Accept	Love Accept	Crush Accept	Friend Accept	Fear Reject	Hate Reject	Jealousy Reject	P.O.'d Reject	Disgust Reject	Love Reject	Crush Reject	Friend Reject
15	-12	-2	-2	-2	-2	-2	3	0	-2	0	1	0	1	0	-2	-2	-1
5	0	0	0	0	3	0	-1	-1	-1	0	0	0	4	0	-2	-2	-2
5	5	3	0	0	0	0	-2	-2	-2	0	4	0	0	0	-2	-2	-2
12	-10	-2	-2	-2	-2	-2	0	0	2	0	0	0	0	0	-1	-1	-1
0	0	2	0	0	0	0	0	0	0	0	0	0	0	0	0	0	0
15	-12	-2	-2	-2	-2	-2	3	0	-2	0	0	0	0	0	-2	-2	1
0	0	2	0	0	0	0	0	0	0	0	0	0	0	0	0	0	0
12	-10	0	0	0	0	0	0	0	2	2	0	0	1	0	-1	-1	-1
12	-10	-2	-2	-2	-2	-2	0	0	2	0	0	0	1	0	-1	-1	-1
7	0	0	0	0	0	0	0	0	1	0	0	0	0	0	-1	-1	-1
10	-8	-1	-1	-1	-1	-1	3	0	-1	0	0	0	2	0	-1	-1	-1
15	-12	-2	-2	-2	-2	-2	3	0	-2	0	1	0	1	0	-2	-2	-1
5	5	3	0	0	0	0	-2	-2	-2	0	0	0	4	0	-2	-2	-2
8	-5	-1	-1	-1	-1	-1	0	0	1	2	0	0	0	0	-1	-1	-1
3	0	5	0	0	0	0	-5	-5	-5	0	5	0	0	0	-3	-3	-3
5	0	3	0	0	0	0	0	0	1	3	1	0	0	0	-1	-1	-1
10	-8	-1	-1	-1	-1	-1	3	0	-1	0	0	0	2	0	-1	-1	-1
0	0	2	0	0	0	0	0	0	0	0	0	0	0	0	0	0	0
15	-12	-2	-2	-2	-2	-2	3	0	-2	0	1	0	1	0	-2	-2	-1
5	2	0	0	0	0	0	0	0	0	0	0	0	0	0	0	0	0
15	-12	0	0	0	0	0	0	0	1	0	2	0	1	0	-3	-3	-2

Social Interaction Directory continued

Interaction	Relationship Level/Stance	Pos/Neg	Availability	Base Prob%	Accept Based on B's	Rel A Accept	Rel A Reject	Rel B Accept	Rel B Reject	Social A Accept	Social A Reject
Tell Joke	Acquaintance	Positive	Mood, Rel, Playful/Serious	50%	Rel, Mood, Neat/Sloppy, Playful/Serious	5	-3	5	-3	8	-5
Tell Tall Tale	Friend	Positive	Mood, Rel, Neat/Sloppy	0%	Rel, Mood, Outgoing/Shy, Active/Lazy, Nice/Grouchy	3	-5	3	-5	10	-8
Threaten	Acquaintance	Negative	Always	60%	Rel, Mood, Neat/Sloppy, Nice/Grouchy	-5	-5	-5	-5	3	0
Tickle	Friend	Positive	Mood, Rel, Playful/Serious	20%	Rel, Mood, Playful/Serious, Nice/Grouchy	3	-5	3	-5	10	-8
Wail	Ghost	N/A	Always	0%	= inverse of B's Logic	0	0	0	0	0	0
Wedgie	Enemy	Negative	Mood, Playful/Serious	75%	Rel, Mood, Outgoing/Shy, Playful/Serious, Active/Lazy, Nice/Grouchy	-8	-10	-8	-10	5	5

Visitor Behavior

Hospitality means tending to your visitor's Needs. This is especially important since visitors always arrive with their Needs fairly low.

> **tip** Since visitors arrive with their Needs depressed, it's a good idea to hold off on socializing until they've had a chance to have a bite to eat and bit of Fun.

Keep good, nourishing food servings available to visitors by making group meals.

Well-cared-for visitors stay for a very long time (until 1:00 a.m.), providing ample opportunity for socializing. Offer them no way to refuel their Needs, however, and they leave abruptly.

> **note** Since acceptance of most social interactions depends in large part on the recipient's Mood, you have another reason to make sure your visitor's Needs are being met.

Since only members of a household may use certain objects (cooking appliances, beds, etc.) it's up to you to provide objects and courtesies that allow your visitors to feed their motives.

◆ Hunger: Serve a meal with multiple portions. It costs more, but this makes six plates of food, more than enough for a small gathering of hungry Sims.

◆ Energy: Equip your house with objects that supply Energy without sleep. The best bet is an espresso machine.

◆ Comfort: Provide lots of comfy places to sit.

◆ Hygiene: Your guests' Hygiene needs can be met with sinks for hand washing. Alternatively, your guests can follow your Sim into the hot tub if he gets in first to set the tone.

◆ Social: You provide this by letting your Sim interact freely with the guests. Guests can also satisfy their Social motive by joining a group object interaction, such as the TV, air hockey table, or the hot tub.

◆ Bladder: Make sure the toilets are clean and easily accessible in roomy bathrooms. More than one bathroom can't hurt, and multiple doors make access easy.

Social B Accept	Social B Reject	Fear Accept	Hate Accept	Jealousy Accept	P.O.'d Accept	Disgust Accept	Love Accept	Crush Accept	Friend Accept	Fear Reject	Hate Reject	Jealousy Reject	P.O.'d Reject	Disgust Reject	Love Reject	Crush Reject	Friend Reject
8	-5	-1	-1	-1	-1	-1	0	0	1	0	0	0	1	0	-1	-1	-1
10	-8	-1	-1	-1	-1	-1	0	0	1	0	0	0	1	0	-1	-1	-1
3	0	3	0	0	0	0	-2	-2	-1	0	4	0	0	0	-2	-2	-2
10	-8	-1	1	-1	-1	-1	0	0	2	0	3	0	1	0	-1	-1	-1
0	0	2	0	0	0	0	0	0	0	0	0	0	0	0	0	0	0
5	5	3	0	0	0	0	-2	-2	-2	0	0	0	4	0	-2	-2	-2

◆ Fun: Furnish your Sim's house with Fun activities. Even better, make them group activities so he or she can socialize with guests while everyone fuels Fun. Note that visitors use many objects on their own initiative but must be invited by a household member to get into joinable activities.

◆ Environment: Keep messes to a minimum and decorate your home with strong Environment score-enhancing objects. Make sure you have plenty of art objects, and keep those trashcans plentiful and accessible.

> **tip** Visitors don't turn on the TV by themselves. Do it for them before they arrive so you don't need to break stride while greeting guests.

Parties

Parties are initiated via phone. Your Sim automatically invites five Sims with whom your Sim has a relationship of 90 or more. If your Sim knows fewer than five Sims at that level, the rest are chosen at random from all other Sims your Sim knows.

Parties begin within moments of the phone invitation.

Within moments, the guests arrive, and the party begins. It ends six hours later, or earlier if two or more Sims depart prematurely. Sims only blow off your party if their Needs aren't being met. Lots must be equipped with toilets, available food (visitors can't use the fridge), a sink for hand washing (visitors can't take baths), and espresso (they can't sleep on beds or sofas) if you want your guests to stay the full six hours.

> **note** While a party is going on, guests' Needs decay more slowly than normal.

If the party goes beyond 2:00 am, the police come and fine your Sim §100. Once your Sim's been fined he or she won't be fined again on the same day, so why not keep the party going for its full duration?

> **tip** For fiscal reasons, therefore, it's always best to start parties no later than 8:00 pm.

The goal of a party is to have a large gathering of Sims in a place where your Sim can keep his or her Needs well tended. This is an optimal relationship-building environment, and a lot of socializing can be done in a very short period.

Chapter 6
Objects

Sims, no matter how lofty their Aspirations, are still materialists at heart. They *love* stuff but not just any stuff—stuff that satisfies their basic Needs and helps them learn new skills. Not that appearance isn't important; the cooler an object is, the better.

This section guides you through the objects that can make your Sim's world a humming, efficient utopia or a dangerous dysfunctional deathtrap.

Objects, Needs, and Skills

Objects serve two primary functions, satisfying your Sims' Needs or improving their skills. When looking to spend your Simoleons, look carefully at what Needs could be filled more efficiently and which skills need work.

Every object's impact on a skill or Need is listed in the catalogue later in this section.

Of course, objects have other functions. Some are just cool to have. And some serve specific functions beyond Needs or skills. Tables, for example, serve no Need or skill function, but life gets pretty difficult without a solid place to sit and eat.

Object Quality and Price

Generally, the more expensive an item is, the more it satisfies its assigned Needs or skills.

The more-expensive skill objects pay off with faster skill development and maybe some Need-feeding ability. Plus, they look really cool.

For Need-satisfying and skill objects, the object's power is indicated in the catalog—the higher the number, the faster or more completely the object satisfies the Need. Often, however, an object's increased value is due to other factors like secondary Need satisfactions (an expensive toilet, for example, feeds both Bladder and Comfort).

For skill-building objects, the price directly reflects the rate of skill acquisition (the cheapest item feeds at the slowest rate and the most expensive one at a higher rate) and the presence of secondary effects (such as multiple skill training, an Environment impact, etc.).

> **note** Occasionally, an object can actually drain a Need. Coffee machines, for example, lower Bladder as they raise Energy.

The Basics

Every smoothly running Sim household needs certain basics for your Sims' eight essential needs. Generally, you can start with the cheapest objects, but sometimes spending a little more money pays off in spades.

Reading while using the toilet is Sim multitasking at its finest.

◆ Hunger: Get a refrigerator. If you don't want to spend all your money on cheap but nutritionally empty snack foods, also look into a countertop and a stove or microwave. A little extra money gets you a food processor or a blender. The better the cooking objects in your Sims' homes, the more ingredients and preparations they can access and the more powerful the food they create.

- Comfort: Make sure you have chairs for dining tables (standing up while eating reduces Comfort) and a good couch for TV watching and the occasional power nap. Your bed provides simultaneous Comfort and Energy, so consider both Needs when selecting one.

- Hygiene: Get a shower. To reduce time spent bathing, extend a little and buy a good one. Stay away from bathtubs early on. Though they offer Comfort, they tend to offer slower satisfaction than a comparably priced shower. Your Sim doesn't need a bathroom sink (instead, shower after every second or third toilet visit), but there must be one for guests to wash up and restore their Hygiene.

- Bladder: You must have a toilet unless you like wetting the floor. A more expensive toilet provides Comfort while you sit. Time on the toilet doesn't have to be wasted. Both playing handheld games and reading magazines while on the toilet can satisfy Fun, and reading can lead to the discovery of recipes and game tips.

- Energy: The floor is no real alternative to even the most awful bed, so get one immediately. An expensive bed lets you refuel on dramatically fewer sleep hours than a cheap one, so this is a good place to splurge.

- Fun: Right off the bat, get a cheap TV to put in front of the couch. It's inexpensive, you can get Comfort at the same time, and it can be a social activity.

- Social: A telephone allows you to invite friends over and even maintain friendships over the landline. A phone is also your lifeline to services like the maid and repairman, as well as the police and fire stations.

- Environment: The best thing you can do for Environment score when money is tight is to let the sun (or the electric equivalent) shine in. Make sure your house has numerous windows and spend freely but wisely on interior lights. Decorations help Environment too, but they can be very expensive for a relatively small boost.

Depreciation

All objects depreciate immediately once placed on a lot. Every day thereafter, the object's resale value drops by a fixed amount per day ("Daily Depreciation") until it reaches a set floor ("Depreciation Limit") below which it can't go. No object is ever worth less than 40 percent of its original value.

> **note** Depreciation isn't an entirely bad thing. It lowers your net worth and that, in turn, lowers the amount of your bills.

Fire Code

The fire code governs how many objects can be placed on a lot.

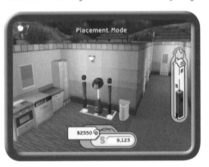

The fire code meter shows how close to capacity the lot is. When it reaches the top, you've violated the fire code.

When you place an object, the fire code meter appears, representing how close the lot is to full capacity. When the red bar hits the top of the meter, the limit is reached. Additional objects can be placed, but with a stern warning and a cost.

When a lot is over its object limit, placing another object generates, upon return to the game, an immediate fire somewhere on the lot.

To avoid this fiery penalty, don't place objects in violation of the fire code. If something needs to be placed, remove some objects or walls from the lot first, then place the new object.

> **note** Placing multiple versions of the same object (for example, six of the same chair around a table) increases a lot's object count less than the same number of different objects (like six unmatched chairs). To avoid running afoul of the fire code in a large house, therefore, use many of the same objects whenever possible. It lets you put more stuff on the lot and provides a decorative continuity too.

Flammability

Your beloved objects can be burned and destroyed if a fire breaks out, reducing them to useless (and Environment score–depressing) ash if not extinguished in time.

Fire isn't totally preventable, but it helps to know what causes it.

- Objects: Objects with open flames (stoves, grills, fireplaces, etc.) carry a chance of igniting any adjacent object. Keep the area around these objects clear if possible.

- Exceeding the Fire Code: If you place objects in a lot that's already at its object capacity (fire code limit), there's a random chance of a fire until the total object count is reduced below the limit.

Fire can, as described, destroy objects, but it can also kill Sims. They can, of course, be returned to life, but it's either expensive or risky.

Fires are extinguished by summoning the fire department. This is done by phone or automatically if there's a smoke detector in the same room as the fire.

The new fire extinguisher object lets your Sims take firefighting into their own hands.

tip There should always be a smoke detector in any kitchen or room with a fireplace.

For faster do-it-yourself fire management, purchase a Snuffit Fire Destroyer. This object, usable only in direct control, snuffs flames in no time flat, usually before the fire department can even arrive. To extinguish flames yourself, use the Extinguish interaction on the fire. It's much slower than the direct control method, but it may just save your objects or housemates if the fire department hasn't been called.

Objects and Building on Lots

You may put your fingerprint on any lot, but you can't make a profit off objects that preexist on the lot. Preexisting objects can be moved, rotated, or deleted, but never sold.

Selling Objects

When you need cash, you can of course sell off (via Buy mode) your items for their current depreciated value. Once an object is placed, you never get back the full purchase price.

Bills

Bills arrive every three days and represent three percent of the depreciated value of objects on the current lot. The more and nicer things you own, the higher your bills.

Watch your mailbox for bills and pay them promptly.

Bills are delivered to your mailbox and due 10 days from receipt. Take them from the mailbox and pay them as soon as possible. After 10 days, an unpaid bill becomes past due, and the Repo Man comes to take objects roughly equivalent to your debt. If there aren't enough objects to cover the bills, the Repo Man takes as many as possible and forgives the remaining liability.

tip In direct control mode, you can take the bills from the mailbox and immediately pay them or set them down somewhere they can be more effectively ignored (if that's your thing).

Object Breakage

Objects eventually break after frequent use; every use brings the object steps closer to a breakdown. Broken objects display a Repair interaction and either work (but with detrimental side effects) or can't be used until fixed.

Getting your Sims' hands dirty repairing things themselves saves repair costs but takes time and (depending on the object) can delivery a painful or fatal shock.

Your Sims can do this themselves (though less than three Mechanical skill points means a good chance of electrocution and death), but this can be slow if you're not high in Mechanical skill. A better use of your time might be to call the Repair Man, who comes and fixes every broken object in your home in a single visit.

When you're self-repairing, the meter above your Sim's head indicates the progress of the repair, not the acquisition of Mechanical skill.

Theft

At night (midnight to be exact) if everyone in the house is asleep or at work, your Sim's home can be invaded by the Thief. He enters and selects the most-expensive accessible item and makes off with it.

To combat this, install a burglar alarm. Note that an alarm protects only single rooms, so full protection requires one in every room with an exterior entrance. The alarm automatically summons the police, who may (or may not) catch the Thief.

If the Thief is apprehended, the object is put back where it belongs.

tip Since outdoors counts as one big room, cheap protection can be had by building single wall segments at the sidewalk corners of your lot and putting alarms on each. Thus, the instant the Thief sets foot on your lot the alarm sounds, sending him into flight.

Object Directory

Object Directory

Object	Category	Price	Asp. Points to Unlock	Hunger	Comfort	Hygiene	Bladder	Energy	Fun	Social	Environment
A.M.P. Wall Lamp	Lighting	§125	—	0	0	0	0	0	0	0	2
AE Arcade Unit	Electronics	§675	—	0	0	0	0	0	6	0	0
Amishim Bookcase	Skill	§250	—	0	0	0	0	0	0	0	0
Art Lamp	Lighting	§325	—	0	0	0	0	0	0	0	1
Astrowonder Telescope	Skill	§500	—	0	0	0	0	0	0	0	0
Athena by Klassick Repro Inc.	Decorative	§5,000	—	0	0	0	0	0	3	0	10
Beetle Yak Rug	Decorative	§5,500	—	0	0	0	0	0	0	0	5
Bel-Air Diner Seat	Seating & Beds	§200	—	0	3	0	0	0	0	0	0
Bel-Air Dining Table	Surfaces	§95	—	0	0	0	0	0	0	0	0
"Big Man" Rifle Replica	Decorative	§450	—	0	0	0	0	0	3	0	5
Bird of Paradise	Decorative	§333	—	0	0	0	0	0	3	0	1
"Birth of Venus" Master Sink	Plumbing	§680	—	0	0	3	0	0	0	0	1
Blade Vision VERY High HD TV	Electronics	§3,500	8,700	0	0	0	0	0	5	0	0
Blue Glow Special	Lighting	§25	—	0	0	0	0	0	0	0	1
Boggs Ole Timey Saloon	Miscellaneous	§3,500	—	0	0	0	0	0	5	0	0
Boggs Saloon Chair	Seating & Beds	§400	—	0	6	0	0	0	0	0	0
Boggs Western Laminate	Surfaces	§410	—	6	0	0	0	0	0	0	1
Bonsai Tree	Skill	§250	—	0	0	0	0	0	0	0	0
"Boom Boom" Floor Lamp	Lighting	§255	—	0	0	0	0	0	0	0	1
Brass Bed	Seating & Beds	§550	—	0	3	0	0	4	6	0	0
Callow Lily	Decorative	§250	—	0	0	0	0	0	1	0	2
Cantankerous Bowel Fish	Decorative	§700	13,500	0	0	0	0	0	3	0	6
"Cerberus" Floor Lamp	Lighting	§245	—	0	0	0	0	0	0	0	1
Chill Lamp	Lighting	§410	—	0	0	0	0	0	0	0	3
Chimeway & Daughters Piano	Skill	§5,000	—	0	0	0	0	0	1	0	0

Object Directory continued

Object	Category	Price	Asp. Points to Unlock	Hunger	Comfort	Hygiene	Bladder	Energy	Fun	Social	Environment
Chocola "Psycho-Active" Drinks	Electronics	§1,500	—	4	0	0	0	3	0	0	0
Chow Bella Bachelor Fridge	Appliances	§750	—	6	0	0	0	0	0	0	0
CiaoTime 360 Moderna Range	Appliances	§500	—	6	0	0	0	0	0	0	0
Cinema Deco Sconce	Lighting	§280	—	0	0	0	0	0	0	0	3
Claymore Ceramic Sink	Plumbing	§230	—	0	0	2	0	0	0	0	0
Club Códe Thrill Light	Lighting	§450	—	0	0	0	0	0	0	0	1
Comic Dehydrator	Miscellaneous	§550	500	0	0	0	0	0	3	0	2
"Concreta" Display Counter	Surfaces	§140	—	4	0	0	0	0	0	0	0
Copper King Kitchen Counter	Surfaces	§280	—	6	0	0	0	0	0	0	1
Cuddlers' Cradle	Seating & Beds	§900	3,400	0	10	0	0	0	0	0	0
"Cupid 2: Revenge of the Toads"	Decorative	§4,000	—	0	0	0	0	0	3	0	9
CyberChronometer Alarm Clock	Electronics	§50	—	0	0	0	0	0	0	0	0
Daddy Warmbums Gas Heater	Lighting	§325	—	0	0	0	0	0	0	0	1
Davey Jones' Crocker	Plumbing	§950	—	0	2	-1	10	0	1	0	0
Decorative Phone Pole	Decorative	§200	—	0	0	0	0	0	0	0	0
Defective Arcade Genie Lamp	Miscellaneous	§6,500	5,300	0	0	0	0	0	0	0	0
Deluxar Counter	Surfaces	§590	—	8	0	0	0	0	0	0	1
Dial-a-While Bird Bath	Decorative	§500	900	0	0	0	0	0	3	0	5
Dialectric Free Standing Range	Appliances	§210	—	4	0	0	0	0	0	0	0
Dig Dog Hotdog Dispensary	Electronics	§1,700	4,600	5	0	0	0	3	0	0	0
"Does it Rock!" Electric Guitar	Skill	§1,500	—	0	0	0	0	0	1	0	0
DreaMaker "Fantasy" Dresser	Miscellaneous	§500	—	0	0	0	0	0	0	0	0
DreaMaker Crash Pad	Seating & Beds	§350	—	0	1	0	0	3	6	0	0
DreaMaker Super Crash Pad	Seating & Beds	§780	—	0	5	0	0	5	6	0	0
Driver Pro 2006: "Chip Shots."	Miscellaneous	§975	2,500	0	0	0	0	0	6	0	0
EconoCool Refrigerator	Appliances	§500	—	4	0	0	0	0	0	0	0
Elementary Memories Dining Chair	Seating & Beds	§80	—	0	3	0	0	0	0	0	0
"Emergency"	Decorative	§175	—	0	0	0	0	0	3	0	2
!!!!Espresso.it.supremo!!!!	Appliances	§450	—	0	0	0	-1	2	0	0	0
Exerto Self-Spot Exercise Machine	Skill	§500	—	0	0	0	0	0	0	0	0
EZ Green Camping Chair	Seating & Beds	§250	—	0	3	0	0	0	0	0	0
EZ Green Camping Counter	Surfaces	§175	—	4	0	0	0	0	0	0	0
Fable Table	Surfaces	§150	—	0	0	0	0	0	0	0	0
Façade King Western Bank	Decorative	§5,000	14,300	0	0	0	0	0	0	0	7
Façade King Western Hotel	Decorative	§5,000	12,800	0	0	0	0	0	0	0	7
Façade King Western Saloon	Decorative	§5,000	20,600	0	0	0	0	0	0	0	7
Façade King Western Store	Decorative	§5,000	19,600	0	0	0	0	0	0	0	7
Faux Llama Trophy	Decorative	§810	—	0	0	0	0	0	3	0	6

Object Directory continued

Object	Category	Price	Asp. Points to Unlock	Hunger	Comfort	Hygiene	Bladder	Energy	Fun	Social	Environment
"Feelin' Dizzy" Designer Counter	Surfaces	§150	—	4	0	0	0	0	0	0	0
"Fists of Bunny" Poster	Decorative	§50	1,500	0	0	0	0	0	3	0	1
Fists of Spite Punching Bag	Skill	§1,500	—	0	0	0	0	-1	0	0	0
"Fitzroy Dreamers" Rock Pool	Plumbing	§8,500	—	0	7	8	0	0	3	0	0
"Floral Fantasy" by Plastiqkue	Seating & Beds	§450	—	0	7	0	0	2	1	0	0
Flourano Glass Lamp	Lighting	§360	—	0	0	0	0	0	0	0	3
Flush Force "Bowls of Steel" 2100	Plumbing	§500	—	0	0	-1	10	0	1	0	0
Flushitol Public Toilet	Plumbing	§500	—	0	0	-1	10	0	1	0	0
Foot Light	Lighting	§215	—	0	0	0	0	0	0	0	1
"Freedom" Swivel Lamp	Lighting	§230	—	0	0	0	0	0	0	0	1
Freedom Vacuum	Appliances	§3,000	22,800	0	0	0	0	0	0	0	0
"Frood" Tree	Miscellaneous	§150	—	0	0	0	0	0	0	0	2
Fruit Punch Barrel	Appliances	§950	1,900	0	0	0	0	0	0	0	0
Furniture Kamp Floor Lamp	Lighting	§335	—	0	0	0	0	0	0	0	2
Furniture Kamp Table Lamp	Lighting	§255	—	0	0	0	0	0	0	0	2
Garden Swing	Seating & Beds	§700	—	0	7	0	0	0	0	0	0
GenoLife Cactus Plant	Decorative	§250	—	0	0	0	0	0	1	0	2
GenoLife Garden Hutch	Miscellaneous	§650	—	0	0	0	0	0	0	0	3
GenoLife Palmetto Hutch	Decorative	§200	—	0	0	0	0	0	1	0	2
Gleep Table Lamp	Lighting	§375	—	0	0	0	0	0	0	0	3
Gold Record	Decorative	§75	—	0	0	0	0	0	3	0	2
Grey Petals' Painting	Decorative	§3,700	—	0	0	0	0	0	3	0	10
"Harmony" Sculpture	Decorative	§900	—	0	0	0	0	0	3	0	4
Hawaiian Fantasy Tiki Torch	Lighting	§210	700	0	0	0	0	0	0	0	1
Hippity-Humpity! Arcade Game	Electronics	§1,500	2,100	0	0	0	0	0	7	0	0
Hydronomic Kitchen Sink	Plumbing	§250	—	0	0	2	0	0	0	0	0
Imagination Helper	Decorative	§150	—	0	0	0	0	0	3	0	1
Independent Expressions, Inc. Easel	Skill	§750	—	0	0	0	0	0	1	0	0
Inverted Vertigo, Cover Art	Decorative	§50	—	0	0	0	0	0	3	0	1
Iterative Dishwasher	Appliances	§550	—	4	0	0	0	0	0	0	0
"It's Reggae, Mon" Poster	Decorative	§50	—	0	0	0	0	0	3	0	1
"Jayded"	Decorative	§125	—	0	0	0	0	0	3	0	2
"Jimmy Three Fingers" Rocket Bench	Skill	§2,000	—	0	0	0	0	0	0	0	0
Kashgar Table Lamp	Lighting	§115	—	0	0	0	0	0	0	0	1
Krampft Industries Hubba Tubba	Plumbing	§950	—	0	5	5	0	0	0	0	0
La Silla Precaria Arm Chair	Seating & Beds	§1,200	—	0	10	0	0	0	0	0	1
Laser Llama Classic Arcade Game	Electronics	§500	—	0	0	0	0	0	5	0	0
Light Therapy Wall Sconce	Lighting	§35	—	0	0	0	0	0	0	0	1
LiquiTonic Blender	Appliances	§200	—	4	0	0	0	0	0	0	0

Object Directory continued

Object	Category	Price	Asp. Points to Unlock	Hunger	Comfort	Hygiene	Bladder	Energy	Fun	Social	Environment
Lowbough Outdoor Table	Surfaces	§450	—	0	0	0	0	0	0	0	0
Lung Dynasty Scroll	Decorative	§3,500	—	0	0	0	0	0	3	0	10
Madcap Miner Metal Detector	Electronics	§1,200	12,000	0	0	0	0	0	0	0	0
"Magic Fingers" Hydraulic Massage	Electronics	§5,000	6,500	0	10	0	0	0	0	0	0
"Manila 1000" Marine Aquarium	Miscellaneous	§500	—	0	0	0	0	0	0	0	4
MaxArts 5pOr3 Gaming Kit	Electronics	§1,135	—	0	0	0	0	0	7	0	0
"ModMan" Office Chair	Seating & Beds	§200	—	0	3	0	0	0	0	0	0
Molotov Antique Table Lamp	Lighting	§275	—	0	0	0	0	0	0	0	2
Molotov Antique Wall Lamp	Lighting	§160	—	0	0	0	0	0	0	0	2
Molotov Antiques Saloon Table	Surfaces	§390	—	0	0	0	0	0	0	0	0
Moneywell Computer	Electronics	§1,300	—	0	0	0	0	0	6	6	0
Montespaghetti Spring	Decorative	§1,200	—	0	0	0	0	0	3	0	8
Moodscape Painting	Decorative	§390	—	0	0	0	0	0	3	0	4
Multiquick Blender	Appliances	§330	—	6	0	0	0	0	0	0	0
Myne Dining Hall Table	Surfaces	§210	—	0	0	0	0	0	0	0	0
Nemo Dining Table	Surfaces	§1,100	—	0	0	0	0	0	0	0	2
Niagara Love Tub	Plumbing	§6,500	6,900	0	0	7	0	0	7	0	0
Nostalgix Gas Range	Appliances	§750	—	8	0	0	0	0	0	0	0
Nostalgix Refrigerator	Appliances	§1,200	—	8	0	0	0	0	0	0	0
Oceana Sofa	Seating & Beds	§1,420	—	0	10	0	0	2	1	0	2
Office Chair	Seating & Beds	§80	—	0	3	0	0	0	0	0	0
Old Thyme Dining Table	Surfaces	§750	—	0	0	0	0	0	0	0	0
Old Thyme End Table	Surfaces	§440	—	0	0	0	0	0	0	0	1
Opticluster Portrait 360	Decorative	§500	—	0	0	0	0	0	3	0	5
Opticluster Promotional Painting	Decorative	§430	—	0	0	0	0	0	3	0	4
Oriental "Master" Bathtub	Plumbing	§1,300	—	0	6	6	0	0	0	0	0
P5 4400SX+ DS	Electronics	§3,900	6,100	0	0	0	0	0	8	6	0
"Painting leisure study 5078643"	Decorative	§300	—	0	0	0	0	0	3	0	7
Pathologie Costume Trunk	Miscellaneous	§5,500	18,600	0	0	0	0	0	0	0	0
People Invaders	Electronics	§710	—	0	0	0	0	0	6	0	0
Peppy Pete's Player Piano	Skill	§6,500	15,900	0	0	0	0	0	1	0	0
Peppy Pete's Slots A' Hoppin'	Miscellaneous	§1,115	—	0	0	0	0	0	2	0	0
"Perspectif"	Decorative	§1,800	—	0	0	0	0	0	3	0	8
Photo Lamp	Lighting	§320	—	0	0	0	0	0	0	0	1
Piazza Amoretto Fountain	Plumbing	§550	3,100	0	0	4	0	0	3	0	0
Pineapple "Hot Rock" Lamp	Lighting	§210	—	0	0	0	0	0	0	0	1
Plaank Bookcase	Skill	§3,000	—	0	0	0	0	0	0	0	3
Ploof Chair by Tameki	Seating & Beds	§750	—	0	6	0	0	0	0	0	0

Object Directory continued

Object	Category	Price	Asp. Points to Unlock	Hunger	Comfort	Hygiene	Bladder	Energy	Fun	Social	Environment
"Polyp"	Decorative	§2,500	—	0	0	0	0	0	3	0	7
"Positive Potential" Microwave	Appliances	§350	—	6	0	0	0	0	0	0	0
Post-Staunton "Strugatsky" Chess Set	Skill	§400	—	0	0	0	0	0	0	0	0
"Procedural" Music System	Electronics	§2,550	9,700	0	0	0	0	0	7	0	3
Prof. Feather's Chicken Checkers	Skill	§5,500	12,100	0	0	0	0	0	9	0	0
Psychonautica's Cerebro-Chess	Skill	§1,200	10,900	0	0	0	0	0	0	0	0
Public Sink	Plumbing	§360	—	0	0	2	0	0	0	0	0
Pure TV	Electronics	§500	—	0	0	0	0	0	3	0	2
Quaffophonic Bar System	Miscellaneous	§2,500	—	0	0	0	0	0	5	0	0
Quattro-Grav Air Tub	Plumbing	§12,000	17,700	0	10	10	0	0	10	5	0
Radioproactive Heating Stove	Appliances	§1,100	11,500	10	0	0	0	0	0	0	0
Rat Race Executive Power Wheel	Skill	§3,000	21,700	0	0	-1	0	-1	0	0	0
Recycled Couch	Seating & Beds	§290	—	0	5	0	0	2	1	0	0
Red Rover Fire Hydrant	Decorative	§50	—	0	0	0	0	0	0	0	0
ResiStall Toilet Stall	Plumbing	§750	—	0	0	-1	10	0	0	0	0
Retro Space-Age Action Pinball	Electronics	§450	3,700	0	0	0	0	0	5	0	0
Roman Lavender	Decorative	§125	—	0	0	0	0	0	3	0	1
Rose Bush	Decorative	§250	—	0	0	0	0	0	1	0	2
RPG "Paladin" Food Processor	Appliances	§200	—	4	0	0	0	0	0	0	0
Rubber Tree Plant	Decorative	§325	—	0	0	0	0	0	1	0	2
Rug Wizard Computer Rug	Decorative	§2,900	—	0	0	0	0	0	0	0	3
Ruggo Boombox	Electronics	§99	—	0	0	0	0	0	2	0	3
"San Carlos" Brass Bed	Seating & Beds	§850	—	0	6	0	0	8	6	0	0
Screaming Death Bonfire	Miscellaneous	§1,300	10,300	0	0	0	0	0	6	0	0
"See Me, Feel Me" Pinball Machine	Electronics	§300	—	0	0	0	0	0	5	0	0
"Self Portrait" by Dandy Slichtensteen	Decorative	§820	—	0	0	0	0	0	3	0	7
Sewage Brothers Resteze Toilet	Plumbing	§300	—	0	0	-1	10	0	1	0	0
Sewer Grate	Decorative	§50	—	0	0	0	0	0	0	0	0
ShagTime Pop Rug	Decorative	§500	—	0	0	0	0	0	0	0	1
Shahrisabz Table Lamp	Lighting	§105	—	0	0	0	0	0	0	0	1
Shojitsu Wall Lamp	Lighting	§155	—	0	0	0	0	0	0	0	2
ShowerMate	Plumbing	§800	—	0	0	10	0	0	0	0	0
ShowHeuristic Hygiene System	Plumbing	§450	—	0	0	6	0	0	0	0	0
Sidestep Lamp	Lighting	§280	—	0	0	0	0	0	0	0	3
Sili-Camp Tent Site	Seating & Beds	§500	—	0	3	0	0	3	6	0	0
Simple Sink	Plumbing	§320	—	0	0	2	0	0	0	0	0
SimSafety V Burglar Alarm	Electronics	§150	—	0	0	0	0	0	0	0	0

Object Directory continued

Object	Category	Price	Asp. Points to Unlock	Hunger	Comfort	Hygiene	Bladder	Energy	Fun	Social	Environment
Single High or Less Bed	Seating & Beds	§300	—	0	1	0	0	2	6	0	0
SirPlus! Metal Desk	Surfaces	§100	—	0	0	0	0	0	0	0	0
SlumberGell Immersion Pod	Miscellaneous	§5,500	26,500	0	0	5	0	10	10	0	0
SmokeSentry SmokeSniffer	Electronics	§100	—	0	0	0	0	0	0	0	0
Snail Shell Shug Rug	Decorative	§350	—	0	0	0	0	0	0	0	1
Snuffit Fire Destroyer	Appliances	§1,000	1,300	0	0	0	0	0	0	0	0
"So Real" Japanese Floor Lamp	Lighting	§330	—	0	0	0	0	0	0	0	2
Soundless Wind Chimes	Decorative	§200	—	0	0	0	0	0	3	0	2
Spielbunnst Lawn Seatery	Seating & Beds	§320	—	0	3	0	0	0	0	0	0
Spin the Bottle	Miscellaneous	§1,625	9,200	0	0	0	0	0	7	0	0
Sprawl-Mart End Table	Surfaces	§65	—	0	0	0	0	0	0	0	0
Sproutch Couch	Seating & Beds	§1,130	2,000	0	10	0	0	2	1	0	2
Street Light	Miscellaneous	§125	—	0	0	0	0	0	0	0	1
Strike-a-Match Air Hockey	Miscellaneous	§950	7,300	0	0	-1	0	0	6	0	0
"Suds du Solei" Imperial Tub	Plumbing	§1,500	—	0	8	8	0	0	0	0	0
Summer Breeze Toilet Hut	Plumbing	§750	4,900	0	0	-1	10	0	0	0	0
Survivall End Table	Surfaces	§140	—	0	0	0	0	0	0	0	0
Sweet Tooth Pinball	Electronics	§650	—	0	0	0	0	0	5	0	0
Telephone Pole	Decorative	§100	—	0	0	0	0	0	0	0	0
"The Chesler" Sofa	Seating & Beds	§550	—	0	7	0	0	2	1	0	0
"The Crate"	Seating & Beds	§560	—	0	6	0	0	0	0	0	0
The Eggalitarian	Seating & Beds	§1,000	2,300	0	10	0	0	0	0	0	1
The Goo of Spring	Decorative	§3,200	—	0	0	0	0	0	3	0	10
The Grillinator "BigBQ"	Appliances	§280	—	4	0	0	0	0	0	0	0
"The Heffe" Raw Hide Rug	Decorative	§2,100	5,700	0	0	0	0	0	0	0	3
The Kitchen Sink	Plumbing	§500	—	0	0	3	0	0	0	0	1
The Love Seat	Seating & Beds	§1,600	—	0	10	0	0	2	1	0	2
"The Plushocrat" Lounge Chair	Seating & Beds	§440	—	0	6	0	0	0	0	0	0
The Sonic Expurgator	Plumbing	§750	—	0	0	8	0	0	0	0	0
The "Saved from the Curb" Couch	Seating & Beds	§200	—	0	5	0	0	2	1	0	0
The "SculpToilette" Porcelain Lavatory	Plumbing	§950	—	0	10	-1	10	0	1	0	0
The "Tahdis" Wardrobe	Miscellaneous	§750	—	0	0	0	0	0	0	0	0
The Think Tank	Decorative	§350	—	0	0	0	0	0	3	0	3
The "Vallarta"	Seating & Beds	§850	—	0	6	0	0	8	6	0	0
The Vibromatic Heart Bed	Seating & Beds	§3,000	2,800	0	8	0	0	10	6	0	0
This is the End Table	Surfaces	§300	—	0	0	0	0	0	0	0	1

Object Directory continued

Object	Category	Price	Asp. Points to Unlock	Hunger	Comfort	Hygiene	Bladder	Energy	Fun	Social	Environment
Tiled Counter	Surfaces	§210	—	4	0	0	0	0	0	0	0
Touch of Teak Dinette Chair	Seating & Beds	§525	—	0	6	0	0	0	0	0	0
Tournament Foosball Table	Miscellaneous	§800	—	0	0	0	0	0	6	0	0
Traffic Light	Decorative	§100	—	0	0	0	0	0	0	0	0
Trampoline	Miscellaneous	§2,100	8,200	0	0	0	0	0	9	0	0
Trottco MultiVid Television	Electronics	§2,250	—	0	0	0	0	0	4	0	2
Trumpet Vine Sconce	Lighting	§45	—	0	0	0	0	0	0	0	1
"Truth" Telescope	Skill	§1,140	4,300	0	0	0	0	0	0	0	0
Turntablitz DJ Booth	Electronics	§5,000	16,800	0	0	0	0	0	7	0	0
"Up" Dining Chair	Seating & Beds	§1,100	—	0	10	0	0	0	0	0	1
U-Probe-It Computing Organism	Electronics	§2,300	15,100	0	0	0	0	0	7	6	0
U-Probe-It Counter Top	Surfaces	§810	—	10	0	0	0	0	0	0	1
U-Probe-It Refrigerating Organism	Appliances	§1,500	7,700	10	0	0	0	0	0	0	0
U-Probe-It Universal Toilet	Plumbing	§950	—	0	10	-1	10	0	1	0	0
U-Probe-It Utility Desk	Surfaces	§970	—	0	0	0	0	0	0	0	0
U-Probe-It Utility Table	Surfaces	§940	—	0	0	0	0	0	0	0	1
"Vagaries of Love."	Decorative	§325	—	0	0	0	0	0	3	0	3
Victorian Flower Urn	Decorative	§100	—	0	0	0	0	0	3	0	1
Wall Mirror	Skill	§100	—	0	0	0	0	0	0	0	0
Wall Skull	Decorative	§900	—	0	0	0	0	0	3	0	7
Weeping Goo Grass	Decorative	§300	—	0	0	0	0	0	1	0	2
Werkbunnst All Purpose Chair	Seating & Beds	§150	—	0	3	0	0	0	0	0	0
"What a Steel" Economy Trash Can	Miscellaneous	§50	—	0	0	0	0	0	0	0	0
"White Fire" Teppanyaki Table	Skill	§9,999	24,000	0	0	0	0	0	0	0	0
White Rabbit Bubble Blower	Appliances	§890	4,000	-1	0	0	0	0	6	0	0
Wicked Breeze Indoor/ Outdoor Shower	Plumbing	§500	—	0	0	6	0	0	0	0	0
Wicker Time Moonlight Sofa	Seating & Beds	§770	—	0	7	0	0	2	1	0	0
Wilderness Gallery Bench	Seating & Beds	§150	—	0	5	0	0	2	1	0	0
Wireless Wall Phone	Electronics	§75	—	0	0	0	0	0	0	0	0
Wurl N' Hurl Gnarlosurf 2000	Miscellaneous	§15,000	27,900	0	0	0	0	-1	10	0	0
Wurl 'N' Hurl Retro Jukebox	Electronics	§500	1,100	0	0	0	0	0	5	0	3
Yamato Dining Table	Surfaces	§340	—	0	0	0	0	0	0	0	0
Yamato "Rack" Double Bed	Seating & Beds	§1,200	—	0	8	0	0	10	6	0	0
Yamato "Stiff Back" Chair	Seating & Beds	§900	—	0	10	0	0	0	0	0	0
Yamato Table Lamp	Lighting	§280	—	0	0	0	0	0	0	0	2
"You Had Me at What's Up"	Decorative	§2,300	—	0	0	0	0	0	3	0	9

Object Catalog
Seating and Beds

Seating and beds allow for replenishment of Comfort and/or Energy, provide a few Fun interactions, and open up several Social interactions if two Sims share an object.

These objects come in several types.

- Moveable Chairs: These dining and desk chairs can be used for sitting at surfaces (tables, etc.).
- Stationary Chairs: These lounge chairs, etc. can't be used at tables but provide more comfort than dining chairs.
- Sofas: Group seating allows Sims to talk and perform romantic Social interactions. All sofas can be searched for loose change, food, a magical Monkey's Paw, or other surprises.
- Beds: Replenish Energy by sleeping or Comfort by relaxing. While relaxing, a Sim can read a book or (if another Sim is in the bed too) perform romantic interactions.

Elementary Memories Dining Chair
- Cost: §80
- Need(s): Comfort 3

Office Chair
- Cost: §80
- Need(s): Comfort 3

Werkbunnst All Purpose Chair
- Cost: §150
- Need(s): Comfort 3

Wilderness Gallery Bench
- Cost: §150
- Need(s): Comfort 5 (Sit), Energy 2 (Power Nap), Fun 1 (Play Game)

"ModMan" Office Chair
- Cost: §200
- Need(s): Comfort 3 (Sit)

Bel-Air Diner Seat
- Cost: §200
- Need(s): Comfort 3 (Sit)

The "Saved from the Curb" Couch
- Cost: §200
- Need(s): Comfort 5 (Sit), Energy 2 (Power Nap), Fun 1 (Play Game)

EZ Green Camping Chair
- Cost: §250
- Need(s): Comfort 3 (Sit)

Recycled Couch
- Cost: §290
- Need(s): Comfort 5 (Sit), Energy 2 (Power Nap), Fun 1 (Play Game)

note Reading in bed can lead to discovery of new recipes.

Single High or Less Bed
- Cost: §300
- Need(s): Energy 2 (Sleep), Comfort 1 (Sleep/Relax), Fun 6 (Read)

Spielbunnst Lawn Seatery
- Cost: §320
- Need(s): Comfort 3 (Sit)

DreaMaker Crash Pad
- Cost: §350
- Need(s): Energy 3 (Sleep), Comfort 1 (Sleep/Relax), Fun 6 (Read)

Boggs Saloon Chair
- Cost: §400
- Need(s): Comfort 6 (Sit)

"The Plushocrat" Lounge Chair
- Cost: §440
- Need(s): Comfort 6 (Sit)

"Floral Fantasy" by Plastiqkue
- Cost: §450
- Need(s): Comfort 7 (Sit), Energy 1 (Power Nap), Fun 1 (Play Game)

Sili-Camp Tent Site
- Cost: §500
- Need(s): Energy 3 (Sleep), Comfort 3 (Sleep/Relax), Fun 6 (Read)

Touch of Teak Dinette Chair
- Cost: §525
- Need(s): Comfort 6 (Sit)

Brass Bed
- Cost: §550
- Need(s): Energy 4 (Sleep), Comfort 3 (Sleep/Relax), Fun 6 (Read)

"The Chesler" Sofa
- Cost: §550
- Need(s): Comfort 7 (Sit), Energy 2 (Power Nap), Fun 1 (Play Game)

"The Crate"
- Cost: §560
- Need(s): Comfort 6 (Sit)

Garden Swing
- Cost: §700
- Need(s): Comfort 7 (Sit)

Ploof Chair by Tameki
- Cost: §750
- Need(s): Comfort 6 (Sit)

Wicker Time Moonlight Sofa
- Cost: §770
- Need(s): Comfort 7 (Sit), Energy 2 (Power Nap), Fun 1 (Play Game)

DreaMaker Super Crash Pad
- Cost: §780
- Need(s): Energy 5 (Sleep), Comfort 5 (Sleep/Relax), Fun 6 (Read)

"San Carlos" Brass Bed
- Cost: §850
- Need(s): Energy 8 (Sleep), Comfort 6 (Sleep/Relax), Fun 6 (Read)

The "Vallarta"
- Cost: §850
- Need(s): Energy 8 (Sleep), Comfort 6 (Sleep/Relax), Fun 6 (Read)

Vamato "Stiff Back" Chair
- Cost: §900
- Need(s): Comfort 10 (Sit)

Cuddlers' Cradle (Unlockable)

- Unlock: 3,400 Aspiration Points
- Cost: §900
- Need(s): Comfort 10 (Sit)

note A pair of Sims can, relationship permitting, cuddle or (if in love) make out on this swing. If there is no romantic relationship, the Sims talk.

The Eggalitarian (Unlockable)

- Unlock: 2,300 Aspiration Points
- Cost: §1,000
- Need(s): Comfort 10 (Sit), Environment 1

"Up" Dining Chair

- Cost: §1,100
- Need(s): Comfort 10 (Sit) Environment 1

Sproutch Couch (Unlockable)

- Unlock: 2,000 Aspiration Points
- Cost: §1,130
- Need(s): Comfort 10 (Sit), Energy 2 (Power Nap), Fun 1 (Play Game)

The Sproutch Couch is quite comfortable, but it's also a living thing that can produce one of the most powerful fruits known to Sim cuisine, the Dangleberry.

To produce this superfruit, however, the couch must be tended just like a plant. It must be watered once per day. If watered twice, it produces the Dangleberries. And, unless you skip a day, it produces another crop every day when watered.

If you skip a day of watering, the Sprouch Couch decays back to its stubbly state. Let it go two days, and it drops down to being just a normal, vegetation-less couch. You need to water it two days in a row to make it fruit again.

La Silla Precaria Arm Chair

- Cost: §1,200
- Need(s): Comfort 10 (Sit), Environment 1

note All double beds are the primary sources for the pinnacle romantic interaction, WooHoo. If you're playing a Romance Aspiration Sim, it's essential to have any one of these.

Yamato "Rack" Double Bed

- Cost: §1,200
- Need(s): Energy 10 (Sleep), Comfort 8 (Sleep/Relax), Fun 6 (Read)

Oceana Sofa

- Cost: §1,420
- Need(s): Comfort 10 (Sit), Energy 2 (Power Nap), Fun 1 (Play Game), Environment 2

The Love Seat

- Cost: §1,600
- Need(s): Comfort 10 (Sit), Energy 2 (Power Nap), Fun 1 (Play Game), Environment 2

The Vibromatic Heart Bed (Unlockable)

- Unlock: 2,800 Aspiration Points
- Cost: §3,000
- Need(s): Energy 10 (Sleep), Comfort 8 (Sleep/Relax), Fun 6 (Read)

note This amore-inspiring bed's romantic powers are activated with the Enable Mojo interaction. It doubles Fun for all in-bed interactions.

Appliances

Appliances generally go in a kitchen. When it comes to food prep objects, the higher the object's Hunger score the more Hunger satisfaction it contributes to the final food product. In the case of refrigerators, the score also represents the breadth of the ingredient selection within.

For more information on how each food-related appliance affects food preparation, see the "Food Creation" chapter.

LiquiTonic Blender

- Cost: §200
- Need(s): Hunger 4
- Skill(s): Cooking

RPG "Paladin" Food Processor

- ◆ Cost: §200
- ◆ Need(s): Hunger 4
- ◆ Skill(s): Cooking

Dialectric Free Standing Range

- ◆ Cost: §210
- ◆ Need(s): Hunger 4
- ◆ Skill(s): Cooking

The Grillinator "BigBQ"

- ◆ Cost: §280
- ◆ Need(s): Hunger 4
- ◆ Skill(s): Cooking

Grills are part of the food creation system but can be used independently of it too. For their role in the food system, see the "Food Creation" chapter.

When used independently (barbeque), grills cost money (§25), spontaneously producing ingredients that are cooked immediately.

Cleaning a grill is very important. Using a clean grill adds a bonus to the resulting food's Hunger satisfaction while a dirty grill contributes to a food's nausea effect.

Grills also have an elevated fire risk when cooking with low Cooking skill.

Outgoing and Active Sims autonomously prefer to use the grill over an indoor stove.

Multiquick Blender

- ◆ Cost: §330
- ◆ Need(s): Hunger 6
- ◆ Skill(s): Cooking

"Positive Potential" Microwave

- ◆ Cost: §350
- ◆ Need(s): Hunger 6
- ◆ Skill(s): Cooking

!!!!Espresso.it.supremo!!!!

- ◆ Cost: §450
- ◆ Need(s): Energy 2, Bladder -1

note Drinking espresso replenishes Energy but at the cost of your Sim's Bladder.

If the machine breaks, it can still make espresso, but the drink will cause nausea.

EconoCool Refrigerator

- ◆ Cost: §500
- ◆ Need(s): Hunger 4

CiaoTime 360 Moderna Range

- ◆ Cost: §500
- ◆ Need(s): Hunger 6
- ◆ Skill(s): Cooking

Iterative Dishwasher

- ◆ Cost: §550
- ◆ Need(s): Hunger 4
- ◆ Skill(s): Cleaning

note Can serve as a countertop for food preparation.

Chow Bella Bachelor Fridge

- ◆ Cost: §750
- ◆ Need(s): Hunger 6

Nostalgix Gas Range

- ◆ Cost: §750
- ◆ Need(s): Hunger 8
- ◆ Skill(s): Cooking

White Rabbit Bubble Blower (Unlockable)

- ◆ Unlock: 4,000 Aspiration Points
- ◆ Cost: §890
- ◆ Need(s): Fun 6, Hunger -1

While sitting at this bubble blower, your Sims enjoy themselves tremendously but get hungrier and hungrier. No one's quite sure why.

PRIMA OFFICIAL GAME GUIDE

note The number of Sims around the bubble blower changes the color of the bubbles.

With more than one Sim arrayed around it, Sims can tell stupid stories to satisfy Social and build relationships with all present.

Fruit Punch Barrel (Unlockable)
- Unlock: 1,900 Aspiration Points
- Cost: §950
- Need(s): None

note This device delivers Hunger satisfaction and can be used in two ways. Your Sim can either drink from a cup or directly from the tap. While drinking from the tap, Sims have the option to pump the keg to squeeze out a bit more juice.

Snuffit Fire Destroyer (Unlockable)
- Unlock: 1,300 Aspiration Points
- Cost: §1,000
- Need(s): None

This object can be hung on a wall and used to put out fires in half the time it takes the firefighters.

This object can only be used in direct control mode. In classic mode, your Sims are unable to interact with it, and switching to classic from direct while carrying it causes your Sim to place it on the ground.

When the object is in hand, your Sims can briefly spray it at the space immediately in front of them (they can't move while spraying), return it to its wall mount, or (if the mount is too far away) drop it on the ground. If there's a fire in the vicinity, your Sim may extinguish it, spraying as long as it takes to put out the blaze.

Radioproactive Heating Stove (Unlockable)
- Unlock: 11,500 Aspiration Points
- Cost: §1,100
- Need(s): Hunger 10
- Skill(s): Cooking

Nostalgix Refrigerator
- Cost: §1,200
- Need(s): Hunger 8

U-Probe-It Refrigerating Organism (Unlockable)
- Unlock: 7,700 Aspiration Points
- Cost: §1,500
- Need(s): Hunger 10

Freedom Vacuum (Unlockable)
- Unlock: 22,800 Aspiration Points
- Cost: §3,000
- Need(s): None

For instantaneous cleanup of puddles, ashes, or trash, mount one of these objects on your wall and fetch it anytime messes appear.

Though it can be used in classic control mode, the vacuum is best handled in direct control mode. Simply wear the unit and walk near messes. The offending (and Environment-depressing) items are immediately dispatched in a fraction of the time of traditional methods.

Surfaces

Surfaces include dining tables, counters, and any other table-like surfaces. Things may, unsurprisingly, be placed upon them.

Counters are an important element of the food preparation system. For more information, see "Food Creation." To remain effective, counters must be cleaned regularly. Dirty counters contribute to the nausea effect of food prepared on them.

Sprawl-Mart End Table
- Cost: §65

Bel-Air Dining Table
- Cost: §95

SirPlus! Metal Desk
- Cost: §100

Survivall End Table
- Cost: §140

"Concreta" Display Counter
- Cost: §140
- Need(s): Hunger 4
- Skill(s): Cleaning

Fable Table
- Cost: §150

"Feelin' Dizzy" Designer Counter
- Cost: §150
- Need(s): Hunger 4
- Skill(s): Cleaning

EZ Green Camping Counter
- Cost: §175
- Need(s): Hunger 4
- Skill(s): Cleaning

Myne Dining Hall Table
- Cost: §210

Tiled Counter
- Cost: §210
- Need(s): Hunger 4
- Skill(s): Cleaning

Copper King Kitchen Counter
- Cost: §280
- Need(s): Hunger 6
- Skill(s): Cleaning

This is the End Table
- Cost: §300
- Need(s): Environment 1

Yamato Dining Table
- Cost: §340

Molotov Antiques Saloon Table
- Cost: §390

Boggs Western Laminate
- Cost: §410
- Need(s): Hunger 6
- Skill(s): Cleaning

Old Thyme End Table
- Cost: §440
- Need(s): Environment 1

Lowbough Outdoor Table
- Cost: §450

Deluxar Counter
- Cost: §590
- Need(s): Hunger 8, Environment 1
- Skill(s): Cleaning

Old Thyme Dining Table
- Cost: §750

U-Probe-It Counter Top
- Cost: §810
- Need(s): Hunger 10, Environment 1
- Skill(s): Cleaning

U-Probe-It Utility Table
- Cost: §940
- Need(s): Environment 1

PRIMA OFFICIAL GAME GUIDE

U-Probe-It Utility Desk

◆ Cost: §970

Nemo Dining Table

◆ Cost: §1,100
◆ Need(s): Environment 2

Plumbing

Plumbing objects provide necessary Bladder and Hygiene satisfaction. Generally, showers and baths are more effective than sinks at satisfying Hygiene.

Claymore Ceramic Sink

◆ Cost: §230
◆ Need(s): Hygiene 2

Hydronomic Kitchen Sink

◆ Cost: §250
◆ Need(s): Hygiene 2

note While using a toilet, Sims can entertain themselves by reading or playing a handheld video game. Reading can lead to the discovery of new recipes.

Sewage Brothers Resteze Toilet

◆ Cost: §300
◆ Need(s): Bladder 10 (Use), Hygiene -1 (Use), Fun 1 (Read, Play Game)

Simple Sink

◆ Cost: §320
◆ Need(s): Hygiene 2

Public Sink

◆ Cost: §360
◆ Need(s): Hygiene 2

primagames.com

ShowHeuristic Hygiene System

◆ Cost: §450
◆ Need(s): Hygiene 6

The Kitchen Sink

◆ Cost: §500
◆ Need(s): Hygiene 3, Environment 1

Flush Force "Bowls of Steel" 2100

◆ Cost: §500
◆ Need(s): Bladder 10 (Use), Hygiene -1 (Use), Fun 1 (Read/Play Game)

Wicked Breeze Indoor/Outdoor Shower

◆ Cost: §500
◆ Need(s): Hygiene 6

Flushitol Public Toilet

◆ Cost: §500
◆ Need(s): Bladder 10 (Use), Hygiene -1 (Use), Fun 1 (Read, Play Game)

Piazza Amoretto Fountain (Unlockable)

◆ Unlock: 3,100 Aspiration Points
◆ Cost: §550
◆ Need(s): Hygiene 5 (Splash), Fun 3 (View/Splash)

note Sims can view this item as they would any decorative object or splash around in it for Fun and a bit of Hygiene.

"Birth of Venus" Master Sink

◆ Cost: §680
◆ Need(s): Hygiene 3, Environment 1

Objects

The Sonic Expurgator
- Cost: §750
- Need(s): Hygiene 8

ResiStall Toilet Stall
- Cost: §750
- Need(s): Bladder 10 (Use), Hygiene -1 (Use)

note Works just like household toilets but without the option to read or play games while your Sims do their business.

Summer Breeze Toilet Hut (Unlockable)
- Unlock: 4,900 Aspiration Points
- Cost: §750
- Need(s): Bladder 10 (Use), Hygiene -1 (Use)

ShowerMate
- Cost: §800
- Need(s): Hygiene 10

U-Probe-It Universal Toilet
- Cost: §950
- Need(s): Bladder 10 (Use), Comfort 10 (Use), Hygiene -1 (Use), Fun 1 (Read/Play Game)

The "SculpToilette" Porcelain Lavatory
- Cost: §950
- Need(s): Bladder 10 (Use), Comfort 10 (Use), Hygiene -1 (Use), Fun 1 (Read/Play Game)

Davey Jones' Crocker
- Cost: §950
- Need(s): Bladder 10 (Use), Comfort 2 (Use), Hygiene -1 (Use), Fun 1 (Read/Play Game)

Krampft Industries Hubba Tubba
- Cost: §950
- Need(s): Hygiene 5, Comfort 5

Oriental "Master" Bathtub
- Cost: §1,300
- Need(s): Hygiene 6, Comfort 6

"Suds du Solei" Imperial Tub
- Cost: §1,500
- Need(s): Hygiene 8, Comfort 8

Niagara Love Tub (Unlockable)
- Unlock: 6,900 Aspiration Points
- Cost: §6,500
- Need(s): Hygiene 7, Fun 7

This two-seater hot tub is just made for romance. If Sims are Outgoing/Shy 8 or higher, they'll get in nude rather than in a swimsuit. Likewise, if the tub already hosts a nude Sim with whom your Sim has a love or crush memory, your Sim will get in nude too.

Sims who meet all memory and relationship requirements can WooHoo in this tub.

"Fitzroy Dreamers" Rock Pool
- Cost: §8,500
- Need(s): Hygiene 8, Comfort 7, Fun 3

note Since this tub is actually a natural spring, it doesn't break or need repair.

Quattro-Grav Air Tub (Unlockable)
- Unlock: 17,700 Aspiration Points
- Cost: §12,000
- Need(s): Hygiene 10 (Get In), Comfort 10 (Get In), Fun 10 (Get In/Admire), Social 5

This futuristic wonder can be used either as a hot tub or an objet d'art. In Spa mode, just switch it on and direct your Sim to climb in; it works just like any other hot tub.

In Art mode, the spa becomes a moving water sculpture that can be viewed for fun.

PRIMA OFFICIAL GAME GUIDE

Electronics

Electronic items are a major source of Fun.

CyberChronometer Alarm Clock

◆ Cost: §50

Once set, it goes off every day one hour before your carpool arrives. Alarm clocks can be especially important when all playable Sims are asleep or at work because it's difficult to catch the carpool when the game's running at triple speed. The alarm clock instantly changes game speed back to normal as it awakens your Sim.

> **note** Prof. Feather's Chicken Checkers functions as an alarm clock too. See later.

Wireless Wall Phone

◆ Cost: §75

Call for services, chat with friends, or invite other Sims over for a visit. It's required to receive random, social, and work-related calls.

Additionally, the phone can be used to initiate parties and make prank calls. There are three possible prank calls, the success of which depends on a different personality trait or, in one case, a Need.

◆ Fake Sweepstakes: Charisma

◆ Fake Names: Creativity

◆ Fart on Phone: Bladder (success of call guaranteed if Bladder less than 50 percent)

Succeeding in a prank call increases Fun while failure causes depletion of Fun.

Ruggo Boombox

◆ Cost: §99

◆ Need(s): Fun 2, Environment 3

When activated, this item plays a random station or the last station played. Stations include:

◆ Alternative	◆ Industrial	◆ Pop
◆ Ambient Dub	◆ Lounge Music	◆ Punk Pop
◆ Bluegrass	◆ Nu Metal	◆ Trance Dance

All stereos allow you to change to specific songs. These are real-world hits rerecorded by the artists in Simlish. Select between:

◆ "Just Let Go (Tommy Sunshine Brooklyn Fire Retouch)," Performed by Fischerspooner

◆ "Another World," Performed by Kitty Shack

◆ "Late Again," Performed by MxPx

◆ "Pressure," Performed by Paramore

◆ "Take Me Home Please," Performed by Reggie and The Full Effect

◆ "Suddenly," Performed by Ryan Ferguson

◆ "Like Light To The Flies (Simlish remix)," Performed by Trivium

Sims can dance to the music but do so uninterestedly if the music isn't to their liking. They at least moderately enjoy the music if they're Playful and Active and their Energy and Mood are relatively high. If not, enjoyment of music is purely random.

SmokeSentry SmokeSniffer

◆ Cost: §100

This sounds when a fire breaks out in the same room as the detector, automatically summoning the fire department. Since most fires begin in the kitchen, that should be the first place you put one.

SimSafety V Burglar Alarm

◆ Cost: §150

The alarm sounds if a burglar enters a room containing one, so place one in each room with an exterior doorway. Alarms wake all sleeping Sims and automatically summon police.

Laser Llama Classic Arcade Game

◆ Cost: §300

◆ Need(s): Fun 5

"See Me, Feel Me" Pinball Machine

◆ Cost: §300

◆ Need(s): Fun 5

Retro Space-Age Action Pinball (Unlockable)

◆ Unlock: 3,700 Aspiration Points

◆ Cost: §450

◆ Need(s): Fun 5

Wurl 'N' Hurl Retro Jukebox (Unlockable)

◆ Unlock: 1,100 Aspiration Points

◆ Cost: §500

◆ Need(s): Fun 5, Environment 3

note See the Ruggo Boombox.

Pure TV
◆ Cost: §500
◆ Need(s): Fun 3, Environment 2

Sims watch TV for fun and randomly select from the available channels.

◆ Food: Enjoyed by all
◆ Horror: Outgoing Sims enjoy while Shy Sims dislike
◆ Music: Enjoyed by all
◆ News: Serious Sims enjoy while Playful Sims dislike

Fixing a broken TV with low Mechanical skill (below 5) can be fatal.

Sweet Tooth Pinball
◆ Cost: §650
◆ Need(s): Fun 5

AE Arcade Unit
◆ Cost: §675
◆ Need(s): Fun 6

People Invaders
◆ Cost: §710
◆ Need(s): Fun 6

MaxArts 5p0r3 Gaming Kit
◆ Cost: §1,135
◆ Need(s): Fun 7

note This holographic game system doesn't require a television. It can be played alone or you can invite other Sims to play with the Call Over interaction. The game supports up to four Sims at a time.

Madcap Miner Metal Detector (Unlockable)
◆ Unlock: 12,000 Aspiration Points
◆ Cost: §1,200

The metal detector can find money, bottle caps, a copy of THE URBZ (which Sims will rebury), food ingredients, or a mysterious Monkey Paw.

Though it can be used in either direct or classic modes, it's best to use this in direct control mode. In classic control mode, your Sim will wander and search automatically until the interaction is cancelled. The chances of finding anything this way is VERY small.

In direct control mode, on the other hand, you can control them while they search, directing them to areas in which objects are likely to be buried. If a buried object is in range, the detector will flash once and let out a single tone. The closer your Sim gets to the buried object, the faster the detector flashes and the more frequent the tones. When your Sim is near enough the object, use the Dig interaction to unearth the underground surprise.

Objects are placed randomly, either indoors or out.

Moneywell Computer
◆ Cost: §1,300
◆ Need(s): Fun 6 (Play), Social (Chat)
◆ Skill(s): Logic (Design Video Game), Charisma (Blog)

Computers can be used for several things.
◆ Find a Job: It contains more daily listings than the newspaper.
◆ Chat: Talk to other Sims for Social Need or invite them over just as on the telephone.
◆ Design video games: Increase Logic. When game is complete, your Sim may sell it for money; price depends on Sim's Logic skill.
◆ Play video game (THE SIMS™ BUSTIN' OUT, THE SIMS™ 2, or SPORE™): This satisfies Fun.
◆ Blog: Increase Charisma. The more often a Sim blogs, the more popular the blog becomes, and the more Fun the Sim gains for blogging. Neglecting a blog decreases popularity, reducing Fun until it can be rebuilt.

Hippity-Humpity! Arcade Game (Unlockable)
◆ Unlock: 2,100 Aspiration Points
◆ Cost: §1,500
◆ Need(s): Fun 7

Chocola "Psycho-Active" Drinks
◆ Cost: §1,500
◆ Need(s): Hunger 4, Energy 3
◆ Buy Cola: Costs §10. Machine normally dispenses drink but may occasionally reject Sim's bill. Drink satisfies Hunger.
◆ Kick Machine: There's a 10 percent chance of getting a free soda.

Dig Dog Hotdog Dispensary (Unlockable)

- Unlock: 4,600 Aspiration Points
- Cost: $1,700
- Need(s): Hunger 5, Energy 3

note This is identical to Chocola "Psycho-Active" Drinks except hot dogs satisfy more Hunger.

Trottco MultiVid Television

- Cost: $2,250
- Need(s): Fun 4, Environment 2

note See Pure TV.

U-Probe-It Computing Organism (Unlockable)

- Unlock: 15,100 Aspiration Points
- Cost: $2,300
- Need(s): Fun 7 (Play), Social 6 (Chat)
- Skill(s): Logic (Design Video Game), Charisma (Blog)

note See Moneywell Computer.

"Procedural" Music System (Unlockable)

- Unlock: 9,700 Aspiration Points
- Cost: $2,550
- Need(s): Fun 7, Environment 3

note See Ruggo Boombox.

Blade Vision VERY High HD TV (Unlockable)

- Unlock: 8,700 Aspiration Points
- Cost: $3,500
- Need(s): Fun 5, Environment 2

note See Pure TV.

P5 4400SX+ DS (Unlockable)

- Unlock: 6,100 Aspiration Points
- Cost: $3,900
- Need(s): Fun 8 (Play), Social 6 (Chat)
- Skill(s): Logic (Design Video Game), Charisma (Blog)

note See Moneywell Computer.

"Magic Fingers" Hydraulic Massage (Unlockable)

- Unlock: 6,500 Aspiration Points
- Cost: $5,000
- Need(s): Comfort 10

This programmable massage table is a great source of Comfort but is best used once your Sim has developed some Logic skill.

When your Sim programs the table, the length and quality of the massage is directly related to Logic skill. Sims with low Logic run the risk of a very rough massage that actually LOWERS Comfort (above Logic 5, all massages are positive).

note A high Logic Sim can completely replenish Comfort with one use of the massage table.

Each massage costs $50.

Turntablitz DJ Booth (Unlockable)

- Unlock: 16,800 Aspiration Points
- Cost: $5,000
- Need(s): Fun 7, Environment 3

Sims may either act as DJ or dance to the sounds coming from the booth.

- Play Music: Turns on default music and lights.
- DJ: Take over the booth as the DJ. From this perch you can change the music to fast, medium, or slow tempo, or skip to the next track. The different speeds dictate how much Fun your Sim gains and how much Energy is being depleted; the faster the music, the more of both.
- Fireworks, Fog, Lasers: Launch special effects. There's a small chance things could go horribly wrong, based on your Sim's level of Creativity skill.

Lighting

Lighting makes spaces easier to see and can enhance Environment score.

Blue Glow Special

- Cost: $25
- Need(s): Environment 1

Light Therapy Wall Sconce
- Cost: §35
- Need(s): Environment 1

Trumpet Vine Sconce
- Cost: §45
- Need(s): Environment 1

Shahrisabz Table Lamp
- Cost: §105
- Need(s): Environment 1

Kashgar Table Lamp
- Cost: §115
- Need(s): Environment 1

A.M.P. Wall Lamp
- Cost: §125
- Need(s): Environment 2

Shojitsu Wall Lamp
- Cost: §155
- Need(s): Environment 2

Molotov Antique Wall Lamp
- Cost: §160
- Need(s): Environment 2

Pineapple "Hot Rock" Lamp
- Cost: §210
- Need(s): Environment 1

Hawaiian Fantasy Tiki Torch (Unlockable)
- Unlock: 700 Aspiration Points
- Cost: §210
- Need(s): Environment 1

Foot Light
- Cost: §215
- Need(s): Environment 1

"Freedom" Swivel Lamp
- Cost: §230
- Need(s): Environment 1

"Cerberus" Floor Lamp
- Cost: §245
- Need(s): Environment 1

Furniture Kamp Table Lamp
- Cost: §255
- Need(s): Environment 2

"Boom Boom" Floor Lamp
- Cost: §255
- Need(s): Environment 1

Molotov Antique Table Lamp
- Cost: §275
- Need(s): Environment 2

Sidestep Lamp
- Cost: §280
- Need(s): Environment 3

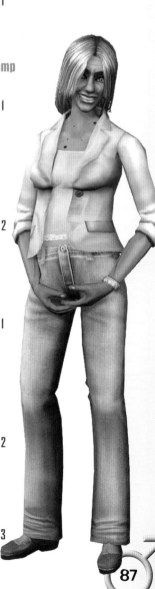

Cinema Deco Sconce
◆ Cost: §280
◆ Need(s): Environment 3

Yamato Table Lamp
◆ Cost: §280
◆ Need(s): Environment 2

Photo Lamp
◆ Cost: §320
◆ Need(s): Environment 1

Art Lamp
◆ Cost: §325
◆ Need(s): Environment 1

Daddy Warmbums Gas Heater
◆ Cost: §325
◆ Need(s): Environment 1

"So Real" Japanese Floor Lamp
◆ Cost: §330
◆ Need(s): Environment 2

Furniture Kamp Floor Lamp
◆ Cost: §335
◆ Need(s): Environment 2

Flourano Glass Lamp
◆ Cost: §360
◆ Need(s): Environment 3

Gleep Table Lamp
◆ Cost: §375
◆ Need(s): Environment 3

Chill Lamp
◆ Cost: §410
◆ Need(s): Environment 3

Club Códe Thrill Light
◆ Cost: §450
◆ Need(s): Environment 1

Decorative

Decorative objects are used to adorn locations and raise Environment score. Viewing some decorative objects satisfies Fun (sculptures and paintings give more Fun than plants). Some objects display images of your Sim (or a custom EyeToy™ image on PlayStation 2).

Inverted Vertigo, Cover Art
◆ Cost: §50
◆ Need(s): Environment 1

Sewer Grate
◆ Cost: §50

Red Rover Fire Hydrant
◆ Cost: §50

"It's Reggae, Mon" Poster
- Cost: §50
- Need(s): Fun 3 (View), Environment 1

"Fists of Bunny" Poster (Unlockable)
- Unlock: 1,500 Aspiration Points
- Cost: §50
- Need(s): Fun 3 (View), Environment 1

Gold Record
- Cost: §75
- Need(s): Fun 3 (View), Environment 2

Traffic Light
- Cost: §100

Victorian Flower Urn
- Cost: §100
- Need(s): Fun 3 (View), Environment 1

Telephone Pole
- Cost: §100

Roman Lavender
- Cost: §125
- Need(s): Fun 3 (View), Environment 1

"Jayded"
- Cost: §125
- Need(s): Fun 3 (View), Environment 2

Imagination Helper
- Cost: §150
- Need(s): Fun 3 (View), Environment 1

"Emergency"
- Cost: §175
- Need(s): Fun 3 (View), Environment 2

Soundless Wind Chimes
- Cost: §200
- Need(s): Fun 3 (View), Environment 2

GenoLife Palmetto Hutch
- Cost: §200
- Need(s): Fun 1 (View), Environment 2

Decorative Phone Pole
- Cost: §200

Callow Lily
- Cost: §250
- Need(s): Fun 1 (View), Environment 2

GenoLife Cactus Plant
- Cost: §250
- Need(s): Fun 1 (View), Environment 2

Rose Bush
- Cost: §250
- Need(s): Fun 1 (View), Environment 2

Weeping Goo Grass
- Cost: §300
- Need(s): Fun 1 (View), Environment 2

"Painting leisure study 5078643"
- Cost: §300
- Need(s): Fun 3 (View), Environment 7

"Vagaries of Love"
- Cost: §325
- Need(s): Fun 3 (View), Environment 3

Rubber Tree Plant
- Cost: §325
- Need(s): Fun 1 (View), Environment 2

Bird of Paradise
- Cost: §333
- Need(s): Fun 3 (View), Environment 1

Snail Shell Shug Rug
- Cost: §350
- Need(s): Environment 1

The Think Tank
- Cost: §350
- Need(s): Fun 3 (View), Environment 3

Moodscape Painting
- Cost: §390
- Need(s): Fun 3 (View), Environment 4

Generally, this painting contains an image of your Sim in his or her current outfit—"Change Picture" selects from five different poses. If you have a PlayStation 2 and a Sony EyeToy™, however, you can customize what appears in this frame (selected from saved Sony EyeToy™ images).

Opticluster Promotional Painting
- Cost: §430
- Need(s): Fun 3 (View), Environment 4

note See Moodscape Painting.

"Big Man" Rifle Replica
- Cost: §450
- Need(s): Fun 3 (View), Environment 5

ShagTime Pop Rug
- Cost: §500
- Need(s): Environment 1

Dial-a-While Bird Bath (Unlockable)
- Unlock: 900 Aspiration Points
- Cost: §500
- Need(s): Fun 3 (View), Environment 5

Opticluster Portrait 360
- Cost: §500
- Need(s): Fun 3 (View), Environment 5

note See Moodscape Painting.

Cantankerous Bowel Fish (Unlockable)
- Unlock: 13,500 Aspiration Points
- Cost: §700
- Need(s): Fun 3 (View), Environment 6

Faux Llama Trophy

- Cost: §810
- Need(s): Fun 3 (View), Environment 6

"Self Portrait" by Dandy Slichtensteen

- Cost: §820
- Need(s): Fun 3 (View), Environment 7

"Harmony" Sculpture

- Cost: §900
- Need(s): Fun 3 (View), Environment 4

Wall Skull

- Cost: §900
- Need(s): Fun 3 (View), Environment 7

Montespaghetti Spring

- Cost: §1,200
- Need(s): Fun 3 (View), Environment 8

"Perspectif"

- Cost: §1,800
- Need(s): Fun 3 (View), Environment 8

"The Heffe" Raw Hide Rug (Unlockable)

- Unlock: 5,700 Aspiration Points
- Cost: §2,100
- Need(s): Fun 3 (View), Environment 3

"You Had Me at What's Up."

- Cost: §2,300
- Need(s): Fun 3 (View), Environment 9

"Polyp"

- Cost: §2,500
- Need(s): Fun 3 (View), Environment 7

Rug Wizard Computer Rug

- Cost: §2,900
- Need(s): Environment 3

The Goo of Spring

- Cost: §3,200
- Need(s): Fun 3 (View), Environment 10

Lung Dynasty Scroll

- Cost: §3,500
- Need(s): Fun 3 (View), Environment 10

Grey Petals' Painting

- Cost: §3,700
- Need(s): Fun 3 (View), Environment 10

"Cupid 2: Revenge of the Toads"

- Cost: §4,000
- Need(s): Fun 3 (View), Environment 10

Façade King Western Store (Unlockable)

- Unlock: 19,600 Aspiration Points
- Cost: §5,000
- Need(s): Environment 7

note This can only be placed outdoors to improve outdoor Environment score.

Façade King Western Saloon (Unlockable)

- Unlock: 20,600 Aspiration Points
- Cost: §5,000
- Need(s): Environment 7

note This can only be placed outdoors to improve outdoor Environment score.

Façade King Western Bank (Unlockable)

- Unlock: 14,300 Aspiration Points
- Cost: §5,000
- Need(s): Environment 7

note This can only be placed outdoors to improve outdoor Environment score.

Athena by Klassick Repro Inc.

- Cost: §5,000
- Need(s): Fun 3 (View), Environment 10

Façade King Western Hotel (Unlockable)

- Unlock: 12,800 Aspiration Points
- Cost: §5,000
- Need(s): Environment 7

note This can only be placed outdoors to improve outdoor Environment score.

Beetle Yak Rug

- Cost: §5,500
- Need(s): Environment 5

Skills

Skill objects can affect Sims' Needs but are primarily intended to build their various skills. Generally, the more expensive an object, the faster it develops skill, especially at higher levels.

Wall Mirror

- Cost: §100
- Skill(s): Charisma

note Practice speaking or kissing to build Charisma.

Bonsai Tree

- Cost: §250
- Skill(s): Creativity

note Prune the tree to expand Creativity.

Amishim Bookcase

- Cost: §250
- Need(s): Fun 6 (Read Book)
- Skill(s): Cooking (Study), Mechanical (Study), Cleaning (Study), Creativity (Write in Journal)

Bookcases are repositories of many important Sim skills but have several other uses as well. From books, your Sims can study to gain skill in Cooking, Cleaning, and Mechanical. Make sure a very comfy chair is the closest chair to the bookshelf. These cram sessions can last a while, and it helps to refresh Comfort simultaneously.

note Reading books can lead to the discovery of new recipes.

Sims can also build their Creative skill by writing in their Journals.

Finally, a Sim can read a good book just for Fun.

Bookshelves work differently in direct vs. classic control modes. In classic mode, you make your selection at the bookshelf itself. In direct mode, your Sim grabs a book from the shelf, then you select what to do with that book.

What your Sim does with a book when finished also depends on the control mode. In direct control, you can direct your Sim to put a finished book down or return it to the shelf. In classic control, Sims' Neat/Sloppy personality trait dictates where they dispose of their used books.

note Leaving books on the floor reduces Environment score, driving down the Mood of any Sims in the room.

Post-Staunton "Strugatsky" Chess Set

- Cost: §400
- Need(s): Fun (Play Paper Football)
- Skill(s): Logic (Play Chess), Mechanical (Play Paper Football)

Playing Chess or Paper Football results in both skill gain and Social interaction between the players (feeding Social Need and building relationships).

Chess builds Logic skill while Paper Football develops Mechanical skill. Playing Chess solo still builds Logic but doesn't feed Social or Fun. Single-player Paper Football, however, DOES NOT develop Mechanical skill and results in less Fun than a real game because, really, it's kind of sad.

Objects

Exerto Self-Spot Exercise Machine
◆ Cost: §500
◆ Skill(s): Body

Sims pump iron to build Body skill. At the outset, select what level of weight to attempt, keeping in mind your Sim's current Body skill—lifting above the Sim's abilities heightens the chance of failure. On the upside, the medium and heavy weight levels develop skill at a faster rate (120 percent for medium and 150 percent for heavy).

tip Generally, Sims with 0–3 Body should lift only light weight. Sims with 4–7 Body should limit themselves to light or medium weight. Strong Sims (Body 8–10) can safely lift at all levels with only a slight chance of failure for heavy weight.

Failure occurs when the Sim fumbles the weights and results in a drop in Energy. If another Sim cheers a player, it doubles the rate of skill development.

Astrowonder Telescope
◆ Cost: §500
◆ Skill(s): Logic

The telescope can be used at night (stargaze) to view heavenly bodies, and during the day (spy) to peek at more earthbound bodies. Both uses build Logic, but the possible consequences differ with the time of day.

When Sims spy, there's a chance that a neighbor (the one on whom your Sim is spying) will arrive on the lot to deliver a good slap.

While stargazing, high Logic Sims have a small chance of discovering a new comet and receiving a large cash prize. For Sims of any Logic, stargazing carries a small chance of alien abduction (fear not, your visit to the saucer only lasts about four hours).

Independent Expressions, Inc. Easel
◆ Cost: §750
◆ Need(s): Fun (Paint)
◆ Skill(s): Creativity

Painting is an excellent way to build Creativity skill and, if your Sim has substantially developed that skill, to make a bit of extra cash.

Your Sim's Creative skill determines both how quickly the painting is completed (the higher the skill, the faster the job) and for how much it sells.

note If you have a PlayStation 2 and an EyeToy™, a painting may be randomly selected from one of your EyeToy™ images.

Once a painting is complete, you must either sell or dispose of it before a new painting can be started. The sale price is directly related to your Sim's Creativity when he or she began the painting and how high it developed by the end.

"Truth" Telescope (Unlockable)
◆ Unlock: 4,300 Aspiration Points
◆ Cost: §1,140
◆ Skill(s): Logic

note See Astrowonder Telescope.

Psychonautica's Cerebro-Chess (Unlockable)
◆ Unlock: 10,900 Aspiration Points
◆ Cost: §1,200
◆ Need(s): Fun (Play Paper Football)
◆ Skill(s): Logic (Play Chess), Mechanical (Play Paper Football)

note See Post-Staunton "Strugatsky" Chess Set.

Fists of Spite Punching Bag
◆ Cost: §1,500
◆ Need(s): -1 Energy
◆ Skill(s): Body

The moves your Sim does while using this Body skill builder depends on current Body skill. The higher the skill, the fancier the moves.

Maximum Body Sims have an additional interaction, Power Move.

If another Sim Cheers your Sim, your Sim's rate of Body skill increase doubles.

note When you can control multiple Sims on a lot, use extra Sims to cheer Sims using the punching bag or wheel objects to double their Body skill rates.

"Does It Rock!" Electric Guitar
◆ Cost: §1,500
◆ Need(s): Fun 1
◆ Skill(s): Creativity

This instrument builds Creativity, and the quality of the music your Sim makes is dictated by the current level of that skill.

While playing, use the Shoot Flame subinteraction to put on a bit of pyrotechnics. There's only a small chance of setting something nearby ablaze.

Sims listening to a guitar player also react according to the player's Creativity skill.

93

"Jimmy Three Fingers" Rocket Bench

- Cost: $2,000
- Skill(s): Mechanical

This workbench is used to build model rockets, develop Mechanical skill, and make a bit of extra cash.

The higher your Sim's Mechanical skill, the faster the rocket gets built, the fancier it looks, and the more money your Sim earns per rocket.

If a rocket is launched indoors, it starts an immediate fire on the nearest flammable object. Just keep it outside, OK?

Rat Race Executive Power Wheel (Unlockable)

- Unlock: 21,700 Aspiration Points
- Cost: $3,000
- Need(s): Hygiene -1, Energy -1
- Skill(s): Body

This Body skill-building device is extremely efficient but requires some maintenance.

Sims may run in the wheel to build Body skill but slowly deplete both Hygiene and Energy. If the wheel is visibly dirty from use, the Hygiene loss is doubled.

Sims' current Body skill dictates how well they run. The lower the skill, the clumsier they are.

If another Sim cheers for the Sim in the wheel, the running Sim's Body skill speed increases. If, on the other hand, a Sim locks the wheel while another is running, the runner falls and loses Comfort.

To clean a dirty wheel, use the Clean Tray interaction.

Plaank Bookcase

- Cost: $3,000
- Need(s): Fun 6 (Read Book), Environment 3
- Skill(s): Cooking (Study), Mechanical (Study), Cleaning (Study), Creativity (Write in Journal)

note See Amishim Bookcase.

Chimeway & Daughters Piano

- Cost: $5,000
- Need(s): Fun 1
- Skill(s): Creativity

Sims can play either traditional classical music or more discordant experimental music to build Creativity skill.

Regardless of the kind of music chosen, the quality of the Sims' music is dictated by their existing Creativity skill. Other Sims can listen and react according to the player's skill.

Prof. Feather's Chicken Checkers (Unlockable)

- Unlock: 12,100 Aspiration Points
- Cost: $5,500
- Need(s): Fun 9 (Play)
- Skill(s): Logic (Practice)

You may choose to play against the chicken just for fun (play) or for both Fun and Logic skill (practice). The chance of beating the chicken increases with your Sim's Logic skill.

note Builds Logic faster than any other object.

If your Sim wins, the chicken lays a Golden Egg that can be used in food preparation. Each Golden Egg goes directly into the Harvested Animals section of your fridge.

tip The Chicken Checkers set can also be used as an alarm clock. Place it in the same room with your Sim's bed and, when set, it functions just like a regular alarm clock.

If Chicken Checkers gets dirty, it depresses Environment score for the room it's in. Clean it regularly to prevent or undo this effect.

Peppy Pete's Player Piano (Unlockable)

- Unlock: 15,900 Aspiration Points
- Cost: $6,500
- Need(s): Fun 1
- Skill(s): Creativity

note Mostly identical to the regular piano, this instrument has an additional player piano option. While it plays, Sims can listen to it for Fun.

"White Fire" Teppanyaki Table (Unlockable)

- Unlock: 24,000 Aspiration Points
- Cost: $9,999
- Skill(s): Cooking

Using this object builds Cooking skill but also costs money.

Other Sims may gather around to watch for Fun and to talk amongst themselves. Their reactions and the flourishes your Sim performs depend on your Sim's Cooking skill. Sims only watch if chairs are placed near the table.

At the end of the performance, food is served that can be eaten for Hunger satisfaction.

Objects

Miscellaneous

These objects play a variety of roles but just don't fit in anywhere else.

"What a Steel" Economy Trash Can
- Cost: §50

note This inexpensive trash can eventually fills up with trash and must be emptied into the curbside can. When it's full, the can depresses Environment score.

Street Light
- Cost: §125
- Need(s): Environment 1

"Frood" Tree
- Cost: §150
- Need(s): Environment 2

note From this tree, your Sims can extract fruits for use in cooking. For full info, see the "Food Creation" chapter.

DreaMaker "Fantasy" Dresser
- Cost: §500

Using this dresser takes your Sims back to Create-a-Sim, where they can alter their look from all available and unlocked clothing.

note Appearance items are unlocked by reaching 100 relationship points with any NPC and by getting promoted to levels 2, 3, 5, 7, 9, and 10 in each career.

"Manila 1000" Marine Aquarium
- Cost: §500
- Need(s): Environment 4

note From this tank, your Sims can extract seafood for use in cooking. For full info, see the "Food Creation" chapter.

Comic Dehydrator (Unlockable)
- Unlock: 500 Aspiration Points
- Cost: §550
- Need(s): Fun 3, Environment 2

This humidor is for serious comic book connoisseurs who want their comic books nice and dry. Functionally, it works just like a bookshelf except it dispenses only comic books that can be read for Fun. No other bookshelf options (skill building, etc.) are available. Certain recipes are only unlocked from reading comics.

GenoLife Garden Hutch
- Cost: §650
- Need(s): Environment 3

note From this garden, your Sims can extract vegetables for use in cooking. For full info, see the "Food Creation" chapter.

The "Tahdis" Wardrobe
- Cost: §750

note See DreaMaker "Fantasy" Dresser.

Tournament Foosball Table
- Cost: §800
- Need(s): Fun 6

Foosball can be practiced alone or played against another Sim.

When challenging another Sim, the bigger the difference in the players' Body skill, the shorter the game may last. The winner is also determined by the difference in Body skill; vast differences result in some gloating.

Regardless of skill, both players get Fun while playing. The winner, however, gets an additional boost in Fun while the loser takes a small hit.

Strike-a-Match Air Hockey (Unlockable)

- ◆ Unlock: 7,300 Aspiration Points
- ◆ Cost: §950
- ◆ Need(s): Hygiene -1, Fun 6

note During a winner's celebration dance, your Sims can start a fight. Body skill difference determines the winner.

Driver Pro 2006: "Chip Shots." (Unlockable)

- ◆ Unlock: 2,500 Aspiration Points
- ◆ Cost: §975
- ◆ Need(s): Fun 6

note After balls are hit from this Fun object, the sound that follows (chosen at random) indicates where (or on what) the ball landed.

Peppy Pete's Slots A' Hoppin'

- ◆ Cost: §1,115
- ◆ Need(s): Fun 2

Playing this slot machine costs money, but the payoff can be huge.

The more your Sims and NPCs play, the bigger the jackpot becomes. If an NPC wins at the machine, however, the jackpot your Sim can win is reduced.

When a Sim wins the jackpot, there's a chance the machine's firework display will start a fire.

Dishonest Sims can cheat, reaching into the machine for money. Their chances of finding something rise with their Mechanical skill. In rare cases, the Sim is injured (reducing Fun and Comfort) or killed in the endeavor.

note Grouchy Sims cheat autonomously, so keep them away from the slots if their Mechanical skill is low.

Screaming Death Bonfire (Unlockable)

- ◆ Unlock: 10,300 Aspiration Points
- ◆ Cost: §1,300
- ◆ Need(s): Fun 6

note May only be placed outdoors.

When Sims sit alone by this massive structure, they can sing, roast a snack (for Hunger), toss in a pinecone, or call other Sims over to join. Tossing in a pinecone creates a big flare that could occasionally cause something nearby to catch fire.

tip Telling a ghost story between midnight and 1:00 am may cause a ghost to appear on the lot.

With at least one other Sim in the circle, Sims can tell ghost or funny stories or sing together. When not otherwise occupied, any Sims around the fire talk as a group for Social and relationship benefits.

Spin the Bottle (Unlockable)

- ◆ Unlock: 9,200 Aspiration Points
- ◆ Cost: §1,625
- ◆ Need(s): Fun 7

This game for up to four Sims requires a spinner and another Sim to kiss. The intensity of the kiss and how much Fun and relationship increases the two Sims experience depend on their current relationship.

Trampoline (Unlockable)

- ◆ Unlock: 8,200 Aspiration Points
- ◆ Cost: §2,100
- ◆ Need(s): Fun 9

note Only one Sim may jump at a time. The higher the Sim's Body skill, the more elaborate the tricks he or she can perform.

Quaffophonic Bar System

◆ Cost: §2,500

◆ Need(s): Fun 5

You can serve either single (§5) or multiple (§25) drinks from this bar. They're more expensive than vending machine drinks, but they also satisfy Fun in addition to Hunger.

While serving multiple drinks, Sims can do two snazzy subinteractions, Juggle Bottles or Behind the Back.

Boggs Ole Timey Saloon

◆ Cost: §3,500

◆ Need(s): Fun 5

note See Quaffophonic Bar System.

Pathologie Costume Trunk (Unlockable)

◆ Unlock: 18,600 Aspiration Points

◆ Cost: §5,500

This enables your Sims to change into a variety of wacky costumes, their jammies, or even to run around in their (pixilated) birthday suits. No matter the choice, your Sims automatically get out of the costume after four hours.

Sims can use the trunk to dress up as a panda, an astronaut, a robot, or a yeti. When Sims are in one of these suits, other Sims may cheer or boo them on sight (depending on the other Sims' personalities). Likewise, if more than one Sim is on the lot in the same costume, they gain or lose Fun, based on their personalities.

SlumberGell Immersion Pod (Unlockable)

◆ Unlock: 26,500 Aspiration Points

◆ Cost: §5,500

◆ Need(s): Hygiene 5 (Sleep/ Meditate), Energy 10 (Sleep), Fun 10 (Meditate)

This alien technology replenishes both Hygiene and Energy while your Sims sleeps. Use it for meditation and you feed both Fun and Hygiene simultaneously.

If the bed gets dirty, it instead DEPLETES Hygiene when used.

tip If a Sim cleans the SlumberGell Immersion Pod when another Sim is using it, the Sim within spins wildly and is forcefully ejected.

Detective Arcade Genie Lamp (Unlockable)

◆ Unlock: 5,300 Aspiration Points

◆ Cost: §6,500

The genie can be used as an information resource or a chance of random good (or ill) fortune.

Talking to the genie results in a curious bit of unfathomable wisdom.

Once per day, you can employ the genie to grant a random wish. The result can be good (free Simoleons, a prepared meal, instant housecleaning, etc.) or bad (fires, sudden Bladder failure, nudity, etc.). Whether the outcome is good or bad is determined by the wisher's Aspiration score. The higher it is, the better the chance of a good wish and vise versa.

Wurl N' Hurl Gnarlosurf 2000 (Unlockable)

◆ Unlock: 27,900 Aspiration Points

◆ Cost: §15,000

◆ Need(s): Fun 10, Energy -1

Sims can either surf or boogie board on this simulator. The higher their Body skill, the more elaborate tricks they perform.

The lower a Sim's Energy, the higher the chance of a wipeout. Since this object itself drains Energy, don't let your Sims ride it too long.

Chapter 7
Characters

The twelve Story mode and four Sims (Freeplay) mode lots that make up your Sims' world provide ample company for your Sims. Knowing them better allows you to establish your Sims' relationships more quickly and efficiently and know generally what to expect when dealing with them and controlling them yourself.

This section exposes the inner workings of all Story mode characters in *The Sims™ 2* and the array of NPC service Sims who make your Sims' lives (mostly) easier.

Story Mode Sims
Betty Buttercup

- Lot: H.M.S. Amore
- Controllable: Yes
- Aspiration: Wealth
- Career/Job: None

Personality

- Neat/Sloppy: 3
- Outgoing/Shy: 10
- Active/Lazy: 0
- Playful/Serious: 10
- Nice/Grouchy: 2

Interests

- Media: 1
- Clothes: 1
- Sports: 2
- Food: 7
- Crime: 0
- Politics: 5
- Space: 8
- Health: 7
- Travel: 0
- Money: 8
- Work: 8
- Weather: 4
- Animals: 3
- Paranormal: 9

Betty Buttercup

Skills

- Cooking: 3
- Mechanical: 0
- Charisma: 0
- Body: 0
- Logic: 0
- Creativity: 0
- Cleaning: 0

Billy Specter

- Lot: Sunset Canyon
- Controllable: Yes
- Aspiration: Wealth
- Career/Job: None

Personality

- Neat/Sloppy: 0
- Outgoing/Shy: 10
- Active/Lazy: 10
- Playful/Serious: 0
- Nice/Grouchy: 0

Interests

- Media: 6
- Clothes: 9
- Sports: 1
- Food: 0
- Crime: 10
- Politics: 3
- Space: 7
- Health: 3
- Travel: 6
- Money: 8
- Work: 3
- Weather: 0
- Animals: 10
- Paranormal: 4

Skills

- Cooking: 3
- Mechanical: 0
- Charisma: 0
- Body: 0
- Logic: 0
- Creativity: 0
- Cleaning: 0

Billy Specter

Candi Cupp

- Lot: Tranquility Falls
- Controllable: Yes
- Aspiration: Wealth
- Career/Job: None

Personality

- Neat/Sloppy: 3
- Outgoing/Shy: 5
- Active/Lazy: 0
- Playful/Serious: 10
- Nice/Grouchy: 10

Interests

- Media: 2
- Clothes: 2
- Sports: 2
- Food: 2
- Crime: 4
- Politics: 9
- Space: 10
- Health: 8
- Travel: 7
- Money: 10
- Work: 2
- Weather: 3
- Animals: 4
- Paranormal: 1

Candi Cupp

Skills

- Cooking: 3
- Mechanical: 0
- Charisma: 0
- Body: 0
- Logic: 0
- Creativity: 0
- Cleaning: 0

Chantel Leer

- Lot: Tranquility Falls
- Controllable: Yes
- Aspiration: Creativity
- Career/Job: None

Personality

- Neat/Sloppy: 5
- Outgoing/Shy: 10
- Active/Lazy: 0
- Playful/Serious: 10
- Nice/Grouchy: 5

Interests

- Media: 9
- Clothes: 5
- Sports: 7
- Food: 8
- Crime: 9
- Politics: 8
- Space: 6
- Health: 7
- Travel: 2
- Money: 5
- Work: 2
- Weather: 7
- Animals: 3
- Paranormal: 5

Chantel Leer

Skills

- Cooking: 3
- Mechanical: 0
- Charisma: 0
- Body: 0
- Logic: 0
- Creativity: 7
- Cleaning: 0

Dina Caliente

- Lot: Jugen House
- Controllable: Yes
- Aspiration: Romance
- Career/Job: None

Personality

- Neat/Sloppy: 5
- Outgoing/Shy: 10
- Active/Lazy: 10
- Playful/Serious: 10
- Nice/Grouchy: 1

Interests

- Media: 2
- Clothes: 1
- Sports: 10
- Food: 0
- Crime: 8
- Politics: 4
- Space: 7
- Health: 10
- Travel: 8
- Money: 3
- Work: 3
- Weather: 7
- Animals: 1
- Paranormal: 5

Skills

- Cooking: 3
- Mechanical: 0
- Charisma: 0
- Body: 0
- Logic: 0
- Creativity: 0
- Cleaning: 0

Dina Caliente

Don Lothario

- Lot: Jugen House
- Controllable: Yes
- Aspiration: Romance
- Career/Job: Science/Lab Cleaner

Personality

- Neat/Sloppy: 5
- Outgoing/Shy: 6
- Active/Lazy: 6
- Playful/Serious: 9
- Nice/Grouchy: 6

Interests

- Media: 5
- Clothes: 5
- Sports: 5
- Food: 4
- Crime: 6
- Politics: 4
- Space: 6
- Health: 6
- Travel: 5
- Money: 4
- Work: 6
- Weather: 4
- Animals: 5
- Paranormal: 5

Skills

- Cooking: 3
- Mechanical: 0
- Charisma: 0
- Body: 0
- Logic: 0
- Creativity: 0
- Cleaning: 0

Don Lothario

Don Treadwell

- Lot: Cliffside Retreat
- Controllable: Yes
- Aspiration: Romance
- Career/Job: None

Personality
- Neat/Sloppy: 5
- Outgoing/Shy: 5
- Active/Lazy: 5
- Playful/Serious: 5
- Nice/Grouchy: 5

Interests
- Media: 8
- Clothes: 7
- Sports: 4
- Food: 3
- Crime: 3
- Politics: 1
- Space: 10
- Health: 7
- Travel: 2
- Money: 0
- Work: 10
- Weather: 5
- Animals: 0
- Paranormal: 10

Skills
- Cooking: 3
- Mechanical: 0
- Charisma: 0
- Body: 0
- Logic: 0
- Creativity: 7
- Cleaning: 0

Don Treadwell

Farah Moonbiscuit

- Lot: Shoreline Trails
- Controllable: Yes
- Aspiration: Creativity
- Career/Job: None

Personality
- Neat/Sloppy: 8
- Outgoing/Shy: 5
- Active/Lazy: 5
- Playful/Serious: 5
- Nice/Grouchy: 5

Interests
- Media: 4
- Clothes: 8
- Sports: 7
- Food: 0
- Crime: 1
- Politics: 2
- Space: 0
- Health: 4
- Travel: 10
- Money: 2
- Work: 6
- Weather: 6
- Animals: 3
- Paranormal: 0

Farah Moonbiscuit

Skills
- Cooking: 3
- Mechanical: 0
- Charisma: 0
- Body: 0
- Logic: 0
- Creativity: 0
- Cleaning: 0

Felicity Usher

- Lot: Rockwell Acres
- Controllable: No
- Aspiration: Romance
- Career/Job: None

Personality
- Neat/Sloppy: 3
- Outgoing/Shy: 10
- Active/Lazy: 5
- Playful/Serious: 10
- Nice/Grouchy: 5

Interests
- Media: 4
- Clothes: 9
- Sports: 8
- Food: 6
- Crime: 10
- Politics: 5
- Space: 5
- Health: 8
- Travel: 10
- Money: 2
- Work: 3
- Weather: 0
- Animals: 5
- Paranormal: 9

Skills
- Cooking: 7
- Mechanical: 0
- Charisma: 0
- Body: 0
- Logic: 0
- Creativity: 0
- Cleaning: 0

Felicity Usher

Gilda Geld

- Lot: Biodome
- Controllable: Yes
- Aspiration: Romance
- Career/Job: None

Personality

- Neat/Sloppy: 4
- Outgoing/Shy: 10
- Active/Lazy: 0
- Playful/Serious: 10
- Nice/Grouchy: 2

Interests

- Media: 9
- Clothes: 9
- Sports: 2
- Food: 1
- Crime: 0
- Politics: 5
- Space: 8
- Health: 1
- Travel: 6
- Money: 9
- Work: 0
- Weather: 3
- Animals: 2
- Paranormal: 7

Gilda Geld

Skills

- Cooking: 3
- Mechanical: 0
- Charisma: 0
- Body: 0
- Logic: 0
- Creativity: 0
- Cleaning: 0

Goopi Gilscarbo

- Lot: Tranquility Falls
- Controllable: Yes
- Aspiration: Knowledge
- Career/Job: None

Personality

- Neat/Sloppy: 5
- Outgoing/Shy: 0
- Active/Lazy: 5
- Playful/Serious: 5
- Nice/Grouchy: 8

Goopi Gilscarbo

Interests

- Media: 8
- Clothes: 9
- Sports: 0
- Food: 10
- Crime: 4
- Politics: 8
- Space: 1
- Health: 7
- Travel: 0
- Money: 0
- Work: 3
- Weather: 1
- Animals: 9
- Paranormal: 3

Skills

- Cooking: 3
- Mechanical: 0
- Charisma: 0
- Body: 0
- Logic: 0
- Creativity: 0
- Cleaning: 0

Hector Fromagero

- Lot: H.M.S. Amore
- Controllable: Yes
- Aspiration: Romance
- Career/Job: None

Personality

- Neat/Sloppy: 3
- Outgoing/Shy: 10
- Active/Lazy: 7
- Playful/Serious: 10
- Nice/Grouchy: 10

Interests

- Media: 2
- Clothes: 0
- Sports: 4
- Food: 5
- Crime: 3
- Politics: 5
- Space: 6
- Health: 7
- Travel: 0
- Money: 5
- Work: 9
- Weather: 3
- Animals: 2
- Paranormal: 8

Skills

- Cooking: 3
- Mechanical: 0
- Charisma: 0
- Body: 0
- Logic: 0
- Creativity: 0
- Cleaning: 0

Hector Fromagero

Helga Mandrake

- Lot: Sunset Canyon
- Controllable: Yes
- Aspiration: Creativity
- Career/Job: None

Personality

- Neat/Sloppy: 5
- Outgoing/Shy: 5
- Active/Lazy: 5
- Playful/Serious: 5
- Nice/Grouchy: 5

Interests

- Media: 5
- Clothes: 6
- Sports: 9
- Food: 0
- Crime: 0
- Politics: 6
- Space: 3
- Health: 1
- Travel: 10
- Money: 4
- Work: 2
- Weather: 9
- Animals: 0
- Paranormal: 10

Helga Mandrake

Skills

- Cooking: 3
- Mechanical: 0
- Charisma: 0
- Body: 0
- Logic: 0
- Creativity: 0
- Cleaning: 0

Isabella Monty

- Lot: Cliffside Retreat
- Controllable: Yes
- Aspiration: Creativity
- Career/Job: None

Personality

- Neat/Sloppy: 3
- Outgoing/Shy: 2
- Active/Lazy: 10
- Playful/Serious: 10
- Nice/Grouchy: 7

Interests

- Media: 5
- Clothes: 7
- Sports: 9
- Food: 0
- Crime: 1
- Politics: 10
- Space: 7
- Health: 2
- Travel: 2
- Money: 9
- Work: 6
- Weather: 3
- Animals: 3
- Paranormal: 8

Isabella Monty

Skills

- Cooking: 7
- Mechanical: 0
- Charisma: 0
- Body: 0
- Logic: 0
- Creativity: 4
- Cleaning: 0

Jasmine Yves

- Lot: Mesa Gallery
- Controllable: Yes
- Aspiration: Creativity
- Career/Job: Art/Studio Assistant (3)

Personality

- Neat/Sloppy: 9
- Outgoing/Shy: 2
- Active/Lazy: 2
- Playful/Serious: 10
- Nice/Grouchy: 6

Interests

- Media: 4
- Clothes: 10
- Sports: 1
- Food: 8
- Crime: 7
- Politics: 4
- Space: 7
- Health: 1
- Travel: 0
- Money: 10
- Work: 9
- Weather: 2
- Animals: 1
- Paranormal: 9

Skills

- Cooking: 3
- Mechanical: 0
- Charisma: 0
- Body: 0
- Logic: 0
- Creativity: 8
- Cleaning: 0

Jasmine Yves

Jessica Jones

- Lot: Biodome
- Controllable: Yes
- Aspiration: Popularity
- Career/Job: None

Personality

- Neat/Sloppy: 3
- Outgoing/Shy: 10
- Active/Lazy: 10
- Playful/Serious: 10
- Nice/Grouchy: 3

Jessica Jones

Interests

- Media: 4
- Clothes: 5
- Sports: 9
- Food: 4
- Crime: 0
- Politics: 8
- Space: 10

- Health: 7
- Travel: 4
- Money: 5
- Work: 10
- Weather: 5
- Animals: 9
- Paranormal: 2

Skills

- Cooking: 3
- Mechanical: 0
- Charisma: 0
- Body: 0

- Logic: 0
- Creativity: 0
- Cleaning: 0

Jessie Rose

- Lot: The Orbit Room
- Controllable: Yes

- Aspiration: Romance
- Career/Job: None

Personality

- Neat/Sloppy: 6
- Outgoing/Shy: 0
- Active/Lazy: 5

- Playful/Serious: 10
- Nice/Grouchy: 7

Interests

- Media: 5
- Clothes: 10
- Sports: 0
- Food: 10
- Crime: 10
- Politics: 7
- Space: 5

- Health: 3
- Travel: 2
- Money: 10
- Work: 7
- Weather: 6
- Animals: 10
- Paranormal: 2

Skills

- Cooking: 3
- Mechanical: 0
- Charisma: 0
- Body: 0

- Logic: 0
- Creativity: 0
- Cleaning: 0

Jessie Rose

John Gray

- Lot: Andromeda Arms
- Controllable: Yes

- Aspiration: Knowledge
- Career/Job: None

Personality

- Neat/Sloppy: 8
- Outgoing/Shy: 8
- Active/Lazy: 8

- Playful/Serious: 8
- Nice/Grouchy: 8

Interests

- Media: 1
- Clothes: 4
- Sports: 2
- Food: 10
- Crime: 9
- Politics: 8
- Space: 10

- Health: 10
- Travel: 0
- Money: 2
- Work: 0
- Weather: 4
- Animals: 10
- Paranormal: 1

Skills

- Cooking: 3
- Mechanical: 0
- Charisma: 0
- Body: 0

- Logic: 0
- Creativity: 0
- Cleaning: 0

John Gray

Jonas W. Bragg

- Lot: Andromeda Arms
- Controllable: No

- Aspiration: Wealth
- Career/Job: None

Personality

- Neat/Sloppy: 10
- Outgoing/Shy: 7
- Active/Lazy: 5

- Playful/Serious: 0
- Nice/Grouchy: 0

Interests

- Media: 4
- Clothes: 1
- Sports: 2
- Food: 6
- Crime: 5
- Politics: 2
- Space: 6

- Health: 2
- Travel: 7
- Money: 8
- Work: 10
- Weather: 5
- Animals: 3
- Paranormal: 10

Jonas W. Bragg

Skills

- Cooking: 3
- Mechanical: 0
- Charisma: 0
- Body: 0
- Logic: 0
- Creativity: 0
- Cleaning: 0

Larry Liu

- Lot: Tranquility Falls
- Controllable: Yes
- Aspiration: Popularity
- Career/Job: Crime/Vandal (1)

Personality

- Neat/Sloppy: 3
- Outgoing/Shy: 10
- Active/Lazy: 10
- Playful/Serious: 7
- Nice/Grouchy: 7

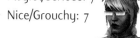

Larry Liu

Interests

- Media: 2
- Clothes: 5
- Sports: 8
- Food: 6
- Crime: 9
- Politics: 3
- Space: 6
- Health: 5
- Travel: 2
- Money: 2
- Work: 0
- Weather: 5
- Animals: 10
- Paranormal: 1

Skills

- Cooking: 3
- Mechanical: 0
- Charisma: 0
- Body: 0
- Logic: 0
- Creativity: 0
- Cleaning: 0

Mary Gray

- Lot: Andromeda Arms
- Controllable: Yes
- Aspiration: Knowledge
- Career/Job: None

Personality

- Neat/Sloppy: 8
- Outgoing/Shy: 8
- Active/Lazy: 8
- Playful/Serious: 8
- Nice/Grouchy: 8

Interests

- Media: 8
- Clothes: 5
- Sports: 6
- Food: 2
- Crime: 3
- Politics: 10
- Space: 5
- Health: 4
- Travel: 2
- Money: 8
- Work: 3
- Weather: 8
- Animals: 10
- Paranormal: 2

Skills

- Cooking: 3
- Mechanical: 0
- Charisma: 0
- Body: 0
- Logic: 0
- Creativity: 0
- Cleaning: 0

Mary Gray

Nelson Longfellow

- Lot: H.M.S. Amore
- Controllable: No
- Aspiration: Popularity
- Career/Job: No

Personality

- Neat/Sloppy: 8
- Outgoing/Shy: 10
- Active/Lazy: 10
- Playful/Serious: 1
- Nice/Grouchy: 7

Interests

- Media: 9
- Clothes: 4
- Sports: 4
- Food: 8
- Crime: 7
- Politics: 0
- Space: 9
- Health: 9
- Travel: 5
- Money: 7
- Work: 7
- Weather: 3
- Animals: 10
- Paranormal: 4

Skills

- Cooking: 3
- Mechanical: 0
- Charisma: 0
- Body: 0
- Logic: 0
- Creativity: 0
- Cleaning: 0

Nelson Longfellow

Nina Caliente

- Lot: Yugen House
- Controllable: Yes
- Aspiration: Romance
- Career/Job: None

Personality

- Neat/Sloppy: 3
- Outgoing/Shy: 8
- Active/Lazy: 0
- Playful/Serious: 9
- Nice/Grouchy: 9

Interests

- Media: 2
- Clothes: 1
- Sports: 7
- Food: 9
- Crime: 9
- Politics: 3
- Space: 4
- Health: 0
- Travel: 3
- Money: 3
- Work: 8
- Weather: 10
- Animals: 2
- Paranormal: 5

Skills

- Cooking: 3
- Mechanical: 0
- Charisma: 0
- Body: 0
- Logic: 0
- Creativity: 0
- Cleaning: 0

Nina Caliente

Noel Howard

- Lot: Biodome
- Controllable: Yes
- Aspiration: Wealth
- Career/Job: Politics/ Congressperson (7)

Personality

- Neat/Sloppy: 10
- Outgoing/Shy: 5
- Active/Lazy: 2
- Playful/Serious: 0
- Nice/Grouchy: 5

Interests

- Media: 0
- Clothes: 9
- Sports: 5
- Food: 9
- Crime: 0
- Politics: 10
- Space: 10
- Health: 0
- Travel: 8
- Money: 1
- Work: 8
- Weather: 2
- Animals: 9
- Paranormal: 6

Noel Howard

Skills

- Cooking: 3
- Mechanical: 0
- Charisma: 6
- Body: 0
- Logic: 7
- Creativity: 6
- Cleaning: 0

Ossie Madison

- Lot: Rockwell Acres
- Controllable: No
- Aspiration: Popularity
- Career/Job: None

Personality

- Neat/Sloppy: 7
- Outgoing/Shy: 6
- Active/Lazy: 1
- Playful/Serious: 3
- Nice/Grouchy: 10

Interests

- Media: 4
- Clothes: 10
- Sports: 4
- Food: 6
- Crime: 9
- Politics: 1
- Space: 4
- Health: 7
- Travel: 9
- Money: 2
- Work: 2
- Weather: 2
- Animals: 1
- Paranormal: 7

Skills

- Cooking: 7
- Mechanical: 0
- Charisma: 0
- Body: 0
- Logic: 0
- Creativity: 0
- Cleaning: 0

Ossie Madison

Patricia Pitts

- Lot: Mesa Gallery
- Controllable: No
- Aspiration: Creativity
- Career/Job: None

Personality

- Neat/Sloppy: 9
- Outgoing/Shy: 8
- Active/Lazy: 7
- Playful/Serious: 6
- Nice/Grouchy: 5

Interests

- Media: 5
- Clothes: 9
- Sports: 5
- Health: 3
- Travel: 1
- Money: 3

Patricia Pitts

- Food: 2
- Crime: 7
- Politics: 5
- Space: 10
- Work: 6
- Weather: 10
- Animals: 8
- Paranormal: 7

Skills

- Cooking: 3
- Mechanical: 0
- Charisma: 0
- Body: 0
- Logic: 0
- Creativity: 0
- Cleaning: 0

Patrizio Monty

- Lot: Cliffside Acres
- Controllable: Yes
- Aspiration: Wealth
- Career/Job: None

Personality

- Neat/Sloppy: 10
- Outgoing/Shy: 0
- Active/Lazy: 0
- Playful/Serious: 0
- Nice/Grouchy: 2

Interests

- Media: 6
- Clothes: 10
- Sports: 7
- Food: 3
- Crime: 10
- Politics: 0
- Space: 4
- Health: 2
- Travel: 0
- Money: 5
- Work: 4
- Weather: 10
- Animals: 1
- Paranormal: 8

Skills

- Cooking: 2
- Mechanical: 0
- Charisma: 0
- Body: 0
- Logic: 0
- Creativity: 0
- Cleaning: 0

Patrizio Monty

Phil Phantasm

- Lot: Orbit Room
- Controllable: Yes
- Aspiration: Wealth
- Career/Job: Business/ Junior Executive (4)

Personality

- Neat/Sloppy: 2
- Outgoing/Shy: 10
- Active/Lazy: 0
- Playful/Serious: 10
- Nice/Grouchy: 0

Interests

- Media: 8
- Clothes: 0
- Sports: 9
- Food: 3
- Crime: 2
- Politics: 5
- Space: 1
- Health: 5
- Travel: 7
- Money: 6
- Work: 7
- Weather: 6
- Animals: 8
- Paranormal: 9

Skills

- Cooking: 3
- Mechanical: 0
- Charisma: 2
- Body: 0
- Logic: 0
- Creativity: 0
- Cleaning: 0

Phil Phantasm

Red S. Hirt

- Lot: Sunset Canyon
- Controllable: Yes
- Aspiration: Popularity
- Career/Job: None

Personality

- Neat/Sloppy: 0
- Outgoing/Shy: 0
- Active/Lazy: 0
- Playful/Serious: 0
- Nice/Grouchy: 10

Interests

- Media: 10
- Clothes: 7
- Sports: 10
- Food: 3
- Crime: 0
- Politics: 6
- Space: 6
- Health: 5
- Travel: 9
- Money: 6
- Work: 5
- Weather: 6
- Animals: 9
- Paranormal: 2

Red S. Hirt

Skills

- Cooking: 3
- Mechanical: 0
- Charisma: 0
- Body: 0
- Logic: 0
- Creativity: 0
- Cleaning: 0

Rico Banana

- Lot: Mesa Gallery
- Controllable: Yes
- Aspiration: Romance
- Career/Job: None

Personality

- Neat/Sloppy: 3
- Outgoing/Shy: 10
- Active/Lazy: 1
- Playful/Serious: 10
- Nice/Grouchy: 7

Interests

- Media: 0
- Clothes: 10
- Sports: 2
- Food: 1
- Crime: 8
- Politics: 8
- Space: 6
- Health: 4
- Travel: 4
- Money: 10
- Work: 8
- Weather: 9
- Animals: 2
- Paranormal: 8

Rico Banana

Skills

- Cooking: 3
- Mechanical: 0
- Charisma: 0
- Body: 0
- Logic: 0
- Creativity: 0
- Cleaning: 0

Sheila Deadbones

- Lot: Sunset Canyon
- Controllable: Yes
- Aspiration: Romance
- Career/Job: None

Personality

- Neat/Sloppy: 5
- Outgoing/Shy: 5
- Active/Lazy: 5
- Playful/Serious: 5
- Nice/Grouchy: 5

Sheila Deadbones

Interests

- Media: 0
- Clothes: 4
- Sports: 1
- Food: 9
- Crime: 4
- Politics: 2
- Space: 1
- Health: 2
- Travel: 9
- Money: 4
- Work: 3
- Weather: 9
- Animals: 10
- Paranormal: 8

Skills

- Cooking: 3
- Mechanical: 0
- Charisma: 0
- Body: 0
- Logic: 0
- Creativity: 0
- Cleaning: 0

Timmy Tool

- Lot: Shoreline Trails
- Controllable: No
- Aspiration: Knowledge
- Career/Job: No

Personality

- Neat/Sloppy: 5
- Outgoing/Shy: 0
- Active/Lazy: 0
- Playful/Serious: 0
- Nice/Grouchy: 6

Interests

- Media: 9
- Clothes: 8
- Sports: 7
- Food: 3
- Crime: 1
- Politics: 1
- Space: 1
- Health: 1
- Travel: 6
- Money: 10
- Work: 1
- Weather: 0
- Animals: 10
- Paranormal: 5

Skills

- Cooking: 3
- Mechanical: 0
- Charisma: 0
- Body: 0
- Logic: 0
- Creativity: 0
- Cleaning: 0

Timmy Tool

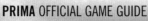
Toothless Joe

- Lot: Jugen House
- Controllable: Yes
- Aspiration: Popularity
- Career/Job: No

Personality

- Neat/Sloppy: 5
- Outgoing/Shy: 2
- Active/Lazy: 10
- Playful/Serious: 10
- Nice/Grouchy: 8

Interests

- Media: 5
- Clothes: 0
- Sports: 5
- Food: 4
- Crime: 9
- Politics: 5
- Space: 1
- Health: 6
- Travel: 6
- Money: 5
- Work: 8
- Weather: 5
- Animals: 2
- Paranormal: 5

Toothless Joe

Skills

- Cooking: 3
- Mechanical: 0
- Charisma: 0
- Body: 0
- Logic: 0
- Creativity: 0
- Cleaning: 0

Torin Namaste

- Lot: Shoreline Trails
- Controllable: No
- Aspiration: Wealth
- Career/Job: None

Personality

- Neat/Sloppy: 5
- Outgoing/Shy: 10
- Active/Lazy: 10
- Playful/Serious: 3
- Nice/Grouchy: 0

Torin Namaste

Interests

- Media: 10
- Clothes: 2
- Sports: 5
- Food: 0
- Crime: 4
- Politics: 7
- Space: 10
- Health: 3
- Travel: 8
- Money: 5
- Work: 8
- Weather: 4
- Animals: 2
- Paranormal: 8

Skills

- Cooking: 3
- Mechanical: 0
- Charisma: 0
- Body: 2
- Logic: 0
- Creativity: 0
- Cleaning: 0

Turk Johnson

- Lot: Orbit Room
- Controllable: Yes
- Aspiration: Creativity
- Career/Job: None

Personality

- Neat/Sloppy: 0
- Outgoing/Shy: 10
- Active/Lazy: 5
- Playful/Serious: 3
- Nice/Grouchy: 7

Turk Johnson

Interests

- Media: 6
- Clothes: 5
- Sports: 3
- Food: 4
- Crime: 1
- Politics: 3
- Space: 5
- Health: 4
- Travel: 1
- Money: 4
- Work: 6
- Weather: 0
- Animals: 0
- Paranormal: 9

Skills

- Cooking: 3
- Mechanical: 0
- Charisma: 0
- Body: 0
- Logic: 0
- Creativity: 0
- Cleaning: 0

Willy Weir

- Lot: Mesa Gallery
- Controllable: Yes
- Aspiration: Wealth
- Career/Job: None

Personality

- Neat/Sloppy: 0
- Outgoing/Shy: 1
- Active/Lazy: 2
- Playful/Serious: 3
- Nice/Grouchy: 4

Willy Weir

Interests

- Media: 2
- Clothes: 5
- Sports: 0
- Food: 2
- Crime: 1
- Politics: 3
- Space: 3
- Health: 8
- Travel: 10
- Money: 0
- Work: 3
- Weather: 2
- Animals: 0
- Paranormal: 2

Skills

- Cooking: 3
- Mechanical: 0
- Charisma: 0
- Body: 0
- Logic: 0
- Creativity: 0
- Cleaning: 0

Wooster Piggins

- Lot: Biodome
- Controllable: Yes
- Aspiration: Knowledge
- Career/Job: None

Personality

- Neat/Sloppy: 10
- Outgoing/Shy: 10
- Active/Lazy: 5
- Playful/Serious: 0
- Nice/Grouchy: 5

Interests

- Media: 7
- Clothes: 3
- Sports: 1
- Food: 3
- Crime: 7
- Politics: 8
- Space: 5
- Health: 9
- Travel: 7
- Money: 6
- Work: 8
- Weather: 2
- Animals: 6
- Paranormal: 5

Skills

- Cooking: 3
- Mechanical: 0
- Charisma: 0
- Body: 0
- Logic: 0
- Creativity: 0
- Cleaning: 0

Wooster Piggins

XHT-F Smith

- Lot: Alien Crash Site
- Controllable: Yes
- Aspiration: Popularity
- Career/Job: None

Personality

- Neat/Sloppy: 0
- Outgoing/Shy: 10
- Active/Lazy: 5
- Playful/Serious: 5
- Nice/Grouchy: 10

Interests

- Media: 9
- Clothes: 6
- Sports: 1
- Food: 1
- Crime: 0
- Politics: 4
- Space: 5
- Health: 9
- Travel: 6
- Money: 7
- Work: 8
- Weather: 3
- Animals: 0
- Paranormal: 5

Skills

- Cooking: 3
- Mechanical: 0
- Charisma: 0
- Body: 0
- Logic: 0
- Creativity: 0
- Cleaning: 0

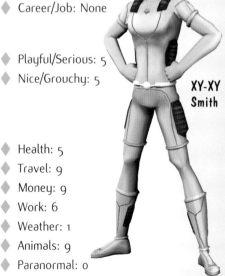

XHT-F Smith

XY-XY Smith

- Lot: Alien Crash Site
- Controllable: Yes
- Aspiration: Knowledge
- Career/Job: None

Personality

- Neat/Sloppy: 5
- Outgoing/Shy: 5
- Active/Lazy: 5
- Playful/Serious: 5
- Nice/Grouchy: 5

Interests

- Media: 9
- Clothes: 2
- Sports: 7
- Food: 3
- Crime: 0
- Politics: 10
- Space: 0
- Health: 5
- Travel: 9
- Money: 9
- Work: 6
- Weather: 1
- Animals: 9
- Paranormal: 0

XY-XY Smith

Skills

- Cooking: 3
- Mechanical: 0
- Charisma: 0
- Body: 0
- Logic: 0
- Creativity: 0
- Cleaning: 0

Service Sims

Thanks to your handy-dandy wall phone, the most loyal and efficient Sim services are only a phone call away. Dial up any of these services when you need them.

> **note** All service NPCs and public servants with the power to fine your Sims for their misdeeds aren't very understanding if your Sims lack the funds to pay the bill/fine.
>
> In all cases, they repossess an object of approximately the value of the outstanding bill or fine. If the NPC has an ongoing service with your Sim (like a maid who comes every day), she cancels the contract.

> **note** There's one further service that can be requested over the phone, but there's no actual NPC who arrives to provide the service.
>
> The Therapist is available over the phone only to provide a way for your Sims to refresh their list of Wants and Fears. More about this service can be found in the "Aspirations" section.

Maid

The maid does the most valuable service in town. Keeping a house clean yourself, even when all Sims are high in Neat, consumes great gobs of time. Even Sims in the first level of their career should feel their time is too valuable for mopping and dishwashing. Better to just call the maid and pay her reasonable fee of §10 per hour.

With Cleaning skill of 10 and a diligent work ethic, she stays until all messes (trash, full trashcans, dirty objects, dishes, food, ashes, unmade beds, and puddles) are cleaned. Therefore, the dirtier the house, the more she costs.

> **note** The Freedom Vacuum can be a substitute for the maid, but it still requires your Sim to break stride to tidy up the place. The Freedom Vacuum is a direct control-only object that instantly picks up any puddles, trash, or ash nearby. It's faster than normal cleaning and available anytime you need it, but it's not as carefree as having a maid and costs the equivalent of three hundred hours of maid service.

Gardener

The potted plants in your Sims' homes, as well as plants used to harvest vegetables and fruits, need watering every few days, or they die. Dead plants kill Environment score, and that's trouble.

To keep your plants nice and producing with no effort on your part, the gardener may just be a sound investment. For §10 per hour every three days, he replants any dead plants and keep everything watered and healthy.

Repair Person

When things are broken and you just don't have the time or the Mechanical skill to do it yourself, call the repair person. She comes over quickly but charges a pretty penny (§50 per hour) to fix any broken items. She stays as long as there's something in need of fixing and charges you when she's done.

Fire Department

When a fire breaks out, you get on the phone to the fire department. Only call them when there is a fire ablaze, though, or you'll be punished with a "tsk-tsk" and a §500 fine.

If there's a smoke detector in the same room as the fire, the fire department comes running automatically.

> **note** The fastest way to fight fires is with the new direct control object, the Snuffit Fire Destroyer. In direct control mode, direct your Sim to take this extinguisher off the wall and go put out the flames yourself. The fire department won't be upset if you finish the job before they get there.

Police

When the Thief invades your home, he swipes one of your Sim's most valuable items. One way to catch the Thief is to call the police as soon as you get the message that the burglar is in your home. Calling the police frivolously, however, gets you in trouble to the tune of a §500 fine.

If the cops catch the Thief, you get your item back and a §500 reward.

You also see the police if your Sims' parties continue after 2:00 am. When the clock strikes 2:00 in the morning, the police come calling and write your Sim a ticket for §100. That's what you get for having too much fun.

> **tip** Once you've gotten nabbed for a late party, the cops don't come back, no matter how long the party goes, so there's no need to break it up once the fine's been assessed.

Sims Who Call on You

There are a few other NPCs who provide a service (of sorts) for your Sims.

Mail Carrier

The mail carrier delivers new bills every three days at 10:00 am. Whenever you pay the bills by putting them in the mailbox (even if the mail carrier isn't scheduled to come), he picks up the mail automatically the next time the clock reaches 10:00 am.

Newsie

The newsie brings the newspaper each morning at 7:00 am. If there are more than five newspapers on the lot, the newsie refuses to deliver any more until you throw enough away to get below five.

Grim Reaper

Whenever a Sim dies, the Grim Reaper comes to visit and ushers the Sim into the netherworld. Dead Sims, however, don't fade away; they immediately become ghosts that wander the lot all day and night. If the deceased was controllable in life, he or she is also controllable as a ghost (but with very different social skills).

Whenever there's a ghost on a lot, the Grim Reaper is always present, wandering the lot and occasionally watering your Sim's plants. He sticks around to be on hand if any ghosts on the lot want to return to life.

Any playable ghost can, at your direction, return to life by either paying the Grim Reaper a resurrection fee or challenging him to a fiddle contest. These transactions are the only interactions available for the Grim Reaper, and they're only available to ghosts. Living Sims can't interact with him at all.

Thief

The Thief comes randomly at midnight if all residents are either asleep or at work and steals the most valuable—purchased by your Sim(s)—item he can physically reach. He can only be stopped by a burglar alarm or the police. If you have neither, he's as good as gone with your valuables.

Repo Man

Fail to pay your bills within 10 days of their arrival, and the Repo Man pays a visit. He takes an item or items with a total depreciated value at or above the amount you owe.

> **note** Once the Repo Man is on the lot, you can't access Buy or Build Catalogs, so there's no way to sell off items or move them to inaccessible locations to keep them from being taken.

Chapter 8

Food Creation

Hunger is the most important and constantly demanding of your Sim's Needs. It's just as essential as Energy but, unlike Energy, it contributes mightily to a Sim's Mood. Want more evidence? It's the only Need that can, if unsatisfied, kill your Sim. More? It's the only Need that gets its own extra section.

How you satisfy your Sim's Hunger is also one of the key differences between playing *The Sims™ 2* and playing it well. The amount of efficiency that can be wrung out of preparing and eating food is absolutely unmatched if you take the time to learn how things function.

This section introduces you to the mechanics of how your Sims can satisfy their Hunger Need and how you can harness the power of the new food creation system to rise to the heights of Sim existence.

note Though the food creation system can be used (albeit a bit awkwardly) in classic control mode, we highly recommend using it exclusively in direct control mode due to its greater efficiency and, above all, control.

Food in General

Your Sims satisfy their Hunger Need by consuming food. Nothing else in the entire game can take its place. The question is not whether to eat, but how much time you're going to consume doing it.

Sims satisfy Hunger by eating. Satisfying it fully in the shortest amount of time, however, is a function of the quality of the food.

Every food object your Sim eats, no matter how it's created, satisfies a fixed amount of Hunger and takes a fixed amount of time to prepare and consume. Efficiency, therefore, arises from creating food with the highest possible Hunger satisfaction and the shortest possible prep and eating time relative to Hunger satisfaction.

This requires balancing. Preparing great food requires two things, time for your Sim to learn to cook and money to purchase the best possible tools. It also requires balancing of satisfaction and time. A snack from the fridge is quicker than making a big meal, but your Sim has to come back for another meal much more quickly.

tip In Story mode, once you have enough money and all the object unlocks you need, buy all the best cooking tools and put them on the lot. Before you leave, sell them back. And when you arrive at the next lot, buy them again. You lose a bit in depreciation, but it's better than just leaving a great fridge behind.

To tame these various issues, it's necessary to understand how the food chain works.

The Food Chain

note There are, as discussed later, two ways to create food, generically and by using the food creation system. The principles discussed here apply to both methods.

By interacting with the fridge, you see all the options of what kind of meal to cook.

Food gets its Hunger satisfaction from several sources.

◆ Inherent: Every generic meal and every ingredient carries in it a quantity of Hunger satisfaction. Generic meals have an assigned satisfaction amount while prepared meals' satisfaction is based on the inherent attributes of the ingredients comprising the meal.

◆ Preparation: How a food is prepared (on a countertop, in a blender, in a food processor, or not at all) adds an additional amount of Hunger satisfaction. All combinations of ingredients have results that skip this step and go directly to the stove.

- Completion: All food combos have results that can be completed on a counter, in a food processor, in the blender, or in the stove. The better (more expensive) the stove, processor, or blender, the greater the added satisfaction.
- Cooking Skill: The Cooking skill (acquired by reading books from the bookshelf and by cooking) of the Sim preparing the food shortens food preparation time and adds additional Hunger satisfaction to the resulting food.

Finished foods tossed into the blender can be consumed very quickly though they lose some of their Hunger satisfaction.

tip Any finished food can be further processed by putting it in the blender. This makes the finished product drinkable and, thus, faster to consume. On the downside, it reduces the Hunger impact of food by 5–10 points (depending on the blender). Still, the time efficiency may be worth it.

note Generic meals and ingredients have defined effects on Hunger satisfaction but also a negative effect on Bladder. Many ingredients also satisfy Energy and carry hidden effects that can dramatically impact your Sim for better or worse.

Meals, Ingredients, and the Refrigerator

With one exception (grilling) all food begins in the refrigerator. All refrigerators feature the same slate of interactions.

- Get Ingredients (Direct Control)/Cook a Meal (Classic Control): This starts the food creation system to make a single serving of a custom food.
- Get a Snack (§5): Your Sim extracts a preprocessed snack that's faster to eat than preparing a full meal but delivers only minimal Hunger satisfaction (especially relative to the time it takes to consume).

- Get Group Meal Ingredients: This starts the food creation system to make four servings of a custom food. All ingredient costs are *tripled*.
- Get Generic Ingredients (§12): This bypasses ingredient selection and makes a generic meal.

note Generic meals have fixed attributes.
- Cost: §12
- Hunger: 40/45/50/55 (depending on the fridge)
- Energy: 5
- Bladder: -20

You can prepare generic meals on the counter (Shabu-Shabu to eat as is or roast and veggies to go in the stove), in the blender (dinner in a cup), in the food processor (casserole or soup) and then the stove, or directly in the stove (roast).

Where you prepare a meal, even a generic one, decides what the final product is.

tip Unless there's only one Sim in the household, always prepare group meals. It takes no extra time but costs more money. However, since a group meal makes four times the amount of food for only three times the cost of a single meal, it's less expensive than letting the other Sims on the lot autonomously make their own single servings of generic meals (which are less nutritious than what you can make with a well-trained and controlled Sim).

Refrigerators differ in two factors, Hunger satisfaction of their contents and in the ingredients available.

Refrigerator Bonuses

The same ingredients and generic meals (except snacks) have different Hunger satisfaction power, depending on the fridge from which they were pulled. In fact, each fridge modifies everything taken from it by a fixed bonus amount.
- EconoCool Refrigerator: 0
- Chow Bella Bachelor Fridge: +5
- Nostalgix Refrigerator: +10
- U-Probe-It Refrigerating Organism: +15

Refrigerators do not alter foods' other Need effects or their special effects (if any).

Ingredient Selection

When using the food creation system, different refrigerators contain different ingredients. The more expensive the fridge, the wider the selection.

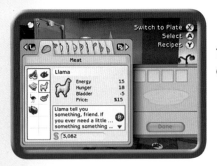

The most expensive fridge offers all ingredients.

note Harvested fruits, vegetables, and animals have the same selection regardless of the fridge. The differences in selection apply only to ingredients "bought" from the fridge.

Food Selection by Fridge

INGREDIENT	CATEGORY	ECONOCOOL REFRIGERATOR	CHOW BELLA BACHELOR FRIDGE	NOSTALGIX REFRIGERATOR	U-PROBE-IT REFRIGERATING ORGANISM
Apple	Fruits			X	X
Banana	Fruits				X
Beef	Meat	X	X	X	X
Beet	Vegetables				X
Broccoli	Vegetables			X	X
Broth	Liquids			X	X
Canola Oil	Oil			X	X
Carrot	Vegetables	X	X	X	X
Celery	Vegetables	X	X	X	X
Cheese	Dairy				X
Cherry	Fruits			X	X
Chicken	Meat	X	X	X	X
Corn Oil	Oils	X	X	X	X
Egg	Dairy	X	X	X	X
Fauxlestra	Oils				X
Juice	Liquids				X
Lamb	Meat			X	X
Lemon	Fruits	X	X	X	X
Lettuce	Vegetables			X	X
Lime	Fruits	X	X	X	X
Llama	Meat				X
Milk	Dairy	X	X	X	X
Oat Flour	Grain				X
Olive Oil	Oils	X	X	X	X
Onion	Vegetables	X	X	X	X
Orange	Fruits	X	X	X	X
Ostrich	Meat				X

Food Selection by Fridge continued

INGREDIENT	CATEGORY	EconoCool Refrigerator	Chow Bella Bachelor Fridge	Nostalgix Refrigerator	U-Probe-It Refrigerating Organism
Peanut Oil	Oils	X	X	X	X
Pork	Meat	X	X	X	X
Potato	Vegetables	X	X	X	X
Rye	Grain			X	X
Sourdough	Grain	X	X	X	X
Strawberry	Fruits				X
Tomato	Vegetables				X
Turkey	Meat			X	X
Water	Liquids	X	X	X	X
White Flour	Grain	X	X	X	X
Whole Wheat Flour	Grain	X	X	X	X
Yogurt	Dairy			X	X

Food Preparation

Ingredients can be eaten directly out of the fridge or go straight to the stove, but more Hunger satisfaction is had with some preparation. Some preparation methods are the final step in the cooking process while others result in a pot of food ready to meet the heat of the stove.

Whether it's at a counter or in a food processor, more Hunger satisfaction is added with a prep stage.

tip It's tempting to skip preparation to save time, but it's not a wise tradeoff, especially early in the game. First, you're losing considerable Hunger satisfaction by not going through more steps. Second, and more important, your Sims develop Cooking skill while cooking, so the more steps they use to make a meal, the more Cooking skill they acquire. Multitasking is way more efficient than making a quick meal, studying cooking at the bookshelf, and having to make another meal sooner because the first wasn't very satisfying. You go longer before the next meal and get more Cooking skill in the same time by fully preparing the meal THEN sitting down to study (or do whatever).

Food can be prepped in or on two things.

◆ Countertops: Food can be prepped for the stove or for uncooked meals on any open countertop or on top of a dishwasher (which acts like a countertop). Hand prepping food on the countertop is slower and adds fewer Hunger points to the process than if you use the food processor. If you can't afford the food processor, or if you desire the food that results from raw prepping, the countertop is all you need.

◆ Food Processor: The food processor is faster, adds more Hunger satisfaction than the countertop, and makes a different variety of foods from the same ingredients. It also acts as a food completion device for an uncooked result.

note When deciding what to do with ingredients once you take them from the fridge, stand your Sim in front of a counter, appliance, or stove to see what interactions are available. In general, if the interaction stars with the word "Prep," it means that using it results in a pot of food to be cooked on the stove. If the interaction starts with "Make," it means selecting it creates a final product.

Completion

Foods can be completed in many different ways.

note Blenders and counters get dirty. If you complete food in a dirty blender or on a dirty counter, it adds +2 to the meal's nausea effect.

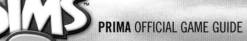

To choose the next step, carry the food to the counter, processor, blender, or stove and choose what you want to make or prep.

Ingredients directly from the fridge can be finished without a preparation step (raw); on the counter; or in the food processor, blender, or stove. These results require no prep and contain only Hunger satisfaction from the ingredients, the fridge, and the device used to complete them.

> **note** Microwave ovens act as stoves as far as the results they produce, but they have some advantages and disadvantages. Cooking foods in the microwave is faster than on the stove, but it adds +1 to the resulting food's nausea effect and deducts -5 from its Hunger satisfaction.

Prepped foods can receive an additional infusion of Hunger satisfaction if prepared on a stove. The amount of Hunger added to the food depends on the quality of the stove—the more expensive it is, the more Hunger satisfaction it imparts.

GRILLING

The Grillinator "BigBQ" grill serves two functions: it can act as a stove for anything extracted from a refrigerator, or, for §25, your Sim can pull a generic BBQ meal from the grill and cook it for a dish that supplies the following:

◆ Hunger: 31   ◆ Energy: 5   ◆ Bladder: -20

Cooking Skill

Cooking skill has several effects on food.

◆ Time: Reduces the time it takes to prep and cook food with all devices and countertops
◆ Hunger Satisfaction: Imparts additional Hunger satisfaction with every step.

◆ Fire: Reduces the chance of fire when using stoves (level 5 or higher makes your Sim accident-proof).
◆ Food Poisoning: Reduces the chance finished product causes fatal food poisoning.
◆ Showmanship: Increases your Sim's flamboyance when using the "White Fire" Teppanyaki Table.
◆ Recipes: Unlocks a new recipe with each level of Cooking skill.

Cooking skill can be learned from books.

Or you could just have your Sims cook A LOT and get all their Cooking skill from time served in the kitchen.

Cooking skill is learned passively from studying Cooking at any bookshelf or learned practically by cooking. The latter is the most efficient since it permits your Sims to produce a meal and develop skill simultaneously.

> **tip** The payoff of having a high-level Cooking Sim early in the game is tremendous. The time and Need efficiency of always having nutritious food to eat is unmatched by any other strategy. Spend more time than you think you should in early lots studying Cooking.
>
> Also, when your Sim arrives at the Cliffside Retreat lot, do a lot of cooking with ingredients harvested from the lot's vegetable garden, fruit trees, and fish tanks. These cost no money, so all the Cooking skill you get doesn't cost a Simoleon.
>
> You might even want to get a roommate (see the "Social Interactions" section) who can focus on Cooking skill and preparing meals while the primary Sim tends to career and satisfying Gold Wants. Since roommates follow your Sim from lot to lot, you only have to train them once. Relying on resident Sims on each lot, by contrast, demands they be trained before they can be of any use.

Ingredients and Meals

Now that you know how the hardware works, let's talk software: the ingredients.

Food ingredients are the raw materials that your Sim uses to make meals. To master the kitchen in *The Sims™ 2*, you must understand how ingredients work and how they are combined.

Ingredient Attributes

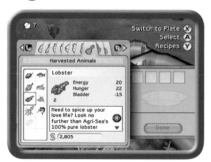

The stats you see in the ingredient selection screen are only small parts of the equation.

Your Sims cook using 64 ingredients, each with its own unique attributes. These attributes come in two forms, basic and special.

Basic Attributes

Every food is identified by several factors.

◆ Type: This lets you know in what drawer of the fridge you can find it and controls how the ingredient is used in food combinations.

◆ Cost: Cost is per individual serving and is the same in every fridge. When making group meals (four servings), ingredients' cost is tripled.

◆ Hunger: This is the number of points toward Hunger satisfaction. This number is altered by the fridge from which the ingredient comes, the objects used in its preparation, the Cooking skill of the chef, and other minor factors.

◆ Energy: This is the amount of Energy Need satisfaction supplied by eating the food.

◆ Fun: Several ingredients are just a hoot to eat and satisfy the Fun Need when consumed. This value isn't shown in the fridge or food descriptions you see onscreen. It also contributes to a food's potential for an Energy boost effect.

◆ Bladder: This is the amount of Bladder Need *depleted* by consuming the food. The greater the amount of Bladder reduction in the foods your Sims eat, the more often they have to visit the toilet. Choose your foods to balance the highest possible Hunger satisfaction with the least possible Bladder depletion, or much of the time you gain with good cooking will be lost in more frequent potty breaks.

When food is prepared, these factors are simply added to determine the food's cost and final attributes.

The types of the ingredients determine what dish actually results, regardless of the specific ingredients. For example, any combination of a grain, a vegetable, and a fruit results in the same dish from each possible prep and completion. Make it in a food processor, and you always get a jam and veggie sandwich. The attributes of the particular sandwich you make, however, depend on the specific ingredients used.

Special Attributes

Every food has at least one special attribute that can combine to make the food even more powerful. Understand how these attributes function and how the resulting food is crafted, and you can create your own edible power-ups.

Love is in the air, or so that heart-spouting dish would suggest. That is evidence of a very special effect.

Most attributes work by accumulation. If the finished product contains 3 or more points in any attribute, the final food is imbued with the attribute's effect. If, therefore, three ingredients feature 1 point of nausea each, the resulting food causes anyone who eats it to immediately vomit. If all ingredients add up to less than 3 points of nausea, the food does not cause nausea.

note Note that food attributes can be increased or reduced by other forces. For example, using a dirty blender or countertop adds 2 nausea points to any food made in it. If, therefore, there is already 1 nausea point in the ingredients, the 2 from the dirty blender convert the food into a food boomerang that tastes even worse coming up than it did going down.

There are five special attributes.

◆ Repulse: Food emits black hearts, and any Sim who eats it is only able to socialize in Archenemy stance for a short time. Description of the final product reads, "While there's nothing about this food that looks improper, there's something about it that makes you feel vaguely angry about it."

◆ Diuretic: Food drips water droplets and, when consumed, depletes the eater's Bladder Need by nearly half (-80). If your Sims are even a bit below medium in that Need, they immediately wet the floor. Description of the final product reads, "Just looking at this makes your stomach gurgle. Something about it just isn't right, but you feel like maybe if you were going to eat it, you should be somewhere near a restroom."

◆ Nausea: Food emits a green haze and, when consumed, causes the eater to immediately vomit. As a side effect, this dramatically depletes Hygiene Need (-60). Description of the final product reads, "Something about it doesn't look quite right, and frankly, that makes you feel a bit sick to your stomach."

◆ Aphrodisiac: Food emits red hearts, and any Sim who eats it socializes with anyone in Lover stance for a short time. Description of the final product reads, "You can't take your eyes off it. It's the most beautiful thing you've ever seen."

◆ Skill Boost: Food emits stars, and anyone who eats it has all skills boosted by 3 levels for a short time. Description of the final product reads, "There's something about this food that just looks perfect. Each piece is perfectly placed, every aspect of it is expertly prepared. Merely being in its presence makes you feel better about yourself."

The description of the finished food provides clues as to its effects.

The visual effect around the food (hearts, stars, etc.) and the food's description confirm which effect, if any, the food contains.

If a food contains no special effects, the description reads, "It looks tasty and well prepared."

Foods may have more than one effect if the ingredients combine for more than 3 points in several attributes. Only the strongest, however, is indicated by the visual effect and the description, so check your ingredients carefully in this book to make sure there isn't a lesser effect that causes problems. Nothing is more unseemly than an aphrodisiac that induces vomiting.

There is one special effect that works a bit differently, the Energy boost. Above and beyond the inherent Energy satisfaction effect of the food, the right combination can offer an even greater pick-me-up.

A food contains an Energy boost if the ingredients' collective Energy, Fun, and Skill boost attributes equal more than 80. If so, the resulting food has an additional +30 boost to Energy Need for a short time. Food with an Energy boost effect emits sparks, and the resulting description reads, "One look at this dish and you know that if you ate it, you could take on the world. Or leap over tall buildings. Well, maybe not the tall buildings thing."

Ingredient Sources

Ingredients come from three sources.

◆ Refrigerators
◆ Harvesting Objects
◆ Other Sources

Refrigerator Ingredients

Most ingredients come from refrigerators. The supply of these ingredients is infinite, but each serving costs a fixed number of Simoleons. The cost triples if your Sim makes a four-serving group meal (what a bargain).

The ingredients available in each fridge depend on the appliance's quality and cost. The more expensive the fridge, the wider the selection of built-in ingredients. To get all possible refrigerator ingredients, you must purchase the U-Probe-It Refrigerating Organism.

Harvesting Objects

Three objects can provide potentially infinite sources of free food.

◆ GenoLife Garden Hutch: Vegetables
◆ "Frood" Tree: Fruits
◆ "Manila 1000" Marine Aquarium: Animals

Scooping fish out of this tank is one of the best ways to cook.

The vegetable garden and the fruit tree function identically. Ripe fruit or vegetables are picked off them and added to refrigerator inventory with the harvest interaction. Both must be watered every day, or the tree stops producing and, if neglected long enough, dies. Dead plants must be replaced with the replant interaction, and the new plant must be watered for two days before it produces again.

The aquarium functions similarly. It also must be cleaned regularly to keep your number of fish consistent. Dirty tanks give less new fish per day.

All harvested ingredients are finite and run out if not restocked. On the plus side, any harvested foods are available to your Sim on any lot they go to, so they never go to waste.

Other Sources

Two extremely powerful foods are obtained from some unexpected places.

Regular games of chicken checkers with a high Logic Sim should supply a steady flow of Golden Eggs.

◆ Dangleberries: Harvested from a well-tended Sproutch Couch. Water it for two straight days and every day thereafter, and it sprouts Dangleberries.
◆ Golden Egg: Won by defeating the chicken in Prof. Feather's Chicken Checkers.

As with other harvested foods, these go automatically into the harvested drawers of the fridge ("Fruits" and "Animals," respectively).

Ingredient Directory

The following table lists every ingredient and its attributes.

note Harvested fruits and veggies qualify as "Fruits" and "Vegetables," respectively, and harvested animals count as "Meat."

Ingredient	Type	Cost	Hunger	Energy	Fun	Bladder	Repulse	Skill Boost	Diuretic	Nausea	Aphrodisiac
Apple	Fruits	§3	14	0	0	-15	0	1	1	0	0
Asparagus	Vegetables	§0	13	0	0	-10	0	1	0	0	0
Avocado	Vegetables	§0	16	0	5	-2	0	1	0	0	1
Banana	Fruits	§3	10	10	10	-2	0	1	0	1	1
Beef	Meat	§6	19	0	0	-10	0	0	0	0	0
Beet	Vegetables	§5	13	0	10	-2	0	0	0	1	0
Bok Choy	Vegetables	§0	12	10	0	-2	0	1	1	0	0
Broccoli	Vegetables	§3	14	5	10	-5	0	1	0	0	0
Broth	Liquids	§5	12	0	0	-5	0	0	0	0	0
Canola Oil	Oils	§5	4	0	0	-5	0	1	1	0	0
Carrot	Vegetables	§3	9	0	10	-2	0	1	0	0	1
Celery	Vegetables	§2	8	10	0	-10	0	0	1	0	0
Cheese	Dairy	§4	11	0	0	-10	1	1	0	1	0
Cherry	Fruits	§6	10	10	0	-2	0	0	0	0	1
Chicken	Meat	§5	16	-2	0	-10	1	1	0	0	0
Chupa-Chupa	Fruits	§0	12	0	10	-2	0	0	0	0	0
Corn Oil	Oils	§2	6	0	0	0	0	0	0	0	0
Dangleberry	Fruits	§0	40	25	25	-25	2	0	0	0	1
Eel	Meat	§0	14	25	10	-15	0	0	1	1	0

Ingredient Directory continued

Ingredient	Type	Cost	Hunger	Energy	Fun	Bladder	Repulse	Skill Boost	Diuretic	Nausea	Aphrodisiac
Egg	Dairy	§2	14	5	0	-5	0	1	0	0	0
Fauxlestra	Oils	§2	5	0	-10	0	0	0	2	1	0
Golden Egg	Meat	§0	15	0	0	-5	1	1	0	1	2
Halibut	Meat	§0	13	10	10	-10	0	1	0	1	1
Jicama	Vegetables	§0	14	0	0	-2	2	1	0	0	0
Juice	Liquids	§3	9	1	15	-10	0	0	0	1	0
Lamb	Meat	§7	20	0	0	-10	0	0	0	0	0
Lemon	Fruits	§2	8	10	10	-2	0	0	0	0	0
Lettuce	Vegetables	§2	7	10	0	-2	0	0	0	1	0
Lime	Fruits	§2	8	10	10	-2	0	0	0	0	1
Llama	Meat	§15	18	15	25	-5	0	1	1	0	2
Lobster	Meat	§0	22	20	15	-15	0	0	0	1	1
Mangosteen	Fruits	§0	11	25	10	-2	0	2	1	0	1
Milk	Dairy	§2	11	0	0	-10	1	1	0	0	0
Mini-Swordfish	Meat	§0	17	15	20	-5	0	1	1	0	2
Oat Flour	Grain	§4	13	10	15	-5	0	1	0	0	0
Olive Oil	Oils	§5	3	0	10	-5	0	1	0	0	1
Onion	Vegetables	§2	12	0	-10	-2	0	0	0	0	0
Orange	Fruits	§2	10	10	10	0	0	0	0	0	0
Ostrich	Meat	§12	12	30	20	-10	0	1	0	0	1
Passion Fruit	Fruits	§0	13	10	0	-2	0	0	0	0	2
Peanut Oil	Oils	§2	2	0	10	-5	0	0	0	0	0
Persimmon	Fruits	§0	13	10	0	-2	0	0	0	0	1
Plum	Fruits	§0	14	10	0	-2	0	2	2	0	0
Pork	Meat	§5	17	10	0	-10	0	0	0	0	0
Portabella Mushroom	Vegetables	§0	13	5	10	-2	0	2	0	0	1
Potato	Vegetables	§2	14	0	0	0	0	0	0	0	0
Purslane	Vegetables	§0	9	0	5	-2	0	2	0	0	0
Red Snapper	Meat	§0	14	10	10	-10	0	1	1	1	1
Rye	Grain	§5	16	0	15	-5	0	1	0	0	0
Shark	Meat	§0	22	20	15	-10	0	0	0	1	2
Sourdough	Grain	§5	14	5	5	-10	1	0	0	0	1
Soursop	Fruits	§0	12	10	0	-2	2	0	2	0	0
Spinach	Vegetables	§0	10	10	0	-2	0	2	0	0	0
Squid	Meat	§0	17	15	25	-5	0	1	1	2	0
Star Fruit	Fruits	§0	13	10	15	-2	0	0	0	0	1
Strawberry	Fruits	§5	13	20	0	-2	0	1	0	0	1
Tomato	Vegetables	§5	14	0	0	-5	0	0	0	0	1
Tuna	Meat	§0	16	15	0	-10	0	1	1	1	0
Turkey	Meat	§4	19	-10	5	-10	1	1	0	0	0
Water	Liquids	§2	2	0	0	-10	0	0	1	0	0
White Flour	Grain	§3	13	0	0	0	1	0	0	0	0
White Truffle	Vegetables	§0	19	0	30	-2	0	1	0	0	2
Whole Wheat Flour	Grain	§4	16	0	10	-5	0	1	0	0	0
Yogurt	Dairy	§5	11	0	10	-5	0	2	0	0	0

Food Combinations and Results

The secret to crafting food with exactly the effects you desire is knowing how they combine.

> **note** You may use only one of each ingredient, but you may use multiple ingredients in the same type. Though the second ingredient of the same type adds its attribute points to the final result, it doesn't determine what the dish actually is. Two pieces of meat completed in the stove make a roast just as if you used one piece. The dish does, however, benefit from the extra attribute points of the additional ingredient.

Generally, food can be made from one to four ingredients, and its effects are the sum of the ingredients' individual attributes, both basic and special. The food's final Hunger satisfaction attribute is increased by the equipment used to prepare it.

The next question, therefore, is *what* to cook. Frankly, you can take any one or combine any four ingredients and get something edible, or you could consider only the ingredients and their effects and make whatever results.

Sometimes, however it's better to know what you're going to get before you select ingredients. There are two sources for this, in-game recipes and this book.

Recipes

Unlocking recipes is challenging, and it helps you get started in the kitchen.

There are 24 unlockable recipes your Sim can discover by reading books, reading magazines on the toilet, skimming comic books, chatting on the computer, reading in bed, and gaining Cooking skill points.

> **note** See the "Unlockables" section to learn how to discover each recipe.

The recipes can be viewed from the ingredient selection screen, and they show you the ingredients required and what equipment you need to get the stated result.

Unlockable Recipes

Recipe Number	Dish	Ingredient 1	Ingredient 2	Ingredient 3	Ingredient 4	Prep	Completion
1	Roast	Beef	—	—	—	—	Stove
2	Sandwich	Beef	Onion	Whole Wheat Flour	—	—	Counter
3	Sweet Vegetable Soup	Carrot	Lime	Passion Fruit	—	Counter	Stove
4	Fruit Shake	Strawberry	Yogurt	—	—	—	Blended
5	Fruitspacho	Apple	Peanut Oil	—	—	—	Processor
6	Salad	Lettuce	Olive Oil	—	—	—	Counter
7	Chef's Salad	Shark	Yogurt	Bok Choy	Plum	—	Counter
8	Ceviche	Halibut	Lime	Corn Oil	—	—	Counter
9	Hors D'Oeuvres	Llama	White Truffle	Fauxlestra	—	—	Counter
10	Soup	Squid	Juice	Milk	—	Processor	Stove
11	Fruit in Pastry	Juice	White Flour	Dangleberry	Corn Oil	Counter	Stove
12	Samosas	Mini-Swordfish	Oat Flour	Soursop	—	Processor	Stove
13	Combo Pizza	Turkey	Cheese	White Flour	Tomato	Counter	Stove
14	Roast & Fruit Sauce	Beef	Whole Wheat Flour	Orange	Fauxlestra	—	Stove
15	Salad-in-a-Cup	Milk	Lettuce	Corn Oil	—	—	Blended
16	Burrito	Beef	Broth	White Flour	Avocado	Processor	Stove
17	Kebabs	Llama	Onion	Chupa-Chupa	—	Counter	Stove
18	Parfait	Cherry	Yogurt	Juice	—	Counter	Stove
19	Fruit Smoothie	Yogurt	Soursop	Fauxlestra	—	—	Processor
20	Gratin Shake	Cheese	Broccoli	—	—	—	Blended
21	Wellington Roast	Beef	Broth	White Flour	Canola Oil	—	Stove
22	Ceviche Puree	Lobster	Lime	Olive Oil	—	—	Processor
23	Cheeseless Pizza	Golden Egg	Oat Flour	Carrot	Soursop	Processor	Stove
24	Casserole	Pork	Golden Egg	Spinach	Dangleberry	Processor	Stove

Though unlocking these recipes provides a sense of accomplishment, you don't really need them to create food. It's much more important to know how the system works so you can independently make these recipes and scores of others. For that, you need to look under the game's hood a bit.

Food Type Combinations

Which food you get from combining ingredients is a result of up to three elements.

◆ Type of Each Ingredient: For determining the result rather than the food's statistics. The specific ingredient within the type isn't important.

◆ Prep Equipment (if any): Counter, food processor.

◆ Completion Equipment (if any): Counter, food processor, blender, stove.

Food Results by Type Combinations and Prep/Completion

Ingredient 1	Ingredient 2	Ingredient 3	Ingredient 4	Raw	Counter Complete	Food Processor Complete
Dairy	—	—	—	Drink	Drink	Drink
Dairy	Grain	—	—	Ingredients	Dough	Dough
Dairy	Grain	Fruits	—	Ingredients	Jam Sandwich	Jam Sandwich
Dairy	Grain	Fruits	Oils	Ingredients	Toast & Jam	Fruit Soup
Dairy	Grain	Oils	—	Ingredients	Raw Dough	Raw Dough
Dairy	Grain	Vegetables	—	Ingredients	Veggie Sandwich	Veggie Sandwich
Dairy	Grain	Vegetables	Fruits	Ingredients	Veggies on Toast	Soup
Dairy	Grain	Vegetables	Oils	Ingredients	Sandwich	Sandwich
Dairy	Fruits	—	—	Ingredients	Fruit Salad	Shake
Dairy	Fruits	Oils	—	Ingredients	Fruit Salad	Fruit Smoothie
Dairy	Oils	—	—	Power Shake	Power Shake	Power Shake
Dairy	Vegetables	—	—	Ingredients	Soup	Soup
Dairy	Vegetables	Fruits	—	Ingredients	Soup	Soup
Dairy	Vegetables	Fruits	Oils	Ingredients	Salad	Power Smoothie
Dairy	Vegetables	Oils	—	Ingredients	Salad	Salad
Grain	—	—	—	Dough	Dough	Dough
Grain	Fruits	—	—	Ingredients	Jam & Toast	Fruit Slurry
Grain	Fruits	Oils	—	Ingredients	Jam Sandwich	Jam Sandwich
Grain	Oils	—	—	Ingredients	Bowl of Dough	Bowl of Dough
Grain	Vegetables	—	—	Ingredients	Veggie Sandwich	Veggie Sandwich
Grain	Vegetables	Fruits	—	Ingredients	Jam & Veggie Sandwich	Jam & Veggie Sandwich
Grain	Vegetables	Fruits	Oils	Ingredients	Leftovers	Pureed Leftovers
Grain	Vegetables	Oils	—	Ingredients	Vegetable Panini	Vegetable Panini
Fruits	—	—	—	Fruits	Fruit	Fruit Smoothie
Fruits	Oils	—	—	Ingredients	Marinated Fruit	Fruitspacho
Liquids	—	—	—	Drink	Drink	Drink
Liquids	Dairy	—	—	Ingredients	Drink	Shake
Liquids	Dairy	Grain	—	Ingredients	Dough	Dough
Liquids	Dairy	Grain	Fruits	Ingredients	Sandwich	Sandwich
Liquids	Dairy	Grain	Oils	Ingredients	Panini	Panini
Liquids	Dairy	Grain	Vegetables	Ingredients	Sandwich	Sandwich
Liquids	Dairy	Fruits	—	Ingredients	Fruit Soup	Fruit Shake
Liquids	Dairy	Fruits	Oils	Ingredients	Soup	Fruit Smoothie
Liquids	Dairy	Oils	—	Ingredients	Creamy Soup	Creamy Soup
Liquids	Dairy	Vegetables	—	Ingredients	Vegetable Soup	Vegetable Soup
Liquids	Dairy	Vegetables	Fruits	Ingredients	Salad	Soup
Liquids	Dairy	Vegetables	Oils	Ingredients	Salad	Veggie Smoothie
Liquids	Grain	—	—	Ingredients	Raw Dough	Raw Dough
Liquids	Grain	Fruits	—	Ingredients	Fruity Dough	Fruity Dough
Liquids	Grain	Fruits	Oils	Ingredients	Jam Sandwich	Jam Sandwich
Liquids	Grain	Oils	—	Ingredients	Dough	Dough
Liquids	Grain	Vegetables	—	Ingredients	Veggie Dough	Veggie Dough
Liquids	Grain	Vegetables	Fruits	Ingredients	Vegetable Sandwich	Vegetable Sandwich

This information can be used so you know how to make a specific dish. If, for example, you wanted to make a pizza, you know you need to combine any meat, any dairy, and any grain, prep it on the counter, and bake it in the stove. This doesn't tell you what the food's attributes are, but you can backward engineer the result by considering the actual ingredients.

The more useful way to employ this information is to design a food that does what you want it to do. For this, use the attribute data in the previous "Ingredient Directory" to determine what ingredients you wish to use, then check the following table to see what (based on their types) they combine to form, using each prep/completion tool.

> **tip** If maximum Hunger satisfaction is essential to any meal you cook, always utilize both the food processor and the stove.

Stove Complete (No Prep)	Counter Prep and Stove Complete	Food Processor Prep and Stove Complete	Blender Complete
Drink	Drink	Drink	Drink
Bread	Bread	Bread	Dough Slurry
Fruity Bread	Fruity Bread	Fruity Bread	Fruity Power Shake
Fruit Foccacia	Fruit Foccacia	Fruit Foccacia	Fruit Shake
Foccacia	Foccacia	Foccacia	Power Shake
Veggie Bread	Veggie Bread	Veggie Bread	Veggie Power Shake
Bread	Veggie Casserole	Veggie Casserole	Veggie Shake
Quiche	Veggie Pizza	Veggie Burrito	Veggie Shake
Fruit Sauce	Fruit Compote	Fruit Shake	Fruit Shake
Fruit Soup	Fruit Soup	Fruit Soup	Fruit Smoothie
Power Shake	Power Shake	Power Shake	Power Shake
Stew	Gratin	Gratin	Gratin Shake
Soup	Casserole	Casserole	Smoothie
Soup	Crudite	Soup	Power Shake
Salad	Salad	Salad	Salad-in-a-Cup
Bread	Bread	Bread	Dough Smoothie
Fruity Bread	Fruity Bread	Fruit Pancake	Fruity Power Shake
Foccacia	Foccacia	Foccacia	Fruit Smoothie
Foccacia	Foccacia	Foccacia	Bread Smoothie
Veggie Casserole	Veggie Casserole	Veggie Casserole	Veggie Power Shake
Bread	Casserole	Casserole	Fruit Smoothie
Vegetable Fruit Foccacia	Vegetable Fruit Foccacia	Vegetable Fruit Foccacia	Smoothie
Foccacia	Foccacia	Foccacia	Vegetable Smoothie
Fruit Soup	Fruit Compote	Fruit Compote	Fruit Smoothie
Fruit Stew	Bowl of Preserves	Bowl of Jam	Fruit Smoothie
Drink	Drink	Drink	Drink
Soup	Soup	Soup	Shake
Bread	Bread	Bread	Drink
Soup	Fruit Bread	Fruit Bread	Fruit Shake
Soup	Foccacia	Foccacia	Smoothie
Dumpling Stew	Veggie Bread	Veggie Burrito	Veggie Shake
Parfait	Parfait	Fruit Shake	Fruit Shake
Soup	Soup	Fruit Smoothie	Fruit Smoothie
Creamy Soup	Creamy Soup	Creamy Soup	Drink
Vegetable Soup	Vegetable Soup	Vegetable Soup	Drink
Salad	Salad	Soup	Smoothie
Salad	Salad	Soup	Veggie Smoothie
Bread	Bread	Bread	Dough Smoothie
Fruity Bread	Fruity Bread	Fruity Bread	Fruity Power Shake
Soup & Bread	Fruit in Pastry	Fruit Compote	Fruit Shake
Foccacia	Foccacia	Foccacia	Power Shake
Veggie Bread	Veggie Bread	Veggie Bread	Veggie Power Shake
Soup & Bread	Veggies & Fruit Sauce	Casserole	Smoothie

Food Results by Type Combinations and Prep/Completion continued

Ingredient 1	Ingredient 2	Ingredient 3	Ingredient 4	Raw	Counter Complete	Food Processor Complete
Liquids	Grain	Vegetables	Oils	Ingredients	Panini	Panini
Liquids	Fruits	—	—	Ingredients	Glazed Fruit	Smoothie
Liquids	Fruits	Oils	—	Ingredients	Fruit Salad	Smoothie
Liquids	Oils	—	—	Ingredients	Soup	Power Smoothie
Liquids	Vegetables	—	—	Ingredients	Veggies & Dip	Gazpacho
Liquids	Vegetables	Fruits	—	Ingredients	Gazpacho	Veggie-Fruitspacho
Liquids	Vegetables	Fruits	Oils	Ingredients	Salad	Drink
Liquids	Vegetables	Oils	—	Ingredients	Salad	Salad
Meat	—	—	—	Meat	Carpaccio	Tartar
Meat	Dairy	—	—	Ingredients	Carpaccio	Carpaccio Soup
Meat	Dairy	Grain	—	Ingredients	Sandwich	Sandwich
Meat	Dairy	Grain	Fruits	Ingredients	Sandwich	Sandwich
Meat	Dairy	Grain	Oils	Ingredients	Panini	Panini
Meat	Dairy	Grain	Vegetables	Ingredients	Chef's Salad	Sandwich
Meat	Dairy	Fruits	—	Ingredients	Fruity Carpaccio	Shake
Meat	Dairy	Fruits	Oils	Ingredients	Leftovers	Pureed Leftovers
Meat	Dairy	Oils	—	Ingredients	Marinated Carpaccio	Shake
Meat	Dairy	Vegetables	—	Ingredients	Sandwich	Sandwich
Meat	Dairy	Vegetables	Fruits	Ingredients	Chef's Salad	Bowl of Stuff
Meat	Dairy	Vegetables	Oils	Ingredients	Chef's Salad	Pureed Leftovers
Meat	Grain	—	—	Ingredients	Sloppy Joe	Sloppy Joe
Meat	Grain	Fruits	—	Ingredients	Sandwich	Sandwich
Meat	Grain	Fruits	Oils	Ingredients	Panini	Panini
Meat	Grain	Oils	—	Ingredients	Panini	Panini
Meat	Grain	Vegetables	—	Ingredients	Sandwich	Sandwich
Meat	Grain	Vegetables	Fruits	Ingredients	Sandwich	Sandwich
Meat	Grain	Vegetables	Oils	Ingredients	Panini	Panini
Meat	Fruits	—	—	Ingredients	Carpaccio	Tartar
Meat	Fruits	Oils	—	Ingredients	Ceviche	Ceviche Puree
Meat	Liquids	—	—	Ingredients	Carpaccio	Carpaccio Soup
Meat	Liquids	Dairy	—	Ingredients	Marinated Carpaccio	Tartar
Meat	Liquids	Dairy	Grain	Ingredients	Sandwich	Sandwich
Meat	Liquids	Dairy	Fruits	Ingredients	Leftovers	Soup
Meat	Liquids	Dairy	Oils	Ingredients	Soup	Soup
Meat	Liquids	Dairy	Vegetables	Ingredients	Chef's Salad	Stew
Meat	Liquids	Grain	—	Ingredients	Sandwich	Sandwich
Meat	Liquids	Grain	Fruits	Ingredients	Sandwich	Sandwich
Meat	Liquids	Grain	Oils	Ingredients	Panini	Panini
Meat	Liquids	Grain	Vegetables	Ingredients	Sandwich	Sandwich
Meat	Liquids	Fruits	—	Ingredients	Fruity Carpaccio	Fruity Stew
Meat	Liquids	Fruits	Oils	Ingredients	Leftovers	Bowl of Soup
Meat	Liquids	Oils	—	Ingredients	Marinated Carpaccio	Tartar
Meat	Liquids	Vegetables	—	Ingredients	Shabu-Shabu	Soup
Meat	Liquids	Vegetables	Fruits	Ingredients	Soup	Soup
Meat	Liquids	Vegetables	Oils	Ingredients	Chef's Salad	Bowl of Soup
Meat	Oils	—	—	Ingredients	Carpaccio	Smoothie
Meat	Vegetables	—	—	Ingredients	Carpaccio	Tartar
Meat	Vegetables	Fruits	—	Ingredients	Hors D'Oeuvres	Ceviche Salsa
Meat	Vegetables	Fruits	Oils	Ingredients	Salad	Pureed Leftovers
Meat	Vegetables	Oils	—	Ingredients	Hors D'Oeuvres	Ceviche Salsa
Oils	—	—	—	Oil	Oil	Frothy Oil
Vegetables	—	—	—	Veggies	Crudite	Slaw
Vegetables	Fruits	—	—	Ingredients	Salad	Salad
Vegetables	Fruits	Oils	—	Ingredients	Salad	Salad
Vegetables	Oils	—	—	Ingredients	Salad	Salad

Stove Complete (No Prep)	Counter Prep and Stove Complete	Food Processor Prep and Stove Complete	Blender Complete
Soup & Bread	Bruschetta	Veggie Burrito	Veggie Smoothie
Fruit Compote	Fruit Compote	Smoothie	Smoothie
Fruit Soup	Fruit Soup	Fruit Soup	Smoothie
Soup	Soup	Soup	Power Smoothie
Stew	Casserole	Casserole	Shake
Soup	Casserole	Casserole	Drink
Soup	Veggies & Fruit Sauce	Soup	Fruit Shake
Salad	Salad	Salad	Salad-in-a-Cup
Roast	Sliced Roast	Meatloaf	Slurry
Roast	Meatloaf	Burrito	Shake
Dumpling Stew	Pizza	Casserole	Power Smoothie
Hawaiian Pizza	Hawaiian Pizza	Hawaiian Pizza	Slurry
Pizza	Pizza	Pizza	Slurry
Combo Pizza	Combo Pizza	Lasagna	Slurry
Roast with Fruit	Roast with Fruit	Meaty-Fruity Soup	Sweet Shake
Roast	Sliced Roast	Soup	Slurry
Roast	Sliced Roast	Soup	Slurry
Roast & Veggie	Roast & Veggie	Burrito	Smoothie
Roast	Chef Salad	Casserole	Slurry
Roast	Sliced Roast	Casserole	Slurry
Calzone	Open-Faced Sandwich	Burrito	Smoothie
Roast	Sliced Roast	Samosas	Slurry
Roast & Fruit Sauce	Pizza	Casserole	Slurry
Wellington Roast	Sliced Wellington	Casserole	Slurry
Roast	Sliced Roast	Burrito	Power Slurry
Cheeseless Pizza	Cheeseless Pizza	Cheeseless Pizza	Drink
Roast & Veggies	Pizza	Casserole	Slurry
Barbeque	Barbeque	Barbeque Sausage	Shake
Roast	Casserole	Casserole	Sweet Slurry
Roast	Stir-Fry	Burrito	Shake
Soup	Soup	Soup	Slurry
Toasted Sandwich	Pizza	Burrito	Slurry
Soup	Roast with Fruit Sauce	Casserole	Slurry
Soup	Soup	Soup	Slurry
Stew	Food	Casserole	Slurry
Soup	Soup	Casserole	Power Meat Smoothie
Roast	Roast with Fruit Sauce	Casserole	Slurry
Wellington Roast	Sliced Wellington Roast	Lasagna	Slurry
Roast	Sliced Roast	Burrito	Slurry
Roast	Roast & Fruit Sauce	Casserole	Leftover Puree
Roast	Sliced Roast	Casserole	Slurry
Seared Roast	Seared, Sliced Roast	Casserole	Shake
Roast	Roast & Veggies	Casserole	Dinner-in-a-Cup
Roast	Sliced Roast	Casserole	Sweet Slurry
Roast	Sliced Roast	Casserole	Slurry
Seared Roast	Seared, Sliced Roast	Soup	Slurry
Roast & Veggies	Stir-Fry	Meatloaf	Slurry
Roast & Veggies	Kebabs	Casserole	Smoothie
Roast	Sliced Roast	Casserole	Slurry
Roast	Sliced Roast	Casserole	Slurry
Oil	Oil	Frothy Oil	Frothy Oil
Veggie Roast	Veggie Stir-Fry	Vegetable Soup	Juice
Sweet Vegetable Soup	Sweet Vegetable Soup	Sweet Vegetable Soup	Shake
Salad	Salad	Salad	Vegetable Smoothie
Warm Salad	Grilled Vegetable Salad	Salad	Salad-in-a-Cup

Chapter 9

Unlockables Index

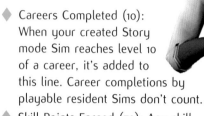

For many players, their sense of success and completion comes from liberating every locked item in a game. Well, if that's you, you've come to the right place: *The Sims™ 2* is chock full of cool unlockables to discover.

> **note** Most unlockables are only released by playing in Story mode, though all unlocked content is also available in any Freeplay Mode households saved in the same saved game file. Objects, on the other hand, can be unlocked in EITHER Story or Freeplay modes.

Unlockables in *The Sims™ 2* include:

◆ Clothing Pieces (76)   ◆ Recipes (24)
◆ Buy Mode Objects (50)   ◆ End Movie
◆ Locations (12)

Unlock Progress

Your success in this endeavor is tracked in Story mode in the Progress panel of the Pause menu. In this view, you can see how many of each item you've unlocked, how many unlockables exist in each category, the percentage completion in each item and in the game as a whole, and your current cumulative Aspiration points.

In Story mode, track your success at unlocking goodies in the Progress panel of the Pause menu.

In addition to the unlockables listed in this section, the Progress panel also tracks other data as well.

◆ Promotions Earned (90): Every step in each career counts toward the total of 90 (10 levels per career) jobs in the game. You earn credit for a promotion when it's attained by your created Story mode Sim only; promotions earned by playable residents don't count.

◆ Careers Completed (10): When your created Story mode Sim reaches level 10 of a career, it's added to this line. Career completions by playable resident Sims don't count.

◆ Skill Points Earned (70): Any skill points earned by your created Sim only are added to this line.

◆ Skills at Maximum (7): When your created Sim reaches level 10 in a skill, it adds one to this count.

◆ Sims Helped (15): There are 15 playable resident Sims who have their own Gold Wants. Switching to them and satisfying their entire chain of Gold Wants satisfies some of your Sim's Gold Wants and can unlock bonus lots. For each Sim helped, one is added to this count.

Appearance/Clothing Items

There are two ways to unlock bonus clothing and adornments.

Locked appearance items are displayed with a gold closed lock until released.

> **note** If an unlocked clothing piece is gender specific and your Sim is from the opposite gender, the unlock doesn't appear when your Sim visits the dresser for a change of clothes. It does, however, appear when you switch control to a Sim of the correct gender and enter the dress or enter Create-a-Sim to create a new Freeplay Sim of the same gender.

NPC Relationship Score (39 Pieces)

You've unlocked new fashion from this Sim!
(A) Go to your wardrobe to try it out!

Getting extremely chummy with NPCs unlocks a piece of their "look."

Build a relationship with an NPC Sim to 100, and a piece of that Sim's wardrobe is unlocked for your Sims' adornment.

Clothing Unlocks

NPC	Home Lot	Unlocked Item
Betty Buttercup	H.M.S. Amore	Fox Stole
Billy Specter	Sunset Canyon	Chaps and Belt
Candi Cupp	Tranquility Falls	Bracelet
Chantal Leer	Tranquility Falls	Fashion Dress/Top
Dina Caliente	Jugen House	Beads Bundle Necklace
Don Lothario	Jugen House	Hair
Don Treadwell	Cliffside Retreat	Waiter's Jacket
Farah Moonbiscuit	Shoreline Trails	Bindi and Necklace
Felicity Usher	Rockwell Acres	Gold-Studded Belt
Gilda Geld	Biodome	Dog Purse
Goopi Gilscarbo	Tranquility Falls	Loafers?
Hector Fromagero	H.M.S. Amore	Shaggy Hair
Helga Mandrake	Sunset Canyon	Horror Hair
Isabella Monty	Cliffside Retreat	Strap Toe Shoes
Jasmine Yves	Mesa Gallery	Dreadlocks
Jessica Jones	Biodome	Scarf (Bundled)
Jessie Rose	The Orbit Room	Silk Belt
John Gray	Andromeda Arms	Round Chrono Watch
Jonas W. Bragg	Alien Crash Site	Army Helmet
Larry Liu	Tranquility Falls	Sweater Vest Shirt

Clothing Unlocks continued

NPC	Home Lot	Unlocked Item
Mary Gray	Andromeda Arms	Dress
Nelson Longfellow	H.M.S. Amore	Captain's Hat and Epaulettes
Nina Caliente	Jugen House	Boots
Noel Howard	Biodome	Round Watch
Ossie Madison	Rockwell Acres	Hat
Patricia Pitts	Mesa Gallery	Andean Hat
Patrizio Monty	Cliffside Retreat	Visor Glasses
Phil Phantasm	The Orbit Room	Glasses
Red S. Hirt	Sunset Canyon	Scarf
Rico Banana	Mesa Gallery	Fur Coat
Sheila Deadbones	Sunset Canyon	Parrot/Peg Leg
Timmy Tool	Shoreline Trails	Sneakers
Toothless Joe	Jugen House	Golf Hat
Torin Namaste	Shoreline Trails	Sandals
Turk Johnson	The Orbit Room	Spiky Hair
Willy Weir	Mesa Gallery	Dashiki Shirt
Wooster Piggins	Biodome	Handlebar Mustache
XHT-F Smith	Alien Crash Site	Space Suit
XY-XY Smith	Alien Crash Site	Space Suit

Career Uniforms (37 Pieces)

Six pieces of each career's signature uniform are unlocked upon promotion of your primary Sim to levels 2, 3, 5, 7, 9, and 10.

Once unlocked, these items are available in Create-a-Sim and the appearance system (by changing clothes in dressers) for any controllable Sim to wear.

> **note** Several of the uniform items are shared between careers. Once unlocked in one career, the same item isn't unlocked by reaching a corresponding level of another career in which it's used. Therefore, reaching level 2 in both the Artist and Fashion careers (both of which unlock the beret) count as only one item in the Progress panel.

Career Uniform Unlocks

Career	Unlocked at Level 2	Unlocked at Level 3	Unlocked at Level 5	Unlocked at Level 7	Unlocked at Level 9	Unlocked at Level 10
Artist	Beret	Glasses	Pointy Shoes	Short Tie	Pea Coat	Feather Boa
Athletics	Jersey	Pants	Shoes	Helmet	Gloves and Pads	Goggles
Business	Bowtie	Vest	Short Tie	Blazer	Bowler Hat	Monocle
Crime	Bowtie	Vest	Short Tie	Blazer	Fedora Hat	Mobster Glasses
Fashion	Beret	Glasses	Pointy Shoes	Short Tie	Pea Coat	Ascot
Law	Army Sweater	Kneepad Pants	Survival Belt	Infrared Helmet	Assault Vest	Police Goggles
Medicine	Rubber Gloves	Medical Cap	Rubber Boots	Smock	Stethoscope	Surgical Binoculars
Military	Army Sweater	Kneepad Pants	Survival Belt	Infrared Helmet	Assault Vest	Infrared Goggles
Politics	Bowtie	Vest	Short Tie	Blazer	Top Hat	Spectacles
Science	Rubber Gloves	Medical Cap	Rubber Boots	Smock	Cybereye	Brain Hat

Buy Catalog Objects

Buy Catalog objects are unlocked by the accumulation of Aspiration points in both Story and Sims (Freeplay) modes.

Whenever any controllable Sim—your Sim or any playable resident Sims—satisfies any kind of Want, points are added to your accumulated Aspiration points. Realization of Fears by any playable Sims, conversely, deducts accumulated Aspiration points.

In the Buy Catalog, locked items are marked with a gold closed lock. The object's description includes the number of Aspiration points you need to release it.

Note that once an object is unlocked, a loss of the necessary Aspiration points—due to occurrence of a Fear—does not relock it. Unlocked objects are unlocked permanently.

> **tip** It's mathematically possible to unlock all objects solely by doing the Gold and Platinum Wants in the eight mandatory Story mode lots. You may, however, need to do several Green (generic/Aspiration-specific) Wants and/or satisfy Gold Wants in at least one of the four optional lots to release all unlocks.

Certainly, however, sidetracking into the optional lots and satisfying the Gold Wants there can speed the pace of object unlocking.

Buy Mode Unlocks

Object	Cumulative Aspiration Points	Object	Cumulative Aspiration Points	Object	Cumulative Aspiration Points
Comic Dehydrator	500	Dig Dog Hotdog Dispensary	4,600	Prof. Feather's Chicken Checkers	12,100
Hawaiian Fantasy Tiki Torch	700	Summer Breeze Toilet Hut	4,900	Façade King Western Hotel	12,800
Dial-a-While Bird Bath	900	Defective Arcade Genie Lamp	5,300	Cantankerous Bowel Fish	13,500
Wurl 'N' Hurl Retro Jukebox	1,100	"The Heffe" Raw Hide Rug	5,700	Façade King Western Bank	14,300
Snuffit Fire Destroyer	1,300	P5 4400SX+ DS	6,100	U-Probe-It Computing Organism	15,100
"Fists of Bunny" Poster	1,500	"Magic Fingers" Hydraulic Massage	6,500	Peppy Pete's Player Piano	15,900
Fruit Bunch Barrel	1,900	Niagara Love Tub	6,900	Turntablitz DJ Booth	16,800
Sproutch Couch	2,000	Strike-a-Match Air Hockey	7,300	Quattro-Grav Air Tub	17,700
Hippity-Humpity! Arcade Game	2,100	U-Probe-It Refrigerating Organism	7,700	Pathologie Costume Trunk	18,600
The Eggalitarian	2,300	Trampoline	8,200	Façade King Western Store	19,600
Driver Pro 2006: "Chip Shots."	2,500	Blade Vision VERY High HD TV	8,700	Façade King Western Saloon	20,600
The Vibromatic Heart Bed	2,800	Spin the Bottle	9,200	Rat Race Executive Power Wheel	21,700
Piazza Amoretto Fountain	3,100	"Procedural" Music System	9,700	Freedom Vacuum	22,800
Cuddlers' Cradle	3,400	Screaming Death Bonfire	10,300	"White Fire" Teppanyaki Table	24,000
Retro Space-Age Action Pinball	3,700	Psychonautica's Cerebro-Chess	10,900	SlumberGell Immersion Pod	26,500
White Rabbit Bubble Blower	4,000	Radioproactive Heating Stove	11,500	Wurl N' Hurl Gnarlosurf 2000	27,900
"Truth" Telescope	4,300	Madcap Miner Metal Detector	12,000		

Locations

The Sims™ 2 Story mode contains twelve lots—eight mandatory and four optional bonus lots. Unlocking each kind is done in similar but not identical fashion.

Mandatory lots are unlocked by satisfying your Sim's Platinum Want on a previous lot, the final major Want after the lot's string of Gold Wants. Your Sim can't travel to the next locked lot in the chain until the Platinum Want is fulfilled.

Once a location is unlocked, your Sim can travel to it via the taxi stand.

Bonus lots are also unlocked by satisfying Wants but not those of your created Sim. Every Story mode lot (except the first) contains at least one playable resident Sim that you can control in addition to your created Sim, and many of these controllable Sims have their own Gold Wants. For most of these resident Sims, satisfying all of their Gold Wants, in turn, satisfies *one of your Sim's Gold Wants* (that is, "Help So-and-So Sim") on the way to the Platinum Want. Four of them, however, are not mentioned in your Sim's Gold Wants at all, and they are the keys to unlocking bonus lots.

For these Sims, satisfying all of their Gold Wants unlocks one of four designated bonus lots. Once unlocked, a bonus lot can be visited anytime. You can depart the progression of mandatory lots to play around on them or save them until you finish all eight mandatory lots. The choice is yours.

note Diverting into the bonus lots can enable you to buy locked objects earlier in the game. Since you rack up extra Aspiration points by satisfying the bonus lot Sims' Gold Wants, you may amass enough points to release unlockable items in, for example, lot six rather than waiting until lot eight.

Lot Unlocks

Lot	Mandatory or Bonus	Unlocked by
Rockwell Acres	Mandatory	Game Start
Shoreline Trails	Mandatory	Satisfy Platinum Want in Rockwell Acres
Cliffside Retreat	Mandatory	Satisfy Platinum Want in Shoreline Trails
H.M.S. Amore	Mandatory	Satisfy Platinum Want in Cliffside Retreat
Mesa Gallery	Bonus	Satisfy All Gold Wants for Hector Fromagero in H.M.S. Amore
Sunset Canyon	Mandatory	Satisfy Platinum Want in H.M.S. Amore
Orbit Room	Bonus	Satisfy All Gold Wants for Billy Specter in Sunset Canyon
Tranquility Falls	Mandatory	Satisfy Platinum Want in Sunset Canyon
Jugen House	Bonus	Satisfy All Gold Wants for Larry Liu in Tranquility Falls
Alien Crash Site	Mandatory	Satisfy Platinum Want in Tranquility Falls
Andromeda Arms	Bonus	Satisfy All Gold Wants for XHT-F Smith in Alien Crash Site
Biodome	Mandatory	Satisfy Platinum Want in Alien Crash Site

Recipes

Though there are myriad ways to combine the various ingredients offered by Sims' refrigerators, there are several tried-and-true recipes that Sims can discover by reading, gaining Cooking skill, or doing various other activities.

Recipes appear in the recipe book in each refrigerator.

Except for default and skill level-based recipe unlocks, all other recipes are unlocked randomly while doing the listed activity. You may have to, for example, read on the toilet several times to unlock the two recipes from that source.

note Recipes (including any unlocked recipes) are available in the recipe book during ingredient assembly.

Several mundane tasks lead to the discovery of recipes.

Ending Movie

The final ending movie, a blooper reel of the game's opening cinematic, is unlocked for your viewing pleasure and amusement by completing the Platinum Want in Biodome, the final mandatory lot.

Once this movie is unlocked, all Story mode lots remain open for Freeplay with your Story mode Sim.

note You can't, however, move a totally new family into the Story mode lots via Freeplay mode. These families can still only inhabit the four designated Freeplay mode lots.

Unlockable Recipes

Recipe Number	Recipe Name	Unlocked By
1	Roast	Default
2	Sandwich	Default
3	Sweet Vegetable Soup	Default
4	Fruit Shake	Read In Bed
5	Fruitspacho	Read In Bed
6	Salad	Read Newspaper
7	Chef Salad	Read Newspaper
8	Ceviche	Read Toilet Magazine
9	Hors D'Oeuvres	Read Toilet Magazine
10	Soup	Read Comic Book
11	Fruit in Pastry	Read Book
12	Samosas	Read Book

Recipe Number	Recipe Name	Unlocked By
13	Combo Pizza	Chat On Computer
14	Roast & Fruit Sauce	Chat On Computer
15	Salad-in-a-cup	Cooking Skill Level 1
16	Burrito	Cooking Skill Level 2
17	Kebabs	Cooking Skill Level 3
18	Parfait	Cooking Skill Level 4
19	Fruit Smoothie	Cooking Skill Level 5
20	Gratin Shake	Cooking Skill Level 6
21	Wellington Roast	Cooking Skill Level 7
22	Ceviche Puree	Cooking Skill Level 8
23	Cheeseless Pizza	Cooking Skill Level 9
24	Casserole	Cooking Skill Level 10

Chapter 10
Build Your Own Abode

Whether you're building from scratch in Freeplay mode or modifying a Story mode lot, it pays to know your way around the Build Catalog.

This section introduces all the tools and objects that make homebuilding and improvement part of the pleasure of controlling your own little virtual people.

Walls and Fences

Walls are the most important part of a building, as they define indoors versus outdoors and delineate one room from the next.

Fences are purely decorative, adoring your Sims' lawns or even any indoor space.

Despite their differences, walls and fences are laid out in exactly the same way.

Drag a straight or diagonal wall.

Select the wall or fence you want to use, place the tool where you wish the wall to begin, press the Tool button, and drag in the direction you wish the wall or fence to run. When you reach the end of the desired run, press the Tool button again, and the section is complete.

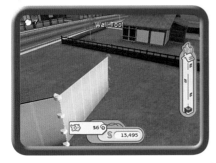

Diagonal and straight walls can't intersect, but they can meet at corners.

Walls and fences can be run parallel or perpendicular to the street or at 45 degree angles. Diagonal and straight runs, however, can't intersect each other.

You can lay out entire rooms at once by holding the Build Room button and dragging out the shape of the room you envision.

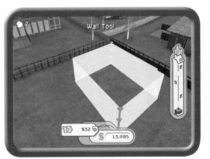

Build an entire room at once with the Build Room button.

note In removal mode, you can press the Change Tools button to switch between various removal tools.

Walls or fences to be removed are marked with red Xs.

Remove walls and fences by entering the Walls & Fences section of the Buy Catalog and pressing the Removal Mode button. Drag the removal tool along the unwanted wall or fence (red Xs appear over sections to be demolished) and press the Tool button to complete. Holding the Build Room button in the removal mode enables deletion of entire rooms at once. The cost of removed walls and fences is refunded.

Walls cost §1 per section while fences vary.

◆ Picket Fence: §10
◆ Friendship Arch Fence: §45
◆ Japanese Fence: §100

Wallpaper

Wallpaper can be applied to any wall segment using the wallpaper tool. Select the wall covering you desire, place the tool at the end of the wall, and drag the length you wish to cover. At the end, press the Tool button again, and it's covered.

tip When demolishing covered walls, strip the wallpaper off first, or you won't get the refund for it.

The Fill Room tool makes papering a breeze.

To paper an entire room at once, position the tool inside a room and press the Fill Room button. To do the same outside, position the tool outdoors. This papers every exterior wall, even in noncontiguous buildings.

Remove wall coverings and return the underlying walls to their bare state by entering the Wallpaper section of the Buy Catalog and pressing the Removal Mode button. Drag the removal tool along the unwanted wallpapered sections (red Xs appear over sections to be stripped) and press the Tool button to complete. Entire rooms can be stripped if you hold the Uncover Room button. The cost of removed wallpaper segments is refunded.

Wallpapers range in cost from §1 to §5 per segment.

tip The more expensive the wallpaper in a room, the higher the Environment score.

Floors

Floors are used to cover the bare grass under your Sims' feet, even in indoor spaces.

Floor coverings can be applied to any indoor or outdoor ground. Select the floor covering you desire and place the tool wherever you want to start placing tile. Press the Tool button once to place a single tile or hold and drag to place a rectangle of tiles. At the end, release the button to apply the tiles.

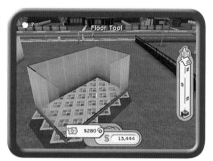

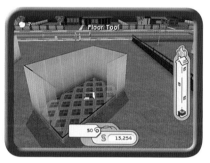

Diagonal rooms automatically cut off corners of floor tiles that run outside the walls.

To carpet an entire room at once, position the tool inside a room, and press the Fill Room button.

note When flooring rooms with diagonal walls, it appears that tiles are placed in the corners outside the walls, but this is only the case before you release the Tool button. The finished floor deletes any portion that's outside the walls.

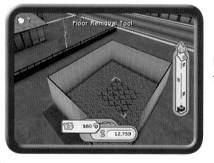

Red Xs mark floor tiles to be removed.

Remove floor tiles and return the underlying ground to its bare state by entering the Floors section of the Buy Catalog and pressing the Removal Mode button. Drag the removal tool along the unwanted floor tiles (red Xs appear over sections to be demolished) and press the Tool button to complete. Entire rooms can be uncovered if you hold the Uncover Room button. The cost of removed floor tiles is refunded.

Floor coverings range in cost from §1 to §5 per segment.

tip The more expensive the floor covering in a room, the higher the Environment score.

Doors

Doors provide access between indoor and outdoor spaces and between indoor rooms.

Doors can't be hung on diagonal walls.

Doors are hung on empty wall segments and can be rotated for the desired swing. Doors can't be placed along diagonal walls.

MAKING DIAGONAL ROOMS

To make a room diagonal, there must be some part of it that features straight walls so that doors may be installed.

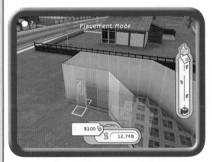

Build a straight room adjacent to a diagonal room and make their walls meet at the corners. You may then put doors on any of the nondiagonal walls.

To solve this problem, run a straight wall up to a corner of the diagonal room. Run another straight wall parallel to the first so it lines up with another diagonal corner. Delete any diagonal walls that separate the two spaces, and you have one big room with both diagonal and straight walls and, most importantly, a way to get in and out.

To remove doors, enter the Doors catalog and press the Grab Mode button. Select the door you wish to delete and sell it just like you would any object in the Buy Catalog.

Doors vary in price.

- ValueWood "Just a Door": §100
- Barred Door: §100
- Door. Catalog # 000001: §100
- Door with Small Window: §100
- Klassick Repro Multi-Frame Door: §100
- Metal Mentality Door: §100
- Coat-of-Many-Layers Door: §100
- Klassick Repro Ornamental Door: §100
- The all new 2005 "Portál": §100
- Mahogany Leaded Glass Door: §100
- Solana Vista Window: §100
- ResisTit Door: §100
- Deko Door: §150
- Door Designs by Todd: §150
- Bulkhead Latch: §200
- Embofree Quality Air Lock Plus: §200
- Boggs Western Door: §200
- Boggs Saloon Doors: §200
- Embofree Quality Air Lock: §200
- Wood-n-Steel Door: §250
- Imprestige Door: §250
- Shojitsu Screen: §250
- Shojitsu Door: §250

Windows

Windows provide light in indoor spaces.

Windows are hung on empty wall segments. They cannot, however, be placed along diagonal walls.

The more windows in a room, the happier the Sims within.

To remove windows, enter the Windows catalog and press the Grab Mode button. Select the window you wish to delete and sell it just like you would any object in the Buy Catalog.

tip More windows mean more light, and that means a higher indoor Environment score. Use as many windows as you can afford.

Windows vary in price.
- Low Rider: §100
- Porthole: §100
- Porthole NextGen: §100
- Peep Hole: §100
- Nautilus Window: §100
- Four Pane Punch: §100
- "The Four Pane": §100
- Practical Window: §100
- Ocular Home Orifice Alpha: §150
- Ocular Home Orifice Beta: §150
- OmniView Horizontal Half Pane: §150
- OmniView Queen Admiral: §150
- Short Pane "Setting Sun" Window: §150
- Tall Pane "Setting Sun" Window: §150
- Gohji Half Pane window: §250
- Gohji Full Pane window: §250
- Molotov Wild West Window Set: §300
- Molotov Pre-Broken Window Set: §300
- Half Imprestige Window: §350
- Imprestige Window: §350

Fireplaces

Fireplaces are wonderful decorative items, and they provide Fun in the form of watching the fire. While watching, your Sim can toast marshmallows for a little bit of Hunger satisfaction.

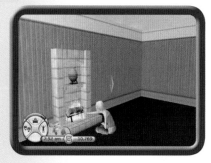

There's nothing quite like roasting marshmallows in front of a roaring hearth.

Fireplaces must be kept clean, or they become a fire hazard. Locate fireplaces along any nondiagonal wall. Be sure, however, to keep flammable objects at least a few feet away from the open flames.

Add and delete them like any Buy Catalog object.
- Minimal Fireplace: §500, Fun 6
- Empire Fireplace: §800, Fun 6

Landscaping

Landscaping plants and shrubs are purely decorative items that can be placed outdoors only.

Want shrubbery? Try a two-level effect with a little path running down the middle.

Add and delete them like any Buy Catalog object.
- Nee Gardens Shrubbery: §50
- Pine Tree: §100
- Cactacaea, aka Cactus: §100
- Pale Birch: §100
- Gnarly Carly Hardwood: §150
- Boxwood Tree: §150
- Cherry Blossom Tree: §150
- Maple Tree: §150
- Willow Tree: §150
- Tree Unit Number Seven: §200
- Shrub: §200

Architectural Tips

- Keep bathrooms and beds near the front of the house to make the before-work routine as close as possible to the street and the carpool.
- A well-functioning house might not really look like a house at all. Do what works best for your strategy, not how you think a house should look.
- Leave plenty of room for Sims to maneuver around each other. A three-tile wide space is much better than a cramped one- or two-tile wide hallway.
- To help facilitate smooth movement of Sims, it's a good idea to make sure that there are at least two doors in every room. If you only have one, it is very easy for an autonomous Sim to engage in an activity (like socializing) right in front of the lone door, trapping Sims inside the room.

Chapter 11
Story Mode

Game Structure

In *The Sims™ 2* Story mode, the goal is to advance your Sims through a series of eight required lots (and, if you're so inclined, four bonus lots) until they complete the final lot and unlock the climactic movie.

Each subsequent lot is unlocked by satisfying a progression of special Wants (Gold Wants). When your Sims reach a new lot, they get their first Gold Want. Satisfying these Wants unlocks the next Gold Want, and so on.

When your Sims satisfy their last Gold Want for a lot, they receive the lot's Platinum Want. Satisfying this final Want unlocks the next lot in the story.

> **note** Completing the Platinum Want in all but the final lot (Biodome) triggers an additional Gold Want, "Visit a New Location." This Want is satisfied when your Sim travels by taxi to the next unlocked lot and is, in each instance, worth 100 Aspiration points.
>
> Since this Want appears for every required lot and isn't part of the chain leading to the Platinum Want, it's not listed in the following lot walkthroughs.

Branching off this linear progression are four bonus lots that provide your Sim with new places to go, new Sims to meet, and more opportunities to amass Aspiration points. You may play these lots any time you want once they're unlocked.

> **note** Since they don't unlock any further lots, there are no Platinum Wants in the bonus lots. Your Sim can, however, satisfy as many or as few of the Gold Wants as you like and may, of course, return to the main lots at any time.
>
> Additionally, visiting the lots and meeting the inhabitants provides a new pool of potential friends for your Sims to get to know—especially useful if they're Romance or Popularity Aspiration. These Sims also become available in any Freeplay lot as well.

Bonus lots are unlocked by helping one of the controllable resident Sims of a required lot satisfy all of his or her Gold Wants. When the Sim's final Gold Want is completely satisfied, the corresponding bonus lot is available via taxi.

Map

PREEXISTING CONDITIONS

Occasionally, a Gold Want requires you to do something you've already done. In most cases, such Wants don't arise at all since they've already been satisfied. In some situations, however, this isn't the case.

Social interactions (which are remembered by the game) and events that can't be easily reproduced (like getting promotions) are credited for Gold Wants, even if they occurred before the Want arose.

Easily repeated actions, however, done before a Gold Want arose do *not* count and must be redone to satisfy the Want. This is the case, for example, with any Gold Want that requires the purchase of an item.

Rockwell Acres

- ◆ Unlocked How: Game Start
- ◆ Non-Playable Resident(s): Ossie Madison, Felicity Usher
- ◆ Playable Resident(s): None
- ◆ Unlocks Lot(s): Shoreline Trails

Primary Sim Gold Wants

Fill Hygiene Need

Locate the shower and use it to fully satisfy the Hygiene Need.

Use Trampoline

Use the backyard trampoline to replenish Fun. When you're done, press the Cancel button.

Meet Someone New

The lot's residents choose this moment to return. Introduce your Sim to either Ossie or Felicity.

Get a New Friend

Develop relationship with either Ossie or Felicity to Friend (at least 40 relationship points).

> **tip** See "Characters" for each resident's personality profile and "Social Interactions" for the ins and outs of social interactions.

Use "Talk" Social on a Sim

Use the Talk interaction on either resident.

Take out Trash

There are several piles of trash on the floor of the house. Pick them up and throw them in the trashcan.

> **note** At this point, your Sim receives the first infusion of money, §2,000.

Platinum Want

◆ Unlocks: Shoreline Trails

Buy a Single Bed Worth at least §50

Go to the Buy Catalog. In the Seating & Beds department, choose the cheapest bed you can find (Single High or Less Bed for §300) and place it anywhere in the house.

> **tip** Once you've satisfied Gold Wants that require you to purchase objects, the objects needn't remain on the lot. To save cash, resell these objects before you prepare to depart the lot.

Shoreline Trails

- Unlocked How: Satisfy Platinum Want in Rockwell Acres
- Non-Playable Resident(s): Timmy Tool, Torin Namaste
- Playable Resident(s): Farah Moonbiscuit
- Unlocks Lot(s): Cliffside Retreat

Primary Sim Gold Wants

Get a Job

Use the newspaper or buy a computer and search the job listings for your Sim's first gainful employment. You may take a job in any profession, but it's best to look for one that fits with your Sim's Aspiration (see "Skills and Careers").

> **note** Job- and skill-related Gold Wants often don't appear when you see them in this walkthrough because, typically, you'll have already satisfied them before the Want arises. In this case, you'll never see job- or skill-related Gold Wants at all.
> If, however, you haven't had the opportunity to tend to your Sim's career or skill, these Wants pop up to focus you on these concerns, and you can't move on until you make a bit more progress.

Alternatively, you could take a job that starts the soonest. If a job begins early in the morning, you've probably missed today's shift and have to wait until tomorrow to satisfy the next Want. Take one that starts later in the day, and you can clear that Want in the next few hours.

> **tip** Newspapers arrive at 7:00 a.m. and contain three random job listings per day. The computer offers the same three plus two more.

Go to Work

Catch the carpool for your Sim's first shift at a new job. Remember, the carpool arrives an hour and a quarter before the shift starts and departs when the shift starts. You may send your Sim to work immediately or wait until just shy of the shift start to satisfy your Sim's Needs to the fullest. Miss the carpool, however, and you have to wait another day to get your next Gold Want.

Gain a Skill Point

Use any skill object on the lot to gain a single skill point. For simplicity's sake, grab a book from the bookshelf and study Cooking; it's the most immediately useful.

Buy an Object

Enter the Buy Catalog and purchase any item for your Sim's new home.

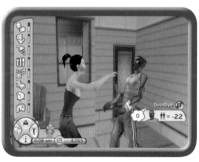

Become Enemies with Torin

Use negative interactions (like "Slap") to drive down relationship score with Torin to Enemy level (-11 or lower).

Reach Body Skill Level 3

Use the Exerto Self-Spot Exercise Machine to develop Body skill to 3.

tip To avoid failure and loss of Energy, only lift light weights until your Sim achieves Body skill of at least 3. Then you can go up to medium weight, which develops Body skill faster.

To speed up Body skill development on this object at any weight level, switch to Farah while your Sim is lifting and have her do the Cheer interaction on the bench. Her support doubles your Sim's rate of skill acquisition.

Perform Surf Trick

Use the surfing simulator in the backyard (choose "Surf" not "Boogie Board") and stay on long enough to do one automatic trick. Once the Want is satisfied, you may exit the object.

tip To reduce the chances of being thrown from the machine, only use the surfing simulator when your Sim's Energy Need is full. Low Energy increases the chances of failure and makes it harder to get the trick you need to satisfy the Want.

Change Clothes

Locate the dresser and use it to change clothes.

tip There's no need to actually change your Sim's clothing or any other appearance element; entering the appearance changing screen and returning to the game satisfies the Want.

Become Friends with Timmy

Raise relationship with Timmy to Friend (40 or higher).

Reach Career Level 2

To be nearly guaranteed a promotion, make sure you have all the skill levels required for the next level and leave for work in the best possible Mood. Check the Careers, Skills & Personalities screen for any skill requirements (they're highlighted on the skill bars) and get your Sim working on those skills ASAP. As for Mood, make sure all of your Sim's Needs are as satisfied as possible when the carpool arrives. The more satisfied the Needs, the better the Mood.

If your Sim has both the skills and the mood and hasn't missed any work days so far, he or she should get the promotion upon return from the shift.

tip The carpool waits for an hour and 15 minutes after it arrives. If your Sim's Mood isn't optimal when the carpool arrives, use the extra time to work on Needs until about 40 minutes past the hour. When that time comes or Needs are as satisfied as they're going to get, head for the carpool.

If, however, your Sim is already in a good Mood when the carpool arrives, take advantage of it and go straight to work.

note Reaching level 2 in a career also unlocks the first of five clothing unlocks that make uniform pieces in each career available. After the promotion, you can change your Sim into any unlocked uniform pieces anytime you like.

Platinum Want

◆ Unlocks: Cliffside Retreat

Beat Torin at Foosball

When your Sim's Fun Need is low, play at the Foosball table and call Torin over to play too. If your Sim wins, you unlock the next lot.

To increase chances of winning, develop your Body skill as high as you can. Torin has Body 2, so the higher your Sim can get above that, the better your chances. For example, if your Sim is Body 2 also, the chances of winning are 50-50. With every level higher than Torin's, the chances of winning increase by five percent. Therefore, having Body skill of 6, for example, ups the probability to 70 percent.

Cliffside Retreat

- ◆ Unlocked How: Satisfy Platinum Want at Shoreline Trails
- ◆ Non-Playable Resident(s): None
- ◆ Playable Resident(s): Isabella Monty, Don Treadwell, Patrizio Monty
- ◆ Unlocks Lot(s): H.M.S. Amore

Primary Sim Gold Wants

Use "Talk" Social on Isabella

Use the Talk interaction on Isabella.

Buy a Dishwasher

The kitchen needs an upgrade, so buy a dishwasher and place it anywhere in the kitchen.

Repair a Stove

Get to work and repair the broken stove.

> **tip** It's slow work if your Sim has low Mechanical skill; take the opportunity to study a bit to speed things up.

Reach Level 3 in a Career

Get another promotion in your Sim's career. For reaching this milestone, you also unlock another piece of that career's uniform.

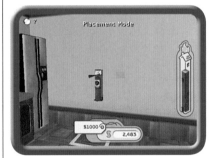

Buy a Fire Extinguisher

No restaurant is up to code without a fire extinguisher, so purchase one from the Buy Catalog (Appliances section). To procure this bit of equipment, you need $1,000 and at least 1,300 Aspiration points (to unlock it).

Build Walls

Enter the Build Catalog and select the wall tool (Walls & Fences). Use it to add a wall to your lot.

> **tip** There's no need to build a whole room, or anything much for that matter. Drag a short section of wall to satisfy this Want.

> **tip** For info on using the wall tool, see "Build Your Own Abode."

Reach Level 4 in a Career

Meet all skill and friend requirements and send your Sim to work in a good Mood to get another promotion.

Platinum Want

◆ Unlocks: H.M.S. Amore

Help Isabella Fulfill Her Gold Wants

Switch control to Isabella and satisfy all her Gold Wants.

Resident Sim Gold Wants (Isabella Monty)

Buy a Table

Enter the Buy Catalog, purchase any table, and place it anywhere on the lot.

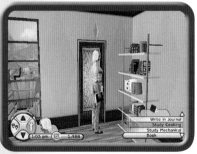

Buy Three Chairs

Go to the Buy Catalog, purchase three chairs, and place them anywhere on the lot.

Gain a Cooking Point

Direct Isabella to the bookshelf or have her cook to elevate her to the next Cooking skill level.

Harvest Squid From Aquarium

Go to the "Manila 1000" Marine Aquarium and harvest seafood to stock the fridge with, among other sea life, squids.

Make a Sandwich

Enter direct control and prepare a meal using the food creation system. To make a sandwich, pick any meat ingredient plus any grain plus water and prepare the resulting food at a counter.

Become Friends with Patrizio

Interact with Patrizio and raise Isabella's relationship score to at least 40.

Buy an Ingredient Source

Enter the Buy Catalog and purchase a GenoLife Garden Hutch, "Frood" Tree, or "Manila 1000" Marine Aquarium.

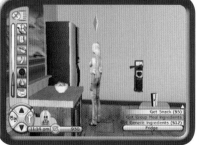

Create a Group Meal

Go to the refrigerator and make a group meal. Go to the fridge and select "Get Group Meal Ingredients." Construct any dish and fully prepare it.

Give Food to Patrizio

When the meal is complete, take a serving, approach Patrizio, use the food, and select the Give Food interaction.

H.M.S. Amore

- Unlocked How: Satisfy Platinum Want at Cliffside Retreat
- Non-Playable Resident(s): Nelson Longfellow
- Playable Resident(s): Betty Buttercup, Hector Fromagero
- Unlocks Lot(s): Sunset Canyon, Mesa Art Gallery (Bonus)

Primary Sim Gold Wants

Reach Level 5 in a Career

Meet all skill and friend requirements and send your Sim to work in a good Mood to be promoted to level 5 in any career.

> **tip** Level 5 promotions unlock the third uniform clothing piece.

Earn §250

Once the Want appears, earn §250 from any source. The quickest source of money is your Sim's job, but you could also search the couches for cash.

Change Clothes

Purchase a dresser from the Buy Catalog and use it to change clothes.

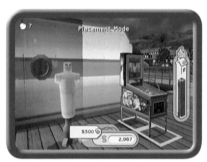

Buy an Object Worth at Least §300

Go into the Buy Catalog and buy any single object worth at least §300.

Buy a Blender

Enter the Buy Catalog and purchase either blender object.

Reach Level 6 in a Career

Continue to go to work in a very good Mood and meet each career level's skill and friend requirement to achieve level 6 in any career.

Platinum Want

- Unlocks: Sunset Canyon

Help Betty Fulfill Her Gold Wants

Switch control to Betty Buttercup and satisfy all of her Gold Wants.

Resident Sim Gold Wants (Betty Buttercup)

Gain a Charisma Point

Go to the Buy Catalog, purchase a mirror, and use it to practice speech or kissing to gain one point of Charisma skill.

Become Friends with Nelson

Betty and Nelson begin as Enemies (-20 relationship points). Interact to rebuild their relationship to the Friend level (40 or more relationship points).

Gain a Body Skill Point

Purchase any Body skill-developing object from the Buy Catalog and rise to the next level of Body skill.

Make Aphrodisiac Meal

To further woo the curmudgeonly captain, prepare a meal that has an aphrodisiac effect. Meals containing ingredients with at least three aphrodisiac effect points have a romance-inspiring impact on anyone who eats them.

For example, purchase a "Frood" Tree and harvest from it. Then, go to the fridge and pull out a passion fruit, a carrot, and a lime. Cook them at the stove to make a meal that could inspire the captain.

Give Food to Nelson

Stand near Nelson, select the food, and do the Give Food interaction. If Nelson accepts, Betty's one step closer to the man of her dreams.

Gain a Charisma Point

Return to the mirror and gain another Charisma skill point.

Buy a Painting

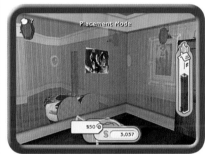

Enter the Buy Catalog and purchase any painting from the Decorations panel. Place it on any eligible wall space on the lot.

Use "Make Out" Social on Nelson

Work Betty's relationship with Nelson to Lover status by raising her relationship score to 75 or higher and doing romantic socials. Next, successfully perform the Make Out interaction.

Marry Nelson Longfellow

Successfully use the Propose interaction to marry Nelson Longfellow. Make sure both Sims' Mood and relationship are top drawer.

Resident Sim Gold Wants (Hector Fromagero)

◆ Unlocks: Mesa Gallery

Use "Make Out" Social on a Sim

Build relationship with any Sim (household Sims are the easiest because they're frequently around) and successfully perform the Make Out interaction.

Play Spin the Bottle

Get a Spin the Bottle object from the Buy Catalog in the Miscellaneous category (unlocked at 9,200 Aspiration points) for §1,625 and play a solo game.

WooHoo with a Sim

Utilize the heart-shaped beds in the ship's cabins to lure a Sim into Hector's amorous web. Relax on the bed, call over a Sim with whom Hector has a strong romantic relationship, and successfully do the WooHoo interaction.

Use "Make Out" on Three Sims

Making out with three Sims may sound easy, but the possibility for jealousy complicates things considerably. First, make out again with the first Sim Hector previously made out with.

Next, develop a relationship with two more visitor Sims when the first Sim is away from the lot. Wait until only one of these Sims is on the lot, and successfully make out. Repeat with the other Sim.

Get Two Sims in the Hot Tub

Direct Hector to climb into the hot tub and coax one other Sim into it with the Ask to Join interaction.

WooHoo with Three Sims

Using the same three paramours, bed each one when the others aren't on the lot.

Sunset Canyon

◆ Unlocked How: Satisfy Platinum Want at H.M.S. Amore
◆ Non-Playable Resident(s): None
◆ Playable Resident(s): Red S. Hirt, Sheila Deadbones, Helga Mandrake, Billy Specter
◆ Unlocks Lot(s): Tranquility Falls

Primary Sim Gold Wants

Take out Trash

Find the outdoor tables and pick up the trash nearby.

Buy a Metal Detector

Go to the Buy Catalog (Electronics section) and obtain a Madcap Metal Detector for §1,200. It's unlocked with 12,000 Aspiration points.

Find Treasure with Metal Detector

In direct control mode, activate the metal detector and wander the lot to locate any hidden object. When you hear the detector start to beep more often, search the immediate area until the beeping becomes almost constant. When you think you've found the spot, press the Select Interaction button. If you're near the treasure, the Dig interaction becomes available. Use it and see what you find.

Wear a Costume

Locate the costume trunk (first building on the left from the entrance) and change into any costume you choose (not nudity or pajamas).

tip Change out immediately if you like.

Serve Meal to Red S. Hirt

Buy a grill, prepare a meal, and give it to Red.

Reach Level 7 in a Career

Continue to advance in any career by achieving level 7.

note This career level unlocks the fourth uniform clothing piece.

Platinum Want

◆ Unlocks: Tranquility Falls

Help Red S. Hirt

Switch control to Red S. Hirt and satisfy all his Gold Wants.

Resident Sim Gold Wants (Red S. Hirt)

tip Many lots don't come with telephones built in, so you have to buy one before you can satisfy any Gold Want that requires it.

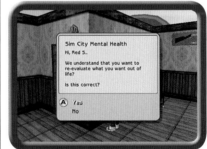

Call the Shrink

Purchase a telephone and use the Services menu to call the Therapist.

Gain Creativity Point

Bang on the piano to gain a point of Creativity skill.

Play the Guitar

Purchase a "Does it Rock!" Electric Guitar (Skill category) for §1,500 from the Buy Catalog and direct Red to play it.

Paint Picture

Sell the guitar and buy an Independent Expressions, Inc. Easel (Skill category) for §750. Direct Red to paint until a picture is completed.

Resurrect Helga

Switch control to Helga and locate the Grim Reaper as he wanders the lot. Either pay him the resurrection fee (§100) for an instant rebirth or challenge him to a fiddle contest until she wins her return to the land of the living.

Fill Social Need

Interact with other Sims until Red's Social Need is completely fulfilled.

Be Loved by Helga

Interact with Helga to achieve the relationship score and Love memories necessary to achieve Lover relationship.

> **tip** Since you can control both Sims, make sure both have high Mood. This can make things go much more quickly.

Kiss Helga

Do any kiss interaction (Make Out, Smooch) to keep the romantic mood going.

Cuddle with Helga in Bed

Purchase a bed, direct Red to relax in it, and call over Helga. Once she's relaxing too, unleash the Cuddle interaction.

Resident Sim Gold Wants (Billy Specter)

◆ Unlocks: Orbit Room (Bonus)

Return to Life

Find the Grim Reaper and either pay the resurrection fee (§100) or challenge him to a fiddle contest.

Dance on Sheila's Grave

Find Sheila Deadbones' tombstone (first from the gate) and do the Dance interaction.

Become Enemies with Helga

Do negative social interactions with Helga to reduce the relationship to Enemy status (-11--30).

145

Become Archenemies with Helga

Continue to act out against Helga to reduce relationship to Archenemy status (-30 or lower).

Throw a Party

Find the telephone and use the Throw Party interaction.

tip Only call for parties at "decent" hours (8:00 am to midnight); calling in the middle of the night will get you nowhere.

Tranquility Falls

◆ Unlocked How: Satisfy Platinum Want in Sunset Canyon
◆ Non-Playable Resident(s): None
◆ Playable Resident(s): Chantal Leer, Larry Liu, Candi Cupp, Goopi Gilscarbo
◆ Unlocks Lot(s): Alien Crash Site, Jugen House (Bonus)

Primary Sim Gold Wants

Use Massage Table

Purchase a "Magic Fingers" Hydraulic Massage Table (Electronics) for §5,000. It's unlocked if you've amassed at least 6,500 Aspiration points.

Use "Talk" Social on Larry

Use the Talk interaction on Larry.

Gain a Mechanical Skill Point

Buy and use any book-shelf (study Mechanical), chess board (play Paper Football against another Sim), or "Jimmy Three Fingers" Rocket Bench to gain one Mechanical skill point.

Build Walls

Enter the Build Catalog and activate the wall tool. Construct a whole room (if you like) or a single wall segment and return to the game.

Buy a Genie Lamp

Go to the Miscellaneous section of the Buy Catalog and purchase a Defective Arcade Genie Lamp (§6,500). It unlocks with 5,300 Aspiration points.

Buy an Object Worth over §300

Buy any object with a minimum price of §300.

Reach Level 8 in Career

Continue up the career ladder to achieve level 8.

Buy an Object Worth over §1,000

Life just gets more expensive; procure any object for §1,000 or more.

Visit Another Location

Use the taxi stand to visit any other unlocked lot. Return when you're ready to resume.

Platinum Want

◆ Unlocks: Alien Crash Site

Help Chantal

Switch control to Chantal Leer and satisfy all her Gold Wants.

Resident Sim Gold Wants (Chantal Leer)

tip One of Chantal's later Gold Wants is to master Creativity skill. Get her started on this ASAP so she's at least close when the time comes. Don't, therefore, get her a job as you probably normally would to bring in extra cash. Her time is better spent on this time-consuming later Want.

Change Clothes

Purchase any dresser and change any element of Chantal's appearance. Return to the game.

Buy a Fountain

Enter the Plumbing section of Buy mode and acquire the Piazza Amoretto Fountain (§550)—unlocked at 3,100 Aspiration points.

Add a Room

Using the wall tool in the Build Catalog, construct a new room on the lot.

tip Build a small rectangle of unfinished walls. The Want is satisfied when you have four contiguous walls; size doesn't matter.

Buy Any Object

You heard what your Sim wants. Buy just for the sake of buying. Get anything and put it anywhere.

Buy Four Lights

Buy four items from the Lighting section of the Buy Catalog and place them anywhere on the lot.

PRIMA OFFICIAL GAME GUIDE

Master Creativity Skill

Chantal's already a very creative person (Creativity 7), but she needs to buckle down and perfect her craft. Get a piano (the most expensive Creativity-developing object) and play until she reaches Creativity 10.

tip If money's tight, let Chantal get her Creativity from the Write in Journal interaction on the bookcase that you placed in the house earlier. It's slower, but it doesn't cost anything extra.

Buy An Object Worth over §500

Pick any item from the Buy Catalog worth more than §500 and place it on the lot.

Get Art Career

Now send Chantal to the newspaper to get her a job in the Artist track. You might want to start doing this a bit earlier in case there are no Artist listings for a couple of days, or buy the house a computer to expand the number of listings each day.

Resident Sim Gold Wants (Larry Liu)

◆ Unlocks: Jugen House

Skip Work

Though it might be against your nature, prevent Larry from making the carpool. His first shift starts at 9:00 AM, so be sure to know where he is at 8:00 am and be ready to override his choice when he decides it's time to go.

Make Prank Call

Use the telephone to make any kind of prank call you want.

Fill Fun Need

Using any Fun object on the lot or from the Buy Catalog, fully satisfy Larry's Fun Need.

Buy an Object Worth at Least §500

Use the Buy Catalog to purchase any object with a price tag of §500 or more.

Play Game with Sim

Purchase any game from the Buy Catalog and direct Larry to play. Then have him call another Sim to join the fun.

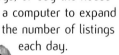

Design a Game

Purchase any computer from the Electronics section of the Buy Catalog and place it on a table with a chair in the right position. Use the Design Computer Game interaction and wait until Larry completes his project. Depending on his Creativity skill, it should sell for a bit of cash.

Be Friends with Chantal

Socialize with Chantal Leer to get a Friend relationship (40 or higher relationship score).

Fill Fun Need

Again, engage Larry in a Fun activity until his Fun Need is completely satisfied.

Make Nauseous Meal

Larry needs to cook a dish that causes nausea. First, the lot needs a basic kitchen—one fridge, one counter, and a stove—placed anywhere you like.

> **tip** To avoid having to add food harvesting objects too, buy the U-Probe-It Refrigerating Organism because it's the only fridge that comes with enough nausea-inducing ingredients.

Next, choose three ingredients with nausea attributes (like lamb, beets, and bananas). Any dish you concoct with these three ingredients causes nausea.

Give Food to Candi

Take the finished dish and serve it to Candi with the Give Food interaction.

Alien Crash Site

- Unlocked How: Satisfy Platinum Want in Tranquility Falls
- Non-Playable Resident(s): Jonas W. Bragg
- Playable Resident(s): XY-XY Smith, XHT-F Smith
- Unlocks Lot(s): Biodome

Primary Sim Gold Wants

Meet an Alien

Have your Sim greet either XY-XY or XHT-F.

Reach Level 9 in a Career

You're almost there. Keep climbing the career ladder to level 9.

> **note** Attaining this level unlocks the fifth uniform piece for a career.

Buy a Computer

Procure any computer from the Electronics section of the Buy Catalog.

Write a Blog

Use the computer and its Blog interaction to publish your Sim's thoughts to the world. Keep at it, and your Sim gains in Charisma too.

Build Walls

Access the Build Catalog and build at least one segment of wall with the wall tool.

Platinum Want

◆ Unlocks: Biodome

Help XY-XY

Switch control to XY-XY Smith to complete all of his Gold Wants.

Resident Sim Gold Wants (XY-XY Smith)

◆ Unlocks: Andromeda Arms

Make Friends with Jonas

Socialize with Jonas (start by apologizing) to raise relationship to Friend (40 or higher relationship score).

Change Clothes

Purchase a wardrobe from the Miscellaneous section of the Buy Catalog. Use the wardrobe to enter the appearance system and, if you like, change XY-XY's appearance. Or just exit out of the screen and return to the game.

Buy an Ingredient Source

Enter the Buy Catalog and purchase a GenoLife Garden Hutch, "Frood" Tree, or "Manila 1000" Marine Aquarium.

Give Food to Jonas

Prepare a meal from the kitchen and bring the food to Jonas. Use the Give Food interaction and hand it to XY-XY's new best friend.

Throw a Party

In honor of interplanetary good feelings, use the phone to throw a party.

Resident Sim Gold Wants (XHT-F Smith)

Get a Job

Look in the newspaper or on the computer for any job.

Earn §200

Either from work or other sources, earn §200.

Buy a Hot Tub

Even though the lot already has a cool alien tub, why not get one your Sim's earthling friends might feel more at home in?

Play Chess

Play a game of chess on the chess board in the living room.

Get a Promotion

Get your Sim's first promotion by sending him to work on time, in a good Mood, and with all skill and friend requirements satisfied.

Earn §400

With this new promotion, it should be no problem to rake in a bit more extra cash.

Buy a Burglar Alarm

Look in the Electronics section of the Buy Catalog and obtain a SimSafety V Burglar Alarm to protect your Sim's new assets.

Read a Book

Purchase any bookcase from the Skills section of the Buy Catalog and read a book for Fun.

Get a Promotion

By continuing to go to work in a good Mood and meeting all skill/friend requirements, that second promotion should be within XHT-F's grasp.

Buy A Rug

To top off the crash site redecoration, buy a lovely rug from the Decorations panel of the Buy Catalog.

Biodome

- ◆ Unlocked How: Satisfy Platinum Wants in Alien Crash Site
- ◆ Non-Playable Resident(s): None
- ◆ Playable Resident(s): Noel Howard, Jessica Jones, Wooster Piggins, Gilda Geld
- ◆ Unlocks: Final Movie

Primary Sim Gold Wants

Use Secret Handshake on Noel

Build relationship above 50 and make sure both your Sim and Noel are in a positive Mood, and the Secret Handshake becomes available. Noel's acceptance depends entirely on his relationship score toward your Sim, so make sure it's as high as possible to improve the odds.

Make a Meal with Energy Boost Effect

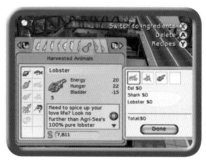

To make foods with Energy boosts, use foods that have high Energy and Fun ratings. If these ratings add up to more than 80 (see "Food Creation"), the food contains an Energy boost.

Harvest some fish from both tanks and make a roast of shark, eel, and lobster. It's also an aphrodisiac, but that's not important right now.

Master Any Career

Get to level 10 in your career, and you're one step closer to greatness.

Help Noel

Switch control to Noel Howard and satisfy all his Gold Wants.

Have at Least §10,000

Get jobs for all controllable Sims and get them working hard every day. Curb your spending and sell any items you have added to the house in order to get family funds up to §10,000.

Platinum Wants

◆ Unlocks: Ending Movie, Story Mode Freeplay.

The final Platinum Want you receive in this level depends on your Sim's Aspiration. Completing the game's final Platinum Want unlocks and plays a secret movie, a funny blooper reel featuring characters from the game.

Wealth: Get Family Funds to §30,000

Using all of the playable Sims, get funds up to §30,000.

Romance: WooHoo with Five Sims

If you haven't amassed five conquests already, develop relationships with and bed five different Sims with the WooHoo interaction.

> **note** The Want is immediately satisfied if you've already racked up five WooHoos with five different Sims.

Knowledge: Master All Skills

Get to level 10 in *all* six skills.

Popularity: Have 20 Friends

Develop relationship to at least Friend (relationship score 40) with 20 different Sims. Remember that relationships decay, so give yourself some headroom by getting all 20 relationships higher than 40.

Creativity: Make Food with a Special Effect

Prove your culinary mettle by constructing a feast with any kind of special effect (Energy boost, aphrodisiac, etc.).

Resident Sim Gold Wants (Noel Howard)

Hire a Maid

Pick up the phone and use the Services menu to hire a maid.

Play Golf

Place a Driver Pro 2006: "Chip Shots." driving range on the lot and hit a few balls.

Buy a Painting Worth Over §1,000

Things are getting pricey, but you can handle it. Venture into the Buy Catalog and purchase any wall painting worth §1,000 or more.

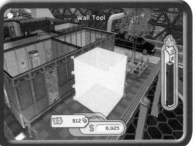

Add a Room

Fire up the Build Catalog and select the wall tool. At the very least, build a small rectangle of unfinished walls. The Want is satisfied when you have four contiguous walls.

Master Charisma Skill

Develop Charisma skill (with a wall mirror or by blogging on a computer) all the way up to its highest level.

Sell a Great Painting

Build Noel's Creativity up to level 9 and paint a picture. The result is a "great" painting. Sell it.

Master Politics Career

Go to work in a good Mood, gain all necessary skills and friends, and get Noel promoted to the top level 10.

Resident Sim Gold Wants (Jessica Jones)

Buy DJ Booth

Using the Electronics section of the Buy Catalog, purchase a Turntablitz DJ Booth (§5,000). This item is unlocked at 16,800 Aspiration points.

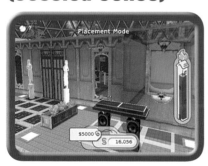

Invite Sim Over

Use the telephone to invite over any Sim Jessica knows. Remember to only call during decent hours (8:00 am to midnight), or you get turned down flat.

Party with an Alien

Call and invite XY-XY Smith. Once he's arrived and greeted, direct Jessica to start the party.

Get Four Sims Dancing

While Jessica uses the DJ booth, attract four Sims to dance to the music or, for a shortcut, direct all other controllable Sims to dance.

Use Fireworks on DJ Booth

Make with the pyrotechnics and use the Fireworks interaction.

Use Laser on DJ Booth

Get the party really moving with the DJ booth's Laser interaction.

153

Mesa Gallery

- Unlocked How: Satisfy all Hector Fromagero's Gold Wants in H.M.S. Amore.
- Non-Playable Resident(s): Patricia Pitts
- Playable Resident(s): Jasmine Yves, Rico Banana, Willy Weir
- Unlocks Lot(s): None

Resident Sim Gold Wants (Jasmine Yves)

Paint a Picture

Paint at one of the easels in the building farthest from the front of the lot to produce one picture.

Sell a Great Painting

Develop Creativity skill up to at least level 9 and use an Independent Expressions, Inc. Easel to produce a "great" painting. When it's done, sell it.

Reach Level 5 in Art Career

Gain the two required Charisma points and send Jasmine to work in a good Mood to get promoted to level 5 in the Artist career (she's already level 4).

Write a Blog

Blog at the nearby computer.

Have Six Friends

Develop four more relationships to, and keep them at, Friend level (above 40).

Have at Least §10,000

Get jobs for all controllable Sims and get them working hard every day. Curb your spending and sell any items you have added to the house in order to get family funds up to §10,000.

Buy a Sculpture

Enter the Buy Catalog and purchase any sculpture from the Decorations panel.

Buy a Painting Worth at least §500

Purchase a painting worth §500 or more from the Decorations panel of the Buy Catalog.

Throw Party

Get on the phone and use the Throw Party interaction.

Wear a Costume

Purchase a Pathologie Costume Trunk ($5,500, unlocked at 18,600 Aspiration points) and change into any costume you choose (not nudity or pajamas).

Get Four Sims Dancing

Using the stereo in the painting studio, get four resident Sims dancing to the tunes.

Play Spin the Bottle

Get a Spin the Bottle object from the Buy Catalog (unlocked at 9,200 Aspiration points) for $1,625 and play a solo game.

Have Three Lovers

Develop relationship with three different Sims to the Lover level. Avoid doing romantic interactions when other Lovers are in the room, or their jealousy will break their Lover status.

Andromeda Arms

- ◆ Unlocked How: Satisfy all XHT-F Smith's Gold Wants in Alien Crash Site
- ◆ Non-Playable Resident(s): None
- ◆ Playable Resident(s): John Gray, Mary Gray
- ◆ Unlocks Lot(s): None

Resident Sim Gold Wants (John Gray)

Buy a Stereo

Buy any stereo from the Electronics section of the Buy Catalog.

Buy a Blender

Buy either blender from the Appliances section of the Buy Catalog.

Buy a Painting

Buy a painting from the Decorations panel of the Buy Catalog.

Buy a Fire Extinguisher

Buy a Snuffit Fire Destroyer from the Appliances section of the Buy Catalog.

Buy an Arcade Game

Buy a Laser Llama Classic Arcade Game, People Invaders, or AE Arcade Unit from the Electronics section of the Buy Catalog.

Buy a Metal Detector

Buy a Madcap Metal Detector from the Electronics section of the Buy Catalog.

Find Bottle Cap with Metal Detector

Use the Metal Detector in direct control mode until you locate a bottle cap anywhere on the lot.

Buy a Television Worth at Least §400

Buy any TV in excess of §400 from the Electronics section of the Buy Catalog.

Buy Ingredient Source

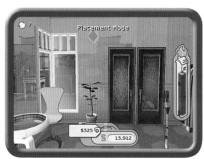

Enter the Buy Catalog and purchase a GenoLife Garden Hutch, "Frood" Tree, or "Manila 1000" Marine Aquarium.

Buy a Decorative Plant

Buy any plant from the Decorations panel of the Buy Catalog.

Buy an Espresso Machine

Buy an !!!!Espresso.it.supremo!!!! from the Appliances section of the Buy Catalog.

Buy a Painting Worth at Least §1,000

From the Decorations panel of the Buy Catalog, purchase a painting worth more than §1,000.

Buy the Kitchen Sink

Buy a Hydronomic Kitchen Sink (§230) from the Plumbing section of the Buy Catalog and place it in an open countertop.

tip Once all the Gold Wants are satisfied, sell back all the new items to regain most of what you spent.

The Orbit Room

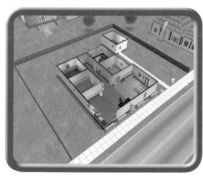

◆ Unlocked How: Satisfy all Billy Specter's Gold Wants in Sunset Canyon

◆ Non-Playable Resident(s): None

◆ Playable Resident(s): Phil Phantasm, Turk Johnson, Jessie Rose

◆ Unlocks Lot(s): None

Resident Sim Gold Wants (Phil Phantasm)

Build a Recording Studio Room

Fire up the Build Catalog and select the wall tool. At the very least, build a small rectangle of unfinished walls. The Want is satisfied when you have four contiguous walls.

Buy a Stereo

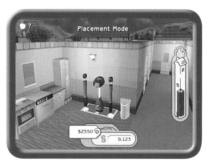

Buy any stereo from the Electronics section of the Buy Catalog.

Invite a Sim Over

Use the telephone to invite any Sim Phil knows (preferably Noel Howard). Remember to only call during decent hours (8:00 am to midnight), or you get turned down flat.

Become Friends with Noel Howard

Interact with Noel to raise relationship to at least 40.

PRIMA OFFICIAL GAME GUIDE

Buy a Computer Worth over §2,000

Purchase any computer costing more than §2,000 from the Electronics section of the Buy Catalog.

Buy a Metal Detector

Buy a Madcap Metal Detector from the Electronics section of the Buy Catalog.

Reach Level 6 in the Business Career

Get Phil promoted to level 6 in Business by meeting all skill and friend requirements and sending him to work in a very good Mood.

Buy an Arcade Game

Buy a Laser Llama Classic Arcade Game, People Invaders, or AE Arcade Unit from the Electronics section of the Buy Catalog.

Throw Party

Use the phone to throw a party.

Dance

Direct Phil to dance to music from the new stereo.

Master the Business Career

Gain all skill and friend requirements and send Phil to work in a good Mood every day to get him promoted to the top of the Business career.

Jugen House

◆ Unlocked How: Satisfy all Larry Liu's Gold Wants in Tranquility Falls
◆ Non-Playable Resident(s): None
◆ Playable Resident(s): Don Lothario, Toothless Joe, Nina Caliente, Dina Caliente
◆ Unlocks Lot(s): None

Resident Sim Gold Wants (Toothless Joe)

Talk Social on a Sim

Use the Talk interaction on any Sim.

Buy a Fruit Punch Barrel

Buy a fruit punch barrel from the Appliances section of the Buy Catalog.

Get a New Enemy

Do negative social interactions with any Sim to reduce the relationship to Enemy status (below -30).

Get Three Enemies

Direct Joe to be a jerk to two more Sims to similarly reduce relationship score to below -30.

Get a New Archenemy

Choose one of the three new Enemies and further berate one until relationship score is reduced below -30, Archenemy status.

tip To make the next Want easier to achieve, make the Enemy a Sim with the lowest Body skill.

Win Fight with a Sim

Perform the Fight interaction with the Archenemy. Victory in fights is based on the difference in Body skill. The farther apart two Sims' Body skill, the more likely the stronger Sim will win.